THE BOOK OF

Crystal Healing

THE BOOK OF

Crystal Healing

A comprehensive guide to this powerful therapy

Emily Anderson

SIRIUS

To Lily.
May your love of crystals continue with the help of this book.

SIRIUS

This edition published in 2023 by Sirius Publishing, a division of
Arcturus Publishing Limited,
26/27 Bickels Yard, 151–153 Bermondsey Street,
London SE1 3HA

Images courtesy of Shutterstock.

ISBN: 978-1-3988-3055-4
AD010240UK

Printed in China

CONTENTS

INTRODUCTION

For centuries, crystals have been used for healing by expert practitioners as well as ordinary men and women wanting a gentle yet effective way to boost health and wellbeing. The right gems used in the right way can alleviate temporary physical symptoms such as headaches, insect bites and stomach upsets, as well as aid more chronic conditions including arthritis, asthma and diabetes. Certain gems get to the root of deeper emotional wounds, including post-traumatic stress, depression or heartbreak, and turn around negative aspects of our mental health that might be holding us back from living our best lives.

By working holistically on all the aspects of your life that may be causing dis-ease, crystals can increase your energy, intuition and joy. By treating the underlying causes of physical issues, crystals can help rid the body of chronic and acute illness. They enable you release fears, harmful beliefs or past-life contracts that are keeping you stuck. Plus they can connect you to your spirit guides, the angelic realm and Source energy to assist with your spiritual growth. They are highly effective healing tools, and they are abundant in our planet.

But how do they actually work? Crystals emit energy according to their crystalline structure, the minerals they're made of, and their colour. Plus, each crystal connects with a certain chakra, or energy centre, in the body's etheric field. Depending on its colour, a crystal can open, clear and activate a chakra into working better and improving your mental, emotional, physical and spiritual health and wellbeing. Crystals work on the premise that everything is connected; if there is balance and clarity in all areas of our lives, ill health can be kept at bay.

These powerful gems vibrate at a frequency that influences the mind, body and spirit through your senses, your aura and the crystal's position on your body or location in your home. Different crystals work on specific issues, all covered in the A–Z section of this book. Each entry includes the chakras and astrological signs connected to the gem as well as various mental, emotional, physical and spiritual issues in our lives that often need to be addressed, and ways to use each crystal to help.

This book will go into more detail on how they are formed, what is meant by 'energy' and 'frequency', and what chakras are all about. But first let's explore a little more about how crystals have been used for healing in the past.

History of crystal use in healing

As far back in history as we know, crystals have been sought after by nobility, used in spell work by witches and mystics, and held in high regard aesthetically and energetically. Until mediaeval times, the garments of soldiers and explorers had empowering amulets of onyx or amazonite woven into them to protect the wearers from harm and help wounds heal quicker. During the Middle Ages, healing gems were placed on saints' shrines and given religious, as well as magical, powers. In St Paul's Cathedral in London, the sapphire on St Erkenwald's shrine was said to cure visitors' eye diseases.

Native Americans believed positive energies from gemstones could be passed from one species to another in what they called a sacred hoop or circle of existence. Such ancient traditional societies believed crystals to be conscious. Their interactive, supportive energies were said to amplify our innate healing and intuitive abilities.

Genesis, in the Old Testament, has one of the earliest references to a healing stone, belonging to Abraham. The stone was reported to cure any sick person who looked at it. *The Papyrus Ebers*, from about 1500BCE, list the healing properties of certain gems. Rubies were thought to help liver and spleen diseases, lapis lazuli was made into eye balm, and emeralds were used for curing dysentery.

Plato, the Greek philosopher (427 to 34BCE), talked of crystals as being made by the stars and planets converting decayed material into the most perfect gemstones, which were then ruled by these planets. If the sun was in a certain constellation or the moon or another planet ascending at the time of engraving a crystal, it would make it even more powerful. Many still believe that certain stones, including moonstone and topaz, strengthen in power during a waxing moon, peaking in healing ability when the moon is full.

Ancient Egyptians, the Chinese and alchemists up until the 18th century added crushed crystals to medicines. Over 200 crystals that could be used in healing were listed in the Greek pharmacist Dioscorides' *De materia medica*. And the first Roman chronicler, Pliny the Elder, includes older crystal teachings in his work *Natural History*, elaborating on the theory that the size and substance of special stones were important in the healing of diseases. Despite the demise of many other traditional-medicine practices, crystal healing remained popular.

Many crystal treatments used across the world today are similar to ancient methods. In Iraq, some 5,500 years ago, according to an ancient medical text, bloodstone was used to treat blood diseases, just as it is nowadays. The ancient Greeks used water infused with blue lace agate and other light-blue gems to soothe sore throats and help speakers communicate from the heart. Today you can buy bottles of water with crystals in them to stop tickly coughs and dry throats. Roman craftsmen made goblets from aquamarine to purify water, which led to physicians recommending it to aid digestion and decrease fluid retention. The Celts used to boil clear quartz in water and drink it to cleanse their systems and increase energy. Dabbing quartz water onto pulse points is still a common remedy for exhaustion.

Mined as long ago as 4000BCE, malachite was used in ancient Egypt as a power stone to channel higher energy to Earth. To help pharaohs be wiser leaders, they lined their headdresses with it. Malachite was also ground into a powder eye shadow believed to enhance vision and spiritual insight. Malachite has been a powerful protection stone since the Middle Ages, when it was thought to shield people from the 'evil eye'. Today it is used to absorb negative energy and pollutants from the environment and the body.

Jet has been used since the Bronze Age in jewellery and ornaments, with the Romans importing it from northwest England to protect them from evil entities. Since then, it's been believed to protect from negative, draining energy, violence or illness. Even Queen Victoria wore jet after the death of her husband, Prince Albert, as it was said to help with grief.

But what exactly are crystals? And how can they help heal everything from dysentery, diabetes and acne to abandonment issues, confusion and depression?

What are crystals?

Crystals are made up of minerals with a specific internal lattice structure that never changes, even if the outward shape is different. They are created over millions of years from molten magma and gases underneath the Earth's crust, and continue to form and metamorphose as the planet shifts and changes, heats up and cools down. They form under enormous pressure, making them some of the most durable materials in the world.

Larger masses, such as quartz, tend to grow slowly, often in underground chambers where a gas bubble allows them to form, sometimes into geodes - domed caves with sparkly interiors - or clusters of points locked together. Others, such as phantom or faden quartz, have stopped and started growing again, creating certain effects in the resulting crystals.

Smaller gems have usually dripped or even exploded into being from volcanic lava, molten rock or meteorites smashing into the Earth's surface. Other minerals solidify in layers between other matter, and are revealed as the surface material breaks down through erosion or excavation. Certain types of crystals are found in specific locations. Turquoise, for example, is found in desert areas, and is created when water interacts with rock containing copper, aluminium and phosphorus. Sedimentary crystals, such as calcite, form closer to the surface when mineralized water trickles through weathered rocks or pushes eroded matter into rivers and streams to make new formations. Many of these often softer crystals are attached to a bedrock, known as the matrix. Drusy crystals grow as tiny sparkly crystals, often of garnet, malachite or dolomite, on a larger, bulkier matrix, often of agate.

From chalcedony and quartz to flint and feldspar, crystals come in varying degrees of hardness - measured by the Mohs Scale of Mineral Hardness - and a vast array of colours depending on their chemical composition. But they all form symmetrically along an internal axis, which can be seen under a microscope. Plus, they all have an internal structure created from geometric shapes, including triangles, squares, hexagons, rhomboids and parallelograms. The pattern these forms create when they lock together gives the generic names of certain crystal types.

However, while outwardly they may seem solid and serene, inside every crystal are atoms - particles rotating around a centre in constant motion. So at a microscopic level, crystals are actually made up of a moving mass of molecules vibrating at a certain frequency. This is what gives each one its own particular energy, which creates an effect when used by humans for healing our minds, bodies and spirits as well as our homes, pets and the planet.

Does size matter?

As living mineral matter, crystals have electromagnetic energy fields; they can absorb, conserve, focus and emit energy depending on their molecular structure. Some work like a magnet, attracting or repelling energy. It may be that a larger crystal transmits more energy, but a smaller crystal can emit energy just as effectively with the right conscious intent and focused direction when you become expert at doing so. Working with smaller stones is simply more practical, especially when you want to place them on the body, or wear or carry them as a talisman.

Most experts and practitioners agree that any size of crystal has healing properties, whatever its shape, rough or smooth. Of course, the ancients would only have used the rough gems found in caves, whereas today you can buy smaller gems, tumbled and polished to smooth shapes. You can get rose quartz in the shape of hearts, clear quartz pyramids and bladed selenite or tourmaline made into a pointed wand. While a crystal wand is an incredible tool for pinpointing dis-ease in a person, and directing energy better, ultimately the external shape matters little when it comes to crystals' powers.

Semiprecious gemstones are just as powerful as rarer, precious gems such as topazes, emeralds, diamonds and sapphires. The healing, protecting and transformative properties of any stone come from the crystal itself and how you work with it. Using them with respect, love and clear, positive intention magnifies their benefits. You just need to make sure they are as close to genuine natural crystals as possible.

Watch out for fakes!

Crystals found in nature have flaws and uneven colouring. They change over time, fading and becoming cloudy or veined. Dyed gems can look obviously dyed in too-bright colours, or more natural, such as howlite dyed to look like turquoise. Many stones, including agate, howlite, jasper, quartz and dalmatian stone, are often dyed to boost their visual appeal and saleability, without taking away anything from their quality. Similarly, the 'aura' type of quartzes, which are bonded with precious metals to add iridescence and shimmery effects, are enhanced by the additions to their energetic frequency. Most rubies and sapphires have been treated in some way to improve their colour, and emeralds often have their fractures filled and clarity improved to make them perfect for jewellery.

Synthetic gems are widely available. They're not strictly fakes; they contain the same chemical properties as raw gems but are created quickly, in laboratories, and often seem more vibrant or uniform in colour. They're cheaper, but they won't hold quite the same quality of energy as natural stones formed over centuries.

Fake crystals are not made of the same materials, and are fairly easy to spot. They can look too perfect and are actually cast from plastic, resin, ceramic or even painted rocks. If there are bubbles in the 'gem', it's likely to be glass. Another method of imitating crystals, particularly opals or rubies, is to make composites, which use the real mineral to coat glass or another rock.

The best way to avoid anything but the genuine item is to buy crystals from reputable shops or trusted experts. Ask the seller where the crystal comes from, and have a good, close look and feel. Check the colour and markings. But, most importantly, sense how it feels to you. Because that's the key to choosing your crystals - being attracted to them and feeling connected to their energy. Then the magic can occur.

How do crystals work?

Science is still deciding exactly how crystals affect illnesses and ailments. But it is known that crystals do indeed vibrate at different frequencies, as well as hold heat and contain an electric charge. This is shown by Kirlian photography, which captures images of the energy field - or aura - radiating from both organic and inorganic substances, including crystals. Plus, there are always new areas of scientific research opening up that may explain more, such as quantum mechanics.

Recent studies into the nature of quartz show that the frequency of light increases as it passes through it. Quartz is used for this aspect of precision and intensity in lasers, as well as other practical applications, such as to keep time in watches and store data in computer chips. Ultrasound machines also use a crystal with an electric charge to produce a sound wave. From this, cutting-edge sound healing technology is being developed, in which a beam of ultrasound can disintegrate tumours deep inside the body, without the need for invasive surgery. The ability of crystals to focus light and energy to heal is what healers and shamans have used throughout history, albeit in less technologically-advanced ways.

As with any type of healing, from herbs to pharmaceutical drugs, crystals seem to enhance the placebo effect — that is, if we believe something will help us then it actually will. Mind over matter is magnified with crystals; if we believe in their power to heal, then they will have a positive effect on our wellbeing. They also seem to amplify our natural healing abilities; focusing attention on the desired outcome eventually enables it to manifest.

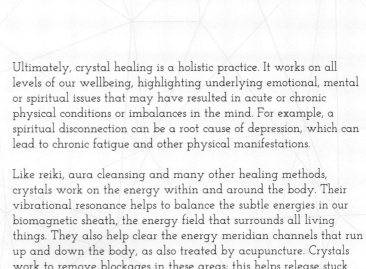

Ultimately, crystal healing is a holistic practice. It works on all levels of our wellbeing, highlighting underlying emotional, mental or spiritual issues that may have resulted in acute or chronic physical conditions or imbalances in the mind. For example, a spiritual disconnection can be a root cause of depression, which can lead to chronic fatigue and other physical manifestations.

Like reiki, aura cleansing and many other healing methods, crystals work on the energy within and around the body. Their vibrational resonance helps to balance the subtle energies in our biomagnetic sheath, the energy field that surrounds all living things. They also help clear the energy meridian channels that run up and down the body, as also treated by acupuncture. Crystals work to remove blockages in these areas; this helps release stuck emotions and clears the way for you to attract optimum health and wellbeing. They also work especially well on energy centres in your body, where two or more meridians cross to make a spinning ball of energy. These are commonly known as *chakras*, the Sanskrit word for wheel.

The chakras

According to Hindu scriptures as well as Tibetan Buddhist and yogic spiritualities, the chakras are spinning wheels of energy within the etheric or spirit body of a human being. They allow energy to flow in and out of the body, and are the areas where we feel the vibes of others and of our environment.

Often depicted as whirling rainbow-coloured circles or lotus flowers, the seven major chakras are positioned from the base of the spine up to the crown of the head. There are believed to be 12 chakras in total, with the Earth star chakra beneath us and the soul star and stellar gateway chakras above the head.

When these wheels become blocked or stagnant, ill health can occur. But when they are vibrating clearly and in alignment with each other, they help raise our frequency, help us attain wellbeing in all levels of our life and even connect with our higher consciousness and guidance from spirit.

Each chakra connects with and affects the health of different organs as well as various aspects of our lives, such as self-expression, security and joy. These chakras, from root to crown, have specific colours, which relate to crystals of the same shade. Some crystals connect to more than one chakra. Crystals can clear, open, activate and balance each chakra by being placed on or near their corresponding energy centre in a simple but effective treatment (described on page 37) that brings clarity, motivation and alignment to our bodies, minds, emotions and spirit.

THE SEVEN MAJOR CHAKRAS ON THE BODY AND THE CRYSTALS THEY CONNECT WITH

1. ROOT - RED

This is located at the perineum, right at the base of the spine. It is linked with the legs, feet, skeleton and large intestine. It represents physical health and the five senses, survival instinct, security and connection to the Earth.

Energetically, this is where kundalini, or life force, energy rises from. If this chakra is blocked, unreasonable anger, as well as pain and discomfort in the related areas of the body, can manifest. When it is clear, you will feel grounded, safe - both physically and to connect with all emotions - and able to move forward in your life.

Crystals to help this chakra: fire agate, bloodstone, cinnabar, red calcite, red garnet, hematite, red or brown jasper, obsidian.

2. SACRAL - ORANGE

Positioned a few centimetres beneath your belly button, the sacral chakra affects the reproductive system, fertility, sexuality and satisfaction. It controls the blood, circulation, bladder and kidneys. It connects with other people and activates your creativity, confidence and self-esteem. It balances your natural urges and desires, happiness and sensual pleasures in the form of eating, drinking and sexual appetite. Disorders involving these areas may include addictions, overindulgence and irritability.

Crystals to assist this chakra: amber, carnelian, chiastolite, chrysoberyl, chrysoprase, orange calcite, lingam, obsidian, rutilated quartz, sardonyx, sunstone.

3. SOLAR PLEXUS - YELLOW

This chakra sits right at the centre of your body, just between the bottom of the breastbone and the navel. It relates physically to the stomach, small intestine, liver, gallbladder and spleen. It controls the digestion of food as well as experiences and emotions, and activates your sense of personal power, uniqueness and integrity. Blockages in this chakra can lead to issues in the related areas of the body and self, including eating disorders, obsessions and too much focus on unimportant details.

Crystals to support this chakra: amber, ametrine, beryl, citrine, marcasite, pyrite, topaz, yellow tiger's eye, yellow zircon.

4. HEART - GREEN/PINK

Sitting in the middle of your chest, close to the heart itself, this chakra supports this organ, along with the lungs, breasts, arms and hands. It represents everything in your life related to love and relationships, including states of compassion, harmony and trust. Your natural healing powers are believed to emanate from this chakra.

When functioning well, it brings a sense of adventure and altruism, and a strong connection with others and the world around you. When out of balance, it can lead to depression and free-floating anxiety, plus ailments in the related bodily areas, such as coughs, lung conditions and heart issues.

Crystals to keep this chakra clear: aventurine, amazonite, moss agate, emerald, green calcite, jade, green and pink kunzite, malachite, peridot, rose quartz, rhodochrosite and rhodonite.

5. THROAT - BLUE

Located in the centre of the throat area, this chakra also connects to the mouth, jaw, ear canals, neck, shoulders, thyroid gland and voice box, and will show dis-ease in any of these areas if blocked. The throat chakra relates to communication, speech and listening as well as a sense of leadership, idealism and freedom. A clear and open throat chakra enables full self-expression of your inner truth, honest ideas and deepest thoughts. Confusion or incoherence can indicate imbalance in this area.

Crystals to balance this chakra: blue lace agate, angelite, apatite, aquamarine, azurite, blue john fluorite, blue calcite, celestite, iolite, blue kyanite, lapis lazuli, sodalite, turquoise.

6. THIRD EYE - INDIGO

Also known as the brow chakra, this spinning wheel of energy sits in the centre of the forehead, just above and right between the eyebrows. It affects the eyes, ears and brain, potentially causing headaches, eye problems, earache and tinnitus if this chakra is out of balance or blocked. Insomnia and nightmares can also occur if this chakra needs clearing. When this chakra is working well, you can expect inspiration, clear thinking and an increase in intuitive skills and psychic insights. Connection to ancient wisdom, the spirit world and the angelic realm can also be enhanced by stimulating this chakra, which helps you tune into clairvoyant messages, prophetic dreams and past-life recollection. It helps your healing powers become more spiritual and supported by a higher power.

Crystals to activate this chakra: amethyst, bornite, fluorite, hawk's eye, labradorite, larimar, lapis lazuli, lazulite, lepidolite, magnesite, merlinite, sugilite, tanzanite.

Many more crystals are connected to the various chakras. See the full A–Z for details on how to use them to clear, open, activate and rebalance the chakras for full health and wellbeing.

7. CROWN - VIOLET/WHITE

The crown chakra is positioned right on top of the head, with the white light of the cosmos pouring into you from above. It connects you to divine consciousness, your higher sense, Source energy and the universe.
It affects the brain, head and psyche, and brings about spiritual growth along with optimum physical, emotional and mental wellbeing. It encourages optimism, imagination and a feeling of oneness with all humanity. Creative spiritual expansion and mystical experiences may occur when this chakra is activated. If stagnant, viruses and infections may linger, along with blocked sinuses, skin and scalp issues, tiredness and anxiety.

Crystals to awaken this chakra: amethyst, beryl, clear fluorite, diamond, howlite, lepidocrocite, novaculite, purple sugilite, any clear or white quartz, moonstone, selenite.

DISCLAIMER

It must be said here, before you start choosing and using crystals as a complementary therapy for healing, that all of the suggestions in this book are not a substitute for conventional medical help. Always consult your doctor before undertaking any alternative treatment to ensure that there are no contraindications for your health.

PART

1

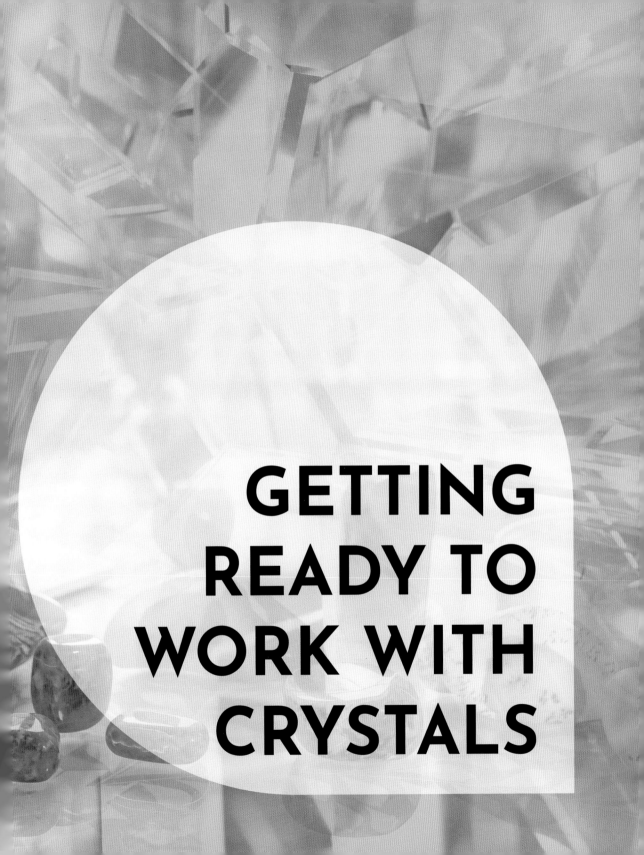

GETTING READY TO WORK WITH CRYSTALS

Choosing the right crystals

Picking the perfect crystals depends on what you want to use them for. If you simply want to meditate with them and expand your awareness of their magical energy, visit crystal shops or mind, body, spirit fairs and browse. You will find that certain crystals attract you more than others. This is why it's best to see crystals in real life, to pick them up, have a good look at them and sense how they feel in your hands. If you find yourself picking one up and you can't put it down, purchase it if you can, as it most likely fits with your needs and desires at this time.

If you can only buy crystals online, you can still feel attracted to a certain type of stone, but until you get it in your hands, you won't know for sure if it's the right one. Make sure any online crystal shop you buy from will take returns if you feel it is not the right one for you after all.

Some crystals may provoke a strong negative reaction in you. You may be repulsed by some, saddened by others. But this emotional response could be triggering something deep within you that you don't like, or have suppressed. Allow whatever feelings are arising to flow through you. Cry, shout or scream if necessary. It may feel uncomfortable, but once these feelings have moved through you, you will feel better.

If you want to work on particular areas of your life, your chakras, or ailments of your own or of others, do your research first. This book lists over 200 crystals and the illnesses and conditions that each gem can help treat, so there are plenty to choose from. As already explained, certain crystals go with certain chakras, which relate to various aspects of dis-ease. So it might be worth getting a set of crystals for all the chakras to start with.

A basic starter selection of general healing stones should include the following as powerful transmuters of auras, emotions and atmosphere:

> **Amethyst** for its calming but also spiritually energizing qualities

> **Citrine** to uplift and bring joy and happiness

> **Rose quartz** to encourage unconditional love to flow for gentle healing

> **Smoky quartz** for grounding spiritual energy and getting rid of stress

> **Clear quartz** is the master healer, clearing and balancing everything while bringing energy to a room, healing session or meditation

Using a pendulum to choose crystals

A pendulum is a crystal or other weight attached to a chain or piece of string that you can use to help you make a decision. Throughout history, pendulums have been used to dowse for water, oil, ley lines and even lost objects or missing people. You can use a pendulum to pick crystals for you, and choose the best treatment from a selection of choices.

Most crystal pendulums are clear quartz, rose quartz or amethyst, but you may find others. If choosing from a crystal shop, hold a few, one at a time, to feel which one you're most attracted to. As with all crystals, you need to cleanse your pendulum's energy before using it and regularly after use to keep it energized. Do this as you would your other gems, via the techniques on pages 22 to 25.

Spend some time forming a relationship with your pendulum by attuning it to your unconscious mind and understanding its 'yes', 'no' and 'maybe' responses. There are a few ways to do this:

◈ Start by taking some deep breaths to centre yourself. Hold your pendulum steady by holding the end of the string loosely between your thumb and index finger and letting it dangle, either with your arm outstretched, if that's comfortable enough, or with your elbow resting on a surface.

◈ Start by asking your higher consciousness or spirit guides to help you receive the clearest answer for the highest good.

◈ **Method 1:** Think of a happy event in your life and see which direction the pendulum moves. It could be clockwise, anticlockwise, forwards and backwards, or left to right. This is the spontaneous positive swing it will give for a 'yes' to a question. Do the same again, but this time think of a sad event in your life and watch how the motion of the pendulum changes. This is the movement it will make when the answer to a question is 'no'.

◈ **Method 2:** Simply ask your pendulum to 'show me a yes' and wait for it to move. Then hold it steady and ask it to 'show me a no' and see the change. This way you can also ask your pendulum to 'show me a maybe,' which could be a possible answer sometimes. See how all the swings differ. Then proceed to ask it questions about which crystals or treatments to choose.

◈ **Method 3:** You may prefer to ask your pendulum to move to questions you know the answers to. So ask it questions with an affirmative answer to get the 'yes' swing, such as 'Do I live in London?' or 'Am I female?' and see which way it moves. Then ask questions to get the 'no' swing, such as 'Do I like bananas?', 'Do I have a dog?' and so on, observing the movement it makes for a 'no'.

- Until you establish a strong relationship with your pendulum, it's worth checking which answers it gives to arbitrary questions first before you ask it more pertinent ones.

- Its movements can change over time, so check the swings for yes and no periodically.

- Make sure you stop the pendulum moving completely after each time of answering.

- It's best not to use your pendulum when you are stressed or tired, as it may give inaccurate answers. Try asking, 'Is now a good time to dowse?' if you're unsure.

ASKING QUESTIONS ABOUT CRYSTALS

Questions for the pendulum can only be those with a yes, no or maybe answer. If you're using a pendulum to help you pick a crystal, formulate your questions correctly, in some of the following ways.

> Should I choose a quartz? Then narrow down the specific quartz you need, for example, phantom, faden or elestial quartz.

> Do I need an amethyst?

> Do I need this particular amethyst? (if in a shop choosing this way)

> Smaller?

> Larger?

> Is calcite the right crystal for me at this time?

> Should it be orange?

> Blue?

> Green?

Dowse for the yes or no answer for each colour until you get to the crystal you need at this time.

If you are using a pendulum to choose a crystal in a shop, you can simply dangle it over a crystal you like and ask it if this is the one you should buy.

Cleansing your crystals

Once you've chosen and purchased your crystals, or if you've been given any as gifts, they need cleansing straight away. In a shop or when given as a present, they will have absorbed vibes from their surroundings and anyone who has handled them. So before you use them you need to thoroughly cleanse them in one of the ways listed below, or as described in the A–Z for specific stones.

Whether you are using crystals for healing or another purpose, they will take in or transmute negative energy, and need to be cleared of it after every treatment, to 'reset' their natural state. At the very least, you should clean them once a month to keep them working at full power. You may see them lose their lustre or colour, or become less bright, or dusty when in need of a good clean.

Some crystals don't need cleaning at all, other than a gentle dust now and then. Azeztulite, citrine and kyanite are all self-cleaning. Carnelian cleans other stones, so it may need the occasionally clean to keep it working well.

Dust sticks to crystals with an electrostatic charge, so if covered in particles, the gem's electromagnetic-frequency (EMF) emitting ability will be reduced. Dust also blocks light photons needed to transmit energy from the crystal to the person in need of its healing. You can easily brush dust off with a small paint or make-up brush, or you can hold many gems under running water, patting them gently with a soft cloth afterwards or letting them air dry. Take care, however, as some are water soluble, such as selenite or sulphur, and must not go in water at all. Others may fade in the sunlight, or even be a fire hazard, such as quartz, which acts like a laser, and focusing light through its point could create a flame.

Check first in the full A–Z in this book that your crystal won't be damaged by the method you choose to clean it. Then enjoy focusing love and attention on your stones by following any of the methods below to keep them clean and crystal clear.

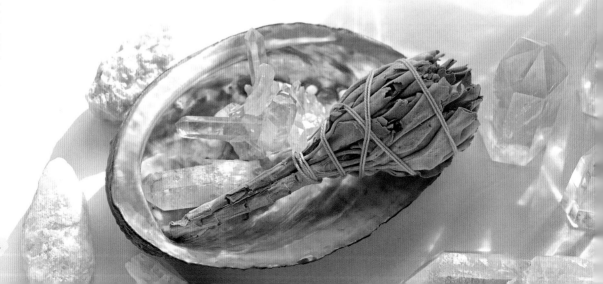

◇ As long as your crystal is hard and not likely to be harmed by water, you can cleanse it quickly by holding it under running water for a few minutes, either from a tap or a river. Or you can immerse it in the sea or a lake for a short while, leaving it longer after heavy use. Be sure to brush off any salt from the sea, in case this affects the crystal.

◇ Recharge your crystals under moonlight or sunlight by laying them out on a cloth or a table underneath the light. But take care where to position gems such as quartz so they don't start a fire. Remember the sun moves in an arc throughout the day.

◇ Cleanse your crystals in a pot of herbs used for healing and purifying, such as rosemary, sage or lavender. A day immersed in any of these scented leaves or flowers will absorb any heavy or unwanted energy.

◇ Try burying your semiprecious stone in the Earth, either in your garden, in an unused plant pot or somewhere you know it will stay undisturbed for two weeks. Cover it with soil when the moon is at its fullest, and uncover it cleansed at the new moon.

◇ Clusters and crystals that are easy to crumble can be buried in rock salt overnight; make sure to brush off every grain of salt afterwards.

◇ You can even use certain gems to clear the energy of others. A piece of carnelian in a bag of tumbled stones will keep them all cleansed. A smaller gemstone can be placed overnight inside a larger geode of amethyst or cluster of quartz.

◇ Stone circles, ancient burial mounds and other sacred sites are the perfect place to perform a crystal cleansing ritual. Take your gems there straight after the sun comes up and lay them out on a flat stone if possible. Quietly meditate on your crystals becoming cleansed, and allow at least half an hour for any undesired energies from them to soak into the sacred stones. The powerful atmosphere from the area will re-energize your gems, ready for their next use.

◇ Smudging with incense, or the smoke from a cleansing bundle of sagebrush or cedar, is an ancient way of cleansing crystals, as well as your aura and the energy in any environment you use for healing sessions. Light your smudge stick and quickly blow it out so it's gently smoking. Pass each of your crystals through the purifying smoke a few times to absorb the cleansing aroma. Waft the smoke anywhere else you want cleansed before putting it out safely.

◇ Using sound can also cleanse crystals. Set out your stones on your altar and chime Tibetan symbols, strike a singing bowl, chant a mantra or drum rhythmically next to them for as long as you wish. This sends healing vibrations washing over them, clearing their energy with the resonance of your voice or the instrument.

◇ If you practise reiki healing, you can hold your crystal in your hands and send this healing energy into them, releasing any negative vibes and clearing their frequency, ready to use again. Similarly, you can visualize them surrounded by light, which will also purify their vibration.

◇ Special crystal-cleansing sprays can also be bought from New Age or crystal shops. One or two drops directly on the gem, or added to an atomizer of water to spray on each stone, should cleanse them effectively.

Charging your crystals with intention

Once your crystals are cleansed, they are ready to be charged with your intention, whether that's to heal others, release past hurts or connect with your higher consciousness. Programming your crystal with what you'd like it to do helps it work better.

First, spend a bit of time sitting with your crystals, tuning into their energy, one by one, simply by holding them in your hands and closing your eyes. You may pick up strong sensations from them, or urges to do something. This is your crystal letting you know what it can do for you to enhance your life or boost your wellbeing. See how this fits with what you want the crystal to help with.

To charge crystals with a desired intention, think for a while about what it is you want your crystal to do. Sit holding your crystal for five to 10 minutes and imagine that thought, intention or goal going deep into the crystal. Ask your crystal to do what is needed for your personal or spiritual growth, or someone else's, and to always work for the highest good for all. Whatever your request from your gems might be, it's always worth adding 'this or something better' so that the path is left up to higher powers and may even surprise you with its brilliance.

Repeat this process every day for two weeks to fully charge your crystal with your intention. In between sessions and when fully charged, you can either place it on your healing altar (see how to make one opposite), meditate further with it, or use it in one of the many healing ways in the next section. You may want to carry it with you, wear it in jewellery or give it to someone to help them. Or it may be part of a crystal healing grid or chakra healing meditation – the healing possibilities are endless. Enjoy trying them all and find which works best for which purpose.

Many crystals love to be charged up under the full moon. This night of maximum lunar light cleanses their energy, but it energizes their purpose and activates their healing qualities even more. Spend the day of the full moon charging your crystals with your intentions, then lay them all out on a pretty cloth for the night.

Preparing a sacred space for healing

Set up a special area to work with your crystals to give the whole process a meaningful, ceremonial feel. Find a space in your home, free from clutter, distractions and technological gadgets, where you will be able to sit calmly and quietly to cleanse, charge, meditate and heal with your gems.

First of all, cleanse the atmosphere of the space by smudging with a smoking sage bundle (as described on page 25). Waft the smoke around the area taking care to hold a dish underneath it to stop lighted ash dropping and starting a fire. If you don't have a sage bundle you can also energy clear with sound by clapping, ringing a bell, banging a gong or twirling some wind chimes. Or you can imagine your sacred altar area filled with white cleansing light.

Next, create a meditation altar to place your crystals on along with other elements for a healing practice such as a seat, soft cushions and blankets. On a low table, a chest of drawers or even an upturned cardboard box, drape a piece of pretty fabric, nothing too busy, and in your favourite colours. On this surface, place your crystals, a pendulum if you have one, some incense, candles or aromatherapy oils, a small, soft brush to clean dust off your gems with, and anything else you want, such as photos, feathers or other trinkets to bring calm, healing vibes to this area. Don't have it too cluttered though!

Special crystals to place on your altar

As well as your starter kit of healing crystals, and any to work on particular chakras or ailments, these gems exude particularly healing atmospheres:

> **Ametrine** has the uplifting and spiritual mixture of amethyst and citrine, bringing both gems' healing vibes to the altar.

> **Peridot** is good for removing emotional blockages as well as space clearing and letting go of anything unwanted in your life.

> **Rainbow fluorite,** with its many colours, elevates different aspects of your life, including good health, heightened intuition, expanded spirituality, increased creativity and calm.

> **Yellow tiger's eye** brings protection and good luck.

If you intend to heal others in your sanctuary, you may need more space to add an upright chair or massage table, or have a clear, clean area on the floor where you or someone else can lie down and receive a crystal healing treatment (see page 40 for methods to heal others). Again, cleanse everything you wish to place in this space so it has a crystal-clear energy. Do the same after every use.

Before healing anyone, including yourself, you need to get really tuned into your crystals. One of the best ways to do this is through meditation. This also develops your spiritual side in a variety of ways, which will help your natural healing abilities expand and improve as well as further enhance your health and wellbeing.

Meditating with crystals

Before using crystals for any healing technique, start your healing journey through meditation. Creating a daily meditation practice brings peace, patience, clarity and relaxation. Add some crystals to that practice and you can develop your spirituality further, heightening your intuition, encouraging telepathy or communing with your higher self, the angelic realm, spirit guides or even your long-dead ancestors. With practice, some crystals can even take you back to see past lives in your mind's eye, or journey to other dimensions by astral travelling. By tuning into crystals' powerful energy in meditation they can enable suppressed emotions to rise to the surface of your awareness to be examined, released and healed, and guide you to solutions to your problems through deeper urges and desires.

Let's start by choosing your favourite crystal or two, the ones you are most attracted to right now, and spend a little time meditating with them.

Meditation is usually done upright, sitting on a chair or kneeling on cushions, whichever is most comfortable. If you can be still enough seated, place an appropriate clear crystal on your crown chakra to connect you to divine consciousness. You could also place your crystals on your meditation altar and gaze at them with eyes gently lowered. A full chakra-cleansing crystal meditation is best done lying down, but that will be explained later. For now, follow the next steps for a simple meditation to connect with your crystals.

◇ Find somewhere quiet where you will not be disturbed and can be comfortable for 10 to 20 minutes or more. Sit upright on a cushion or a chair, or lie down if you'd rather – but try not to fall asleep.

◇ Take each crystal in your hand separately and set an intention for it in this meditation. Visualize the intentions in detail in your mind and imagine this charging up your crystal with purpose to help you.

◇ Position your chosen crystals as you wish. You can continue holding the crystals in your hands, one in cupped hands or one in either or each hand. Your dominant hand, usually the right, is your giving hand, while your non-dominant hand, the left for most people, is your receiving hand. Choose the best for each crystal depending on whether the energy required is being sent to you or you are transmitting it out to the world. Or you can place them on or near the corresponding chakras they clear and strengthen to start exploring how this works.

◇ Feel the gem's energy permeate your body and the space around you. You may want to imagine it is filling your body and aura with light sparkling from the crystal in the same colour. If placed on the chakras, imagine the coloured light cleansing and clearing each one so it is sparkling and bright.

◇ Now, close your eyes and relax. As with all meditation, begin by focusing on your breathing. Allow yourself to take some lovely deep breaths in, and some slow breaths out. Inhale. Exhale.

Allow the energy of the crystal to have an effect – but don't force it or worry if you can't feel it. Just continue relaxing and breathing deeply and see what unfolds. You may get a strong sense to do something new in your life, you might hear messages from beings in other dimensions, or you could even have visions of past-life experiences. Or it may just feel peaceful. Just witness it all, without judgment, knowing you are safe.

When you feel like you've come to the end of your meditation, count down from 10 to one to bring your awareness back into the room. Wriggle your fingers and toes or have a stretch, keeping your eyes closed. Now, imagine your feet are like the roots of a tree going deep into the ground. Your body is strong and rooted to the Earth. Hold this visualization for a few minutes to strongly ground your energy back into the present moment.

When you're ready, move slowly from your position and carry on your day. Have a notebook nearby to note down any experiences you had that resonate, or any questions that may have arisen. You may find yourself having sudden realizations or healing epiphanies about issues in your life.

After working with a crystal for a specific purpose, thank it for its help if you've finished the work or ask it to keep acting on your behalf, either when you use it again for the same purpose, or just while you carry on your day, leaving it on your altar or wherever its energy is needed.

Keep meditating with your favourite crystals and you will gain a stronger sense of purpose. You may connect with a particular spirit guide or angel that will help you. Your dreams may become more vivid, with clear messages or symbolism in them, remembered easily on waking. Your ability to sense what's about to happen or what someone is going to say or do may be stronger. Your connection with others, your creativity and your destiny will become better than they have ever been. All because you took the time to simply be with some of the most powerful life-changing tools on our planet.

MEDITATING WITH CRYSTALS

PART

2

HEALING WITH CRYSTALS

Different ways to heal with crystals

There are many ways of using crystals to heal, from meditating with them on your chakras to putting them on places of aches, pains and ailments. You can absorb crystal energy by carrying one with you all day in a pocket or sleeping with one under your pillow. Creating a healing grid of crystals to sit or lie in the centre of can be beneficial, as can placing them in your home to exude energy into the atmosphere. You can drink water in which crystals have soaked overnight or add gems to your bathwater and soak in their power. The list is endless, and the methods are as gentle as they are powerful.

As well as using this guide, use your intuition to help you choose the right crystal and where to place it. If you or someone else wants help with a physical condition, simply place a small stone, already charged up as described in the previous section, on the area or hold it close to it for as long as you can. Use your mind to amplify its power by imagining its healing energy working its way to the problem or bathing it in healing light that is the colour of the crystal.

Using crystals for diagnosis

Crystals can also be used to diagnose what might be wrong, which area needs more crystals, or whether a problem may have a deeper emotional, spiritual or mental cause that can also be explored.

If you're unsure about where a pain is coming from, you can use a crystal pendulum to scan your body, or someone else's, to get to the root of the problem. Ask the pendulum a series of questions to narrow down a health issue, area of pain or treatment. It can be asked about any aspect of your health and wellbeing, from which foods are best to whether you need a vacation. Remember to ask it questions that need a *yes* or *no* answer. But don't rely too much on your pendulum to make decisions for you. Still use your intuition, wisdom and reason to work out what's best for you, and remember to seek medical attention for any health concerns.

Crystal wands made of selenite or tourmaline are great tools for diagnosis too. Slowly move a wand along the body. You may feel the wand vibrate or pulse, or it may dip down when it reaches an area that needs treating. You can then send healing energy along the wand into the affected area simply by intending it or visualizing it.

Wands can also be used to unwind pain or discomfort in the body. Simply rotate it counter-clockwise to lift away any dis-ease in the problematic or painful area. In the same way, you can use crystals to stimulate points on the feet, just like in reflexology, sending their energy up the meridians in the body. Larimar is great for this, as it goes straight to the place in need of its pressure on the soles of your feet, which relates to an area in your body to be treated.

Getting started: healing yourself

Before you start any healing you may want to ask for support and protection from divine sources such as the angels, God, Goddess, spirit guides or your higher consciousness to work through you for the highest good. Hold your crystal in your hands and place it to your heart, filling it with love and asking that it do what's in the highest interest for you or your patient.

Through meditation, by holding the healing crystal in your hands, you can absorb its powerful energy. While sitting quietly, taking some deep breaths, let out all negative thoughts and feelings as you exhale. As you breathe in, imagine the crystal's positive light filling your whole body. Visualize this energy as a soothing, warm liquid radiating from your heart to fill you up, expanding out into your aura, filling an egg-shaped area 18 inches from your body in all directions. Sit peacefully in your elliptical aura feeling your crystal's energy making you whole and happy.

Once a week, try sitting inside a circle of different coloured crystals laid out on the floor. See each of the rainbow of colours coming into your aura and being absorbed by your body for a full top-up of their energy. Red crystals will energize you, green will nurture you, and orange boosts creativity. Pink will fill you with love, blue helps clear communication, and purple links to higher realms. Afterwards, ground yourself and ask for protection from a black crystal such as jet or obsidian.

Crystal grids

Creating a crystal grid from three or more gems is a powerful way to amplify their healing and protective energy. Don't forget to cleanse and charge them first using any of the previously mentioned methods. Then position your chosen crystals in any geometric pattern such as a circle, square or rectangle.

Sit or lie down, and surround yourself with them to feel the effects on yourself; or position them around a pet's bed, on top of a photograph of someone or something, or on an area of land that needs healing. Make a grid in your home by placing crystals in the corners of a room or the whole house. It can be a good way to protect an area from harmful radiation or other energetic pollution.

Making a triangle-shaped grid works to neutralize negative energy and attract positive vibes. Lying in a five-pointed star shape, using the head, outstretched hands and feet as the five points, works to protect, increase energy and call in love. Any geometric shape can be created with crystals to heighten their energy, and many gems included in this directory are good to use in a crystal grid.

Use a grid of crystals around you to keep you grounded while you undertake a spiritual journey or out-of-body experience to another dimension or to experience past lives. Grid large, smoky elestial quartz or raw labradorite around you as you sit or lie down to guard you from negative energy or unwanted spirits when you travel to other realms.

A grid can be used for a focused-energy healing session, in which case the crystals are then removed and cleansed. Or you can set up a permanent grid, in your home or for distance healing. If you are leaving crystals in place, you will need to cleanse and recharge the stones once a week.

Rose-quartz love grid to strengthen relationships and fill hearts with love

> Make a grid surrounding a central significant stone that is larger than or different from the rest. This love grid uses a large rose-quartz crystal in the middle, and 12 smaller tumbled stones of rose quartz or any other gem associated with love or attraction, or clear quartz to amplify a particular energy (see the A–Z for details).

> Set up this grid on a table or your meditation altar, or in the far right-hand corner of your bedroom, which is associated with love in feng shui.

> Arrange the smaller stones in an infinity symbol, symbolizing everlasting love. It should look like a sideways figure of eight, with six gems looping round on one side of the large central crystal and six on the other side.

> Spend some time tracing the figure of eight with your finger or a crystal wand and thinking of the love this grid will bring into your life. Imagine your and another's hearts expanding with affection and compassion. See loving events playing out in your mind's eye. Feel how wonderful this will feel in your whole body.

> Leave this love grid set up as long as you need to, cleansing, charging and setting it up again weekly if necessary.

Clearing and activating the chakras

A classic chakra healing with crystals involves lying down comfortably on your back for between 10 and 30 minutes with some crystals placed on your body, clothed and under a blanket if you need extra warmth.

Consult the chakras section of this book, or use the A-Z to note which crystals connect with the energy centres along your spine. The lower chakras are more about physical and emotional aspects of our lives, while the upper ones relate more to spiritual expansion. For example, clear crystals such as quartz or selenite activate the crown chakra, opening you up to higher consciousness, the angelic realm and spirit guides. Purple or indigo gems such as amethyst, ametrine and fluorite work on the third eye chakra, which stimulates your connection to your inner self and intuition, and brings your innate psychic skills to the fore. Red and brown gems work on the root chakra, to ground you to the Earth and keep you safe. You need a crystal for each chakra for this healing session. If you enjoy it, you can do it once a week if you like.

Place the different coloured crystals on top of or next to their corresponding chakras. You may want to place a red or brown gem on the floor just below the root chakra, and a clear or violet crystal just above the top of the head, also on the ground. Leave the gems for as long as you wish - half an hour is ideal - for them to cleanse, balance and energize your entire mind, body and spirit as you rest, focusing only on your breathing.

You may see in your mind's eye or imagine the different colours of the crystals pouring their bright, sparkling energy into your chakras, releasing blocks, clearing their energy and helping them spin smoothly and quickly in a counter-clockwise direction. You may feel your vibration raising, and you may hear, see or sense messages from spirit or guidance from your soul. Or you may drop off to sleep. Whatever happens, the crystals will be working their magic, and you are safe.

When finished, remove the stones carefully and hold a black crystal such as obsidian, jet or black tourmaline to ground your energy for a few minutes. Have a drink of water to refresh, and note how the treatment made you feel and any messages or urges you received.

If you want to intensify a particular chakra's treatment, you can position four quartz points around the coloured gem on a chakra to magnify its energy. You may want to do this if you know a certain chakra is very blocked or stagnant, if you are having related physical or emotional symptoms, as this will get its energy spinning clearly once again.

Healing using the minerals in crystals

Some crystals contain minerals widely known to help balance and benefit the body. Malachite, for example, contains copper, which is used to reduce inflammation and prevent swelling. Others contain iron, magnesium and calcium. To absorb traces of minerals from crystals, they can be worn on the body, carried with you in a pouch or in your pocket, or drunk as an elixir unless indicated otherwise. Malachite, again, is toxic when ingested, as are a few others; check the A–Z.

Always make sure the crystal you want to use is safe for drinking, as some are not suitable, may be toxic, or will dissolve in water. Some have trace minerals that are beneficial in small doses, but care needs to be taken when ingesting them. See the full crystal A–Z for details.

Many crystals can be made into an elixir or gem essence by simply soaking the stone in water overnight (see details opposite). You can then either drink the crystal water for a full-body healing or, depending on the gem, use it topically to treat certain skin conditions. For example, an amber elixir can be used both ways: drunk to relieve constipation or applied to cuts and grazes as an antiseptic. A foot soak of warmed marcasite elixir can soften corns, while drinking aragonite essence can soothe achy muscles. Drinking essence of shattuckite is a beneficial tonic for the body, helping combat many minor illnesses.

You can also drink an infusion of a crystal to imbibe its qualities, such as rose-quartz essence to encourage unconditional love, or a shungite elixir for protection from EMFs from mobile phones and computers.

Alternatively, bathe in any gem essence to soak in their vibes. Just add the crystal elixir, or a few small stones, to your bathwater and relax as you imbibe the minerals or energy described in the A–Z for each crystal. Again, make sure it is safe to do so before you soak in a crystal's essence.

MAKING CRYSTAL ELIXIRS

◇ Choose the piece of crystal you want to use that is safe and suitable to be immersed in water.

◇ Cleanse it using the method suitable for that gem (see page 25), making sure dust is removed with running water or by brushing it off.

◇ Charge the crystal with the intention you have for it, to allow that energy to filter out into the water.

◇ Place the stone in a glass container or bottle and fill it with water; pure mineral or distilled water is best, but filtered tap water is fine.

◇ Put a lid on the receptacle and leave it overnight, either in the refrigerator or, according to ancient Celtic tradition, from sunset to sunset on the night of a full moon. Charging the elixir by the light of the full moon adds extra power.

◇ While this process is happening, focus your intention on what you want the gem essence to heal or help with.

◇ After 24 hours, the crystal elixir is ready to be used, as required, over the next 24 hours.

MAKING AN ELIXIR USING THE INDIRECT METHOD

Crystals such as malachite or sulphur that are toxic to ingest or will completely dissolve in water must not be made into elixirs. But they can still be made into a gem essence using what's called the *indirect method*. This is where you place a stone in a glass container and then stand the container in another container of spring water so the stone does not touch the water but picks up its vibrations through the glass.

See each crystal's entry to find out whether it can be made into an elixir.

Elixir experiment

See if you can tell the difference between different types of crystal elixirs in taste and effect on your energy and wellbeing.

> Take three glasses of water and place a different crystal in each one overnight.

> Use a plain glass of water as a control, then sip from the three other glasses to see if, for example, the quartz elixir tastes fresher than the regular water, or an amethyst essence tastes more metallic.

> Do certain crystal waters quench your thirst quicker? Or make you feel calmer or more energized?

Healing others

You can use any of the above methods to heal others, near and far. Contact healing is when the person being healed is present. It doesn't mean you make contact with the crystal and their body; usually the gem is held a few centimetres from the body, always fully clothed; or the crystal can be placed on their clothed body at the chakra points.

This simple crystal healing process for other people or pets is similar to reiki healing, but crystals amplify and direct the energy.

◇ Start by asking any guides or angels to assist with this healing. Take a few deep breaths and tune into your patient's energy.

◇ Use your intuition to choose the right crystals for them.

◇ Sense the energy of the crystal regarding where it wants to be positioned and for how long.

◇ You may want to hold it in a certain area or move it gently and continuously over your patient.

◇ Visualize the crystal's colour and energy radiating into your patient, filling them with light and healing what needs to be healed.

◇ When you are done, say a few words of thanks to your higher power and the crystal for its work.

◇ Remember to cleanse it well after every healing session, as it is likely to have absorbed energy.

Distance healing

You can also use crystals to send healing energy from a distance to people, groups or animals, as well as to oceans, the Earth or areas of the world that need help. Choose green or brown crystals, such as moss agate or jade, to heal the land or forests and the creatures that dwell there. Blue gems, including aquamarine or blue coral, work wonders on the waters of the world and the fish that swim in them. Tiger's eye or leopard-skin jasper help endangered species stay healthy and strong. Or choose a crystal intuitively to send the best energy to the person or people you want to help.

◈ Hold a crystal in your hands.

◈ Focus on filling the stone with prayers and intentions to heal whatever you've chosen to help. Visualize the person, people, animal or place you are going to send the healing energy to, in a neutral way.

◈ Say your wish for their health and wellbeing out loud, repeatedly, into the crystal, or chant a healing mantra for it to absorb.

◈ Inhale deeply and imagine the light from the crystal filling you up. Exhale any darkness. Continue to breathe in light until you are full of sparkling, positive, healing energy.

◈ Now, send this healing light to your chosen subject as you breathe out, still saying the healing prayer or mantra in your mind.

◈ Visualize the healing taking place, and the person, pet or area shining with health and vitality. Do this for as long as you wish, up to half an hour.

◈ You could also place the charged crystal on a photo of the absent friend, animal or place to be healed and leave it there for as long as you want it to work its magic.

Crystal rituals and remedies to heal common physical ailments

In each crystal entry in the A-Z there is a full description of all the physical issues and ailments each gem can help with, along with how to use them. But here are a few common problems and simple crystal remedies.

Don't forget, all health issues need to be talked through with a medical professional. These remedies are only intended to be supplementary to conventional medicine, not instead of.

Acne
An elixir of amber can be applied topically to the affected area. Or any of the following crystals can be worn daily or held next to the worst spots: amethyst, amber, angel wing or clear selenite, blue smithsonite, jade or white topaz.

Backache
Put selenite under the mattress at night or lie on your stomach for half an hour with a piece of selenite placed wherever the discomfort is on your spine.

Colds
Carry or wear blue moss agate, carnelian, fluorite, jet, rose quartz or topaz. Lithium quartz also helps.

Constipation
Drink an elixir of amber. Hold lepidolite, moonstone or ruby to the abdomen until it has an effect. If chronic, carry these gems with you daily or wear all the time.

Earache
Use a quartz crystal wand and rotate slowly in clockwise circles near the entrance to the ear.

Exhaustion
Brown aragonite, tanzanite, vanadinite or yellow quartz can be held, worn or carried in a pocket.

Headaches
Depending on the cause, different crystals will help. A double-terminated quartz on the crown chakra can alleviate symptoms, as can holding an amethyst, elestial quartz, peach aventurine, scenic quartz or sugilite on the place where the pain is worst.

Insomnia
Hold a piece of smooth, tumbled malachite in your hand an hour before you want to go to sleep, while cleaning your teeth and getting ready for bed. This should improve your sleep from the first night, and certainly see it go back to a normal pattern within two weeks.

Pregnancy
For any uncomfortable symptoms carry or wear chrysocolla, Kambamba stone, unakite or white moonstone. Chrysocolla also assists in the healthy development of the baby.

Toothache
Amethyst, aquamarine, Blue John fluorite, dolomite, howlite and magnesite can help with teeth problems by wearing, carrying or holding to the skin next to any pain.

Crystal rituals and remedies to heal common emotional issues

Crystals are especially good at assisting with emotional and mental issues, as they can help you get to the root of a problem. Many enable you to fully experience feelings - even long-suppressed - so you are able to release the hold they have on you and heal. In the A-Z, you will find more details, but here are a few common issues and treatments. Remember to talk to your doctor about any serious emotional or mental health concerns.

Anger

If not fully felt at the time, anger can get stuck in our bodies and turn into resentment. It needs to be felt and then released for us to move on with our lives. Hold a piece of carnelian in your hand to calm and ground you while any anger in your system rises to be fully experienced until it dissipates. Snowflake obsidian also allows for a quick release of anger.

Anxiety

This emotion connects to the root chakra and it comes out of fears about your security or safety. So red or brown gems, such as garnet or jaspers, can help alleviate everything from extreme phobias and obsessions to social anxiety or niggling everyday worries. Sit quietly, holding any root chakra-connected crystal, and imagine its colour brightening and supporting the root area. Light blue or green gems can also calm stressful experiences. Try holding, or carrying in a pocket, green aventurine, blue apatite, Preseli bluestone, blue or green quartz or blue lace agate to quell anxieties about going for a job interview or catching a train, for example.

Depression

Many crystals are said to help lift depression, including aqua aura, blue sapphire, bowenite, jet, kunzite, lapis lazuli, lepidolite, lithium quartz, malachite, quartz, tiger's eye and zircon. Just spending some time with them in a meditative state will have positive benefits on your mood. When worn as jewellery or carried daily, amber, in particular, can elevate your mood, while smoky quartz will absorb negative feelings and replace them with more upbeat emotions. These stones will need cleansing daily.

Grief

Carry a piece of black obsidian in a pocket to absorb this powerful emotion. Amethyst, Apache tears, black onyx, rose quartz, smoky quartz and spirit quartz can all help ease the pain. Sit holding one of these gems in your non-dominant (receiving) hand and say, 'I take comfort from the divine / God / Source during this time of grief.' Allow feelings to flow naturally until they subside. Do this as often as you need to to fully feel grief and let it flow through you, however painful, rather than stagnate into depression.

Trauma

Emotional or physical trauma can be hard to get over and often takes a multifaceted approach. While healing, send yourself unconditional love by lying on your back for 10 to 20 minutes with a piece of rose quartz on your heart chakra. Allow its gentle, pink, loving energy to fill your heart with peace. Carrying a piece of black tourmaline in a pocket at all times can take away many of the negative feelings of post-traumatic stress disorders. Cleanse these crystals regularly.

Loneliness

Lack of self-worth can be at the root of loneliness, an area covered by the solar plexus chakra. Sit in meditation holding a piece of tiger's eye to this area for 10 minutes or more. The rose-quartz infinity grid on page 36 can be made with some clear quartz gems as well, to amplify its energy to attract love and supportive friendships. Carry a piece of rutilated or snowflake quartz, jasper, mookaite, or uvarovite placed in a pocket to ease lonely feelings.

Mood swings

Whether due to hormonal changes or stress, erratic moods can be intense and destabilizing. Wearing a piece of sodalite in a necklace every day helps balance the thyroid and parathyroid in charge of hormones. Smoky quartz also keeps emotions on an even keel, especially if placed in a pocket near the sacral chakra every day. When you feel your mood changing, use the (ideally smooth) crystal as a touchstone to centre the mind on the present moment.

Negative thinking

Carry a piece of black tourmaline in a pocket to absorb negative energy from a constant train of unhelpful thoughts, and work with smoky quartz often to stop this harmful pattern of thinking. Both gems also soak up others' negative vibes directed towards you.

Healing home life with crystals

Choose the right crystals for certain areas of your home and they will help protect you from harm, bring peace or energize, as needed. Cleansed before use, programmed with conscious attention and positioned in the right place, they can help with countless areas of your life. Blue lace agate is said to calm children, while a large piece of selenite in a house can generate a peaceful, positive atmosphere to smooth relationships. Other gems encourage better organization, cooperation among groups, calmer pets and stronger, healthier plants and crops in your allotment.

Crystals can also help our health by protecting us from the harmful effects of EMFs and increased radiation from modern technology, which many people are sensitive to. Placing shungite, black tourmaline or smoky quartz between you and your device, or sticking pieces to your mobile phone, can soak up any potentially damaging energy.

Certain gems also work their magic according to *feng shui*, the ancient Chinese art of energy flow in the home. With this, your house or room is divided into different sections that reflect various areas of your life. For example, the left corner of your room is the career and wealth area, so you want gems such as citrine and jade here, creating dynamic and successful energy, workwise.

However you want to use crystals in your home, choose intuitively, keep them cleansed and ask them to work for you in the areas where they are needed most. Touch them every time you walk past. Pick them up often - whenever you're in need of a boost or some balance, calm or energy. Make them part of your life to receive maximum benefits from their powerful blessings.

HOUSEHOLD PROBLEM, CRYSTAL SOLUTION

For most household problems, there's crystal that can help.

Messy, chaotic house
Fluorite organizes inside and out to bring harmony and structure to your daily life and help clear your clutter.

Arguments
Blue lace agate on your coffee table or dining table eases conversations and stops anyone saying anything they might later regret. Or place a large piece of amber in your living space to guard against conflict, transform negative vibes into positive, and dispel sadness or anxiety.

Noisy neighbours
Put rose quartz next to the wall between you and your annoying neighbours to calm their shouting and push peace in their direction.

Hyperactive children or pets
Purple fluorite helps dogs behave better when out and about, and helps children calm down, while moss agate balances both when placed in their bed.

Unhelpful teenagers
Place amazonite in their bedroom to help them get out of bed at a reasonable time and live a healthier lifestyle. Ametrine will do the same, plus keep teens out of trouble.

Alleviating nightmares
A piece of jet in the room, or held to soothe someone before bed, quashes bad dreams.

Dying plants
If your pot plants are affected by central heating and look like they're wilting, place moss agate crystals in the soil. Fluorite can mend damaged plants; pass it over the affected area, then bury the stone in the pot.

Technology making you lethargic or ill
If you're affected by EMFs, wear shungite or schorl (black tourmaline) or stick a disc of either to the back of your mobile phone. You can also create a special grid of protection with shungite, black tourmaline or smoky quartz by placing small pieces of them in the corner of each room in your home to transform negative energies. Try joining the crystals up in your mind or using a quartz wand to protect your entire home.

KEY CRYSTALS FOR EACH AREA OF YOUR HOME

At the front door
This is a key place to put crystals to keep away unwanted visitors and attract good vibes only. To protect the whole home from harmful energies, place smoky quartz, black tourmaline or jet in the doorway. To attract only good vibes, place carnelian just inside the front door; if it's abundance you're after, use citrine.

Living room
A large piece of rose quartz or jade in your living space will bring love and harmony throughout the home. Place a wand of selenite on the coffee table to fill the place with positive light. Tiger's eye placed in a prominent position will help bring harmony to turbulent family relationships. Labradorite will inject some fun into your home if you've been stuck in a rut.

Dining room
Amber or carnelian on the dining table will help stimulate healthy appetites. Citrine in the centre of the room is said to keep conversation positive while you eat, as well as assisting with digestion. Orange calcite here will create lively debate but keep it upbeat and respectful.

Kitchen
To stimulate creative, confident cooking with ease, choose carnelian for the kitchen surface. Red jasper is also energizing, and will wake you up in the morning as you make your breakfast.

Bedroom
For a deep sleep, place a small, smooth stone of amethyst or moonstone under your pillow or bed. Or put a piece of rose quartz on your bedside table. Alternatively, soak an amethyst in water overnight and drink before bedtime.

To improve your love life, turquoise balances the sexes and stimulates romantic love. If you want to attract creativity and calm, along with strength and alertness, place a piece of turquoise on both sides of the bed.

Office
To combat stress, a black obsidian sphere or dish of smaller tumbled stones will rebalance your workload. To enhance creativity, place clear quartz or celestite on your desk, but balance it with lapis lazuli so you don't work too late. Citrine in your wallet, on your financial documents and in the career area (far left corner from the door) will attract success, as will turquoise used in the same way.

Bathroom
Keep a dish of your favourite crystals here to add to bathwater. Jade will restore your tired body, and rose quartz soothes frayed nerves. Clear quartz added to your bath will energize, and turquoise will bring inspired ideas while you soak.

Garden
Green aventurine helps roots fill with energy and boosts plant growth, as does moss agate planted with your crops. Charge a clear quartz with your intention to grow a beautiful garden, or as a reminder to water your plants regularly, and place the crystal in your outside space to work its magic.

Divining with crystals

According to the written history of early Mesopotamia, using crystals for guidance goes back at least 5,500 years - possibly further, if ancient graves are anything to go by. Prehistoric people have been found buried with pouches of gems, crystal balls and polished crystal mirrors used for scrying, while the ancient Greeks would use agate or jet to determine who was guilty of a crime.

You can use crystal spheres, pendulums or a bag of smaller stones to help you divine what the future has in store so you can prepare, plan and even raise your vibration to match - or deflect, as the case may be.

◈ Cleanse your divination crystals before use.

◈ Whichever method you choose, first make sure to clear your mind of worries or expectations. You need to be able to focus fully on what comes through in the present moment and what your intuition is telling you. Tune into your guides or a higher power for assistance if you wish.

◈ Take the time to carefully formulate the question you want to ask. Keep it as simple as possible and as close as possible to the core of what you want to know.

◈ Hold your crystals and connect with their energy. Allow them to harmonize with your energy so you can work together to get the best guidance. Ask them to show you the truth of the matter, clearly and with a timescale if necessary.

◈ Keep an open mind about the answer. Everything is possible. It might not be what it seems initially. Note down whatever comes to mind or is suggested by the crystal so you can look back later and see if, on reflection, it makes more sense or is linked to what actually happened.

◈ Take time to process your new realizations or answers so you can make the right decision going forward.

Scrying with crystal balls

Crystal balls have long been seen as tools of personal wisdom, enabling sensitives to see into the future and make sense of the past. Scrying in crystal balls grew especially popular in 15th-century Europe, when people believed they could see angels or spirits in them to help divine the future. The most famous insight was that of Queen Elizabeth I's astrologer Dr John Dee, who warned her of the Spanish Armada invasion after looking into an obsidian ball.

Whatever stone they are made from, crystal spheres connect with the crown chakra and activate our psychic and clairvoyant powers, enabling us to access the akashic records, where everything from the past, present and future is recorded.

HOW TO READ A CRYSTAL SPHERE

◇ First relax, ideally by candlelight, or using the light of the sun or moon to reflect into your crystal ball as you hold it.

◇ Allow your energies to harmonize.

◇ Ask the question you would like an answer to.

◇ Now, sense any feelings or impressions, see images or words that come to mind initially. Don't worry if at first you get nothing.

◇ Next, place your ball down on a silk or velvet cloth.

◇ Gently soften your gaze and look at your crystal sphere. It may appear to cloud over, but keep looking gently until any images appear inside the ball or in your mind. The different images may have significant meanings, or together they may make a story that serves as an answer to your question.

◇ When you've finished, disconnect from the ball's energy and ground yourself in the present moment by taking a few deep breaths. Cover the sphere with a cloth when not in use.

◇ Make a note of what you saw and what you think it may represent. What feelings or thoughts arise? The insights you gain may be subtly guiding you in the right direction.

◇ You can also do a similar reading with three smaller spheres. Hold them one at a time to examining past, present and future. For hidden insights into your past, or glimpses of former lives, look into an amethyst, rose quartz or calcite ball. Then, to give guidance on the present connected to the past just seen, choose a sphere made of citrine or clear quartz. Finally, look into a beryl or smoky quartz crystal ball to see future opportunities or potential.

Which crystal for which zodiac sign?

Each astrological sign has a few crystals that work best with it because they emanate a similar energy or one that gives your astro personality a boost. Choose gifts for yourself, family and friends from the appropriate gems to boost your astrological traits. Wear them as jewellery or place them in prominent positions in your home to let their planetary influence fill your rooms.

ARIES
21 March - 20 April
Aventurine, Apache tears, bloodstone, diamond, hematite, jasper, pyrite.

TAURUS
21 April - 21 May
Chrysanthemum stone, desert rose selenite, emerald, rose quartz, rhodonite, indicolite quartz, peridot.

GEMINI
22 May - 21 June
Ametrine, citrine, epidote, green aventurine, howlite, lazulite, Preseli bluestone.

CANCER
22 June - 22 July
Menalite, moonstone, pearl, ruby, selenite, shungite, sodalite.

LEO
23 July - 23 August
Amber, carnelian, citrine, clear quartz, fire opal, tiger's eye, topaz.

VIRGO
24 August - 22 September
Amazonite, blue sapphire, limonite, moss agate, smithsonite, sugilite, yellow aragonite.

LIBRA
23 September - 23 October
Ametrine, blue quartz, celestite, citrine, lapis lazuli, opal, rose quartz.

SCORPIO
24 October - 22 November
Apache tears, black obsidian, flint, Himalayan diamond, coral, labradorite, malachite.

SAGITTARIUS
23 November - 21 December
Azurite, dioptase, iolite, labradorite, ruby, rhodochrosite, turquoise.

CAPRICORN
22 December - 20 January
Aragonite, black onyx, garnet, jet, smoky quartz, tiger's eye, tourmaline.

AQUARIUS
21 January - 18 February
Amethyst, angelite, blue lace agate, bowenite, fuchsite, moldavite, sugilite.

PISCES
19 February - 20 March
Aquamarine, beryl, blue lace agate, blue jasper, jade, kyanite, fluorite.

Final thoughts

As you can see, there are many wonderful ways to use crystals to heal your life - not just by treating the body and mind, but by using them to expand your spirituality, heal your home and even take a peek into a hopefully healthy, joyful and fulfilling future. Using them in service to others adds to this fulfilment, helping friends and family, healing your pets and sending positive vibes across the planet. You can work with as many or as few as you wish, tuning into them whenever you feel the need. In time, they will become your go-to tools for positive transformation and will enhance your life in ways you hadn't even imagined when you first began this healing journey with crystals.

PART
3

A–Z OF CRYSTALS FOR HEALING

Agate

TYPE OF CRYSTAL Agate is a soft and waxy type of chalcedony formed from microscopic pieces of quartz in the United States, Brazil, India, Africa and the Czech Republic. Clear or milky-white agate is often banded with other colours, or sometimes patterned, and comes in different shapes including rough or polished stones, smooth rounded gems and polished slices. Many commercial agates may be dyed to enhance their colour, although this gives them no additional healing properties.

CHAKRA CONNECTION Depends on the colour (see individual agates below)

ASTRO AFFILIATION Depends on type (see following entries)

HEALING by bringing balance

Mind Agate improves focus, concentration and analytical skills, highlighting hidden details, all of which leads to good problem-solving. Slowly but steadily, agate brings about self-acceptance, increases confidence and encourages speaking your truth. It releases resentment and bitterness towards others. Agates are grounding stones, encouraging intellectual, emotional and physical balance, as well as a sense of safety and calm after trauma. Memories may be stimulated with this crystal, which heals any anger connected to them and gives you the courage to carry on.

Body Agate draws your attention to issues getting in the way of your wellbeing. It has a powerful cleansing effect, clearing up digestive issues and eyesight problems. The gem assists colon and pancreas functions and eases symptoms of gastroenteritis, irritable bowel syndrome and stomach pain. It boosts the lymphatic and circulation systems and strengthens blood vessels, calming varicose veins and other skin disorders. The pancreas and uterus are also supported by agates.

Spirit This stone stabilizes sexual energy and helps bring faithfulness and emotional security to relationships. Used for quiet contemplation, its many layers can reveal formerly unknown information and buried memories, bringing to light anything upsetting your overall wellbeing. Agate strengthens the aura, cleaning out any unwanted negative energies from your energetic field. It enhances your protection and helps with channelling and further spiritual development. Agate raises your consciousness and tunes you into the collective one-ness of all life.

How to use Wear it close to the body, as jewellery or in a pocket. Hold in either hand in meditation or place on the appropriate chakra (depending on type). Place on the abdomen while lying down in meditation to stimulate digestion and relieve tummy troubles. Place pink agate, in particular, on the heart centre to allow love into your life and promote affection between parent and child. Place green agate between those in a dispute, or carry or wear it to a discussion, to bring about resolution.

Agate - banded, pink or grey

TYPE OF CRYSTAL Also called Botswana Agate, as that's where it is commonly found, this type of agate has clearly defined bands alternating white with grey or pink. It is also obtained from South Africa, Morocco, the Czech Republic, Brazil and the US.

CHAKRA CONNECTION Sacral, heart, third eye, crown

ASTRO AFFILIATION Taurus, Scorpio

HEALING by seeing both sides to a story

Mind A mind-stimulating stone, banded agates, especially pink, help lift malaise, depression and stress. These crystals enable you to see the broader perspective of problems as well as focus on relevant details, helping you find wise and creative solutions and not get caught up in repetitive, destructive or obsessive thoughts. Banded agates help resolve conflict with others and block toxic emotions coming your way, increasing mental and emotional wellbeing.

Body Traditionally, this agate has been used to detox and heal from physical, mental or emotional poisoning or toxicity, as it absorbs negative energies. It eliminates fatigue and supports the nervous system, so it can be beneficial to those suffering from ME or post-viral exhaustion. It supports the healthy expression of sexuality and natural sensuality, and boosts fertility. The skin, chest and brain, as well as the circulation and nervous systems, benefit from treatments with this crystal. It also assists anyone wanting to stop smoking.

Spirit This nurturing stone brings universal love, heightens femininity and inspires creative endeavours. It activates the crown chakra, bringing higher consciousness down into the physical realm. Gazing into its bands during meditation can take you into past lives or other realities for multi-dimensional, deep soul healing. On your third eye, it cuts any mental cords to anyone who ever had authority over you, such as a guru, teacher or parent, bringing that power back to you. A banded agate gem can be programmed to protect you and your family from the unwanted energies of others - in this life or in the spirit world - and encourage supportive, non-smothering love.

How to use Hold on the appropriate chakra or area of the body. Meditate while holding or sitting in front of and gazing into the bands. Place on third eye to cut cords to people. Use in a healing grid (see page 35 on how to make one). Can cause dizziness; remove if so.

Agate - blue lace

TYPE OF CRYSTAL A light blue and white banded variety of agate from South Africa, Brazil and Australia.

CHAKRA CONNECTION Throat and third eye

ASTRO AFFILIATION Pisces

HEALING communication

Mind Blue lace agate encourages clear thinking and calm, honest communication of your innermost thoughts and deepest feelings, removing the self-judgment that can often come from parental control in childhood. It balances fluctuating emotions, enabling you to express them in healthy ways and feel at peace again. Neutralizing angry thoughts and words, it can even sort out stammers and help public speaking go smoothly.

Body Blue lace agate is great for sore throats and assists with any issues connected to the voice, neck and shoulder areas, plus thyroid and lymph problems. Particularly good for improving eyesight, an elixir (see how to make this on page 39) of this gem soothes and cools tired eyes, and is said to treat brain-fluid imbalances and hydrocephalus. This stone is also believed to ease arthritis pain and release fluid retention. It supports the healing of broken bones and fractures, trapped nerves, issues with capillaries and skin growths. Blue lace agate also lessens inflammation, infection and fever, as well as boosting the healthy functioning of the pancreas. In sound-healing sessions, it can direct sound to the place on the body that's in need of healing.

Spirit Nurturing and supportive, this gentle gem encourages tranquillity and raises your vibration by connecting you to communication from the spiritual realms. This enables expression of deeper insights and inspiration from higher dimensions. Blue lace agate unblocks the throat chakra, releasing habitual patterns of repressing feelings, such as anger or jealousy, for fear of being judged or abandoned. Let blue lace agate dissolve these old ways of being, which may have left you feeling emotionally suffocated, so you can fully share your true authentic self. It is especially good for helping men tap into their sensitive sides.

How to use Place on the throat or third eye area when lying down in meditation to clear these chakras. In seated meditation, hold a piece of blue lace agate in your receiving (non-dominant) hand to bring about calm, or in your giving (dominant) hand if you need to communicate with gentle honesty and respectful truth. To calm nerves and help with public speaking, carry in your pocket, or wear in a necklace, as close to the throat as possible, or in earrings, or place on the lectern from which you are about to speak.

Agate - fire

TYPE OF CRYSTAL Fire agate is a fairly rare orange or brownish-red swirling and pearlescent stone found in the United States, India, Brazil, Iceland, Morocco and the Czech Republic. Its flashes of 'fire' are caused by the thin layers of limonite within it.

CHAKRA CONNECTION Root chakra

ASTRO AFFILIATION Aries

HEALING security issues

Mind Fire agate gets rid of any fears you may have about your safety, reassuring you that all is well, even in troubled times. Hold a piece of fire agate in your hands to encourage deep introspection and the chance for any inner issues to come to awareness for healing. This crystal can combat cravings and help release you from the hold of addictions and destructive tendencies.

Body With a strong connection to the Earth, this agate has powerful grounding qualities to bring security and support in troubled times. It is good for restoring your zest for life, especially after energy burnout, plus it renews sexual fire and appetite. Fire agate is also thought to reduce the hot flushes of menopausal women and take away heat from the body, such as with sunburn or fever. It helps with stomach problems and heals the nervous, endocrine and circulatory systems. This agate also assists the eyes, improving sight and night vision.

Spirit Fire agate creates a protective shield around the body, which sends harmful intentions back to their source and clears blockages in your auric field. This earthy stone aids relaxation, bringing the body into a state of calm for deeper and more transformative meditations. This helps with development of the consciousness. As well as assisting with the physical eyes, it helps increase your inner vision and intuition.

How to use You can wear fire agate for longer periods than other crystals - in jewellery, for example. Place on the body wherever you need healing, while lying down, or position next to the root chakra to stimulate overall energy levels.

Agate - moss

TYPE OF CRYSTAL This translucent mossy green or blue stone ranges from light to dark green, as well as blue, red or yellow, with white, grey, brown or black flecks and branching patterning like moss. Found in India, Australia and the United States, it is generally sold as small tumbled stones.

CHAKRA CONNECTION Heart (green moss agate), throat (blue moss agate)

ASTRO AFFILIATION Virgo

HEALING connection with nature

Mind Moss agate can alleviate depression by helping you appreciate nature and see beauty everywhere, releasing stress and fear, and giving you renewed hope, trust and optimism. It helps you understand the reason behind difficulties you may have and inspires new ideas to help move forward. This stone enables intellectuals to access their intuitive side, and encourage sensitives to practically channel their energy into a project. As with all agates, it brings balance to emotions and improves communication and self-expression.

Body This stone can quicken recovery time and improve the prognosis for long-term illnesses. It's a good gem for midwives to work with, as it is believed to bring about a smooth delivery and diminish pain. Moss agate lessens sensitivities to weather and other environmental issues you may be affected by. Drinking a gem essence of this agate assists a detox by boosting circulation, encouraging good lymphatic movement and eliminating toxins. It treats colds and flus by giving the immune system a nudge and taking down a high temperature. It also reduces inflammation and helps you rehydrate. Applied as an elixir, it can soothe skin issues, such as fungal infections.

Spirit Moss agate supports new beginnings of any kind and attracts love and prosperity by connecting you to the abundant flow of nature. It improves self-esteem and activates your positive personality characteristics, helping you get along better with other people. The stone encourages spiritual growth and promotes giving something another try if you've felt unmotivated for a while.

How to use Place on the heart when lying down in meditation, or hold in either hand when seated. Position a piece of moss agate on or touching the affected area of the body. If you're gardening, carry a piece of moss agate in a pocket to improve your green-fingered abilities, and place around plants to improve their growth.

Agate - tree

TYPE OF CRYSTAL Also known as dendritic agate, this stone is transparent, brown or green with fern-like markings similar to tiny trees. It is found in the United States, Brazil, Morocco, the Czech Republic, Iceland and India, and sold in small shaped and polished pieces.

CHAKRA CONNECTION Heart

ASTRO AFFILIATION Taurus

HEALING by attracting abundance

Mind This gem enriches your connection with the Earth and the true abundance of nature. Holding it helps you be more present in the moment rather than in your head. It makes you stay calm, centred and stable in times of turbulence, and shows you the higher perspective to overcome problems by seeing them as character-building challenges that you have the strength and perseverance to get though. It is a stone to use for the long term, as its effects can take time.

Body Chakra imbalances can be rectified with tree agate, helping alleviate subtle symptoms of disease. It can also help align the skeleton and bring pain relief if placed on the affected area of the body. With its fern-like tendrils, tree agate's energy resonates with any bodily systems that branch,

including the nerves and blood vessels. It can give circulation a boost and soothe the nervous system, even clearing up conditions such as neuralgia and capillary deterioration. It activates the immune system and thymus gland function, especially when taped overnight on the chest area in front of the heart, where this gland sits.

Spirit Tree agate encourages a peaceful environment, both external and internal. It can help you enjoy the magic of every moment. Like a tree, this agate enables you to stay connected with your roots as you develop and raise your consciousness. It also helps open and align the chakras, connecting you with the higher realms for further spiritual expansion, protecting you from negativity both in yourself and from others. With its strong connection to nature, it

also encourages communicating with plants and trees, helping you attune to what they need to thrive or want to share with you.

How to use Place in plant pots to boost the health of houseplants, or sow along with fruit and vegetable crops outdoors to increase yield. Position or hold on the injured or blocked area of the body or chakra system. Wear as jewellery for a long while to get best results over time.

Alexandrite

TYPE OF CRYSTAL Gritty green chrysoberyl, which shines red under some lights, is found rarely, in small masses and sometimes crystals, in the US, Brazil, China, Russia, Ireland and parts of northern Europe.

CHAKRA CONNECTION Heart

ASTRO AFFILIATION Scorpio

HEALING by seeing both sides

Mind Alexandrite marries the head and the heart, so you can be rational and intuitive at the same time, thoroughly assessing your own and others' emotions. The way this stone looks as if it is two colours at the same time reflects its ability to help you see both sides to a story so you can glean a more informed and illuminated perspective. This stone rebuilds confidence and self-esteem by helping you realign with who you are deep inside. It grants willpower to anyone who wears it.

Body Used as a purifier, this stone supports longevity and youthfulness, helping combat dementia, Alzheimer's and Parkinson's disease. It's good for lessening the side effects of leukaemia and boosting the overall health of the glandular and nervous systems. Alexandrite can soothe inflammation as well as relieve tension in the neck. It also supports the pancreas, spleen, liver and male reproductive organs.

Spirit This unusual crystal encourages dreaming, fires up the imagination and inspires creativity. It can help you access your past lives and other esoteric knowledge through meditation. It will attune you to your inner voice to bring about a blissful inner transformation that could lead to good fortune.

How to use Hold or place on or next to the relevant area, or use in a healing grid (see page 35 for how to create one). Worn over the heart, it is said to bring luck in love and grace to the wearer.

Warning: Alexandrite contains aluminium, so do not make into an elixir to drink.

Amazonite

TYPE OF CRYSTAL Also sometimes called Amazon jade or Amazon stone, amazonite is a usually opaque, blue-green/ light turquoise type of microcline, a variety of feldspar. Its colour comes from copper or lead, but its mineral makeup is considered stable and not toxic. It is found in masses in Russia, Canada, the US, Brazil, India, Austria, Namibia, Zimbabwe and Mozambique. It often has veins of white or gold, along with an opalescent lustre, and can be bought in various sizes, sometimes tumbled.

CHAKRA CONNECTION Heart, throat and third eye

ASTRO AFFILIATION Virgo

HEALING by filtering unwanted energy

Mind Amazonite serves to filter all information going into the mind and combine it with intuition to bring balance to your thoughts. It helps you see both sides to an issue or take in other points of view, while also calming the brain's constant chatter. This soothing stone will help you heal from emotional trauma, taking away any worries, fears or negativity from your life. It can even help those with schizophrenia find peace.

Body This stone protects the body from the effects of geopathic stress, microwaves and EMF radiation from mobile phones, Wi-Fi routers and other technological gadgets. It is also good for bone issues such as osteoporosis, calcium deposits and deficiencies, as well as tooth decay, and easing muscle spasms. It supports the smooth running of the nervous system.

Spirit A crystal to bring balance to your masculine and feminine sides, Amazonite assists in manifesting universal love and raising the consciousness of humankind. This green gem opens the heart chakra to promote unconditional love; the throat chakra to encourage heartfelt, loving communication; and the third eye to connect you to your inner vision. Place on these areas in meditation to enhance.

How to use Drink as an elixir to help with calcium-related issues as well as for spiritual development. Stick a piece of Amazonite to your mobile phone or place a chunk between you and any device to protect you from harmful EMFs. Wear in a necklace or earrings for the same effect. Sitting or lying down in meditation, hold a piece in your non-dominant (receiving) hand to bring peace into your life, or in your dominant (giving) hand to take away stress.

Tip Cleanse amazonite in a mint infusion to fully recharge its powers.

Amazonite has been used for healing and good fortune for centuries. It is believed to have featured on the breastplates of warrior women in the matriarchal Bronze Age tribe of Amazonians. Easy to carve, this crystal was made into beads and other jewellery by the early Mesopotamians, and into a scarab ring in King Tutankhamen's tomb. Found growing in slabs, the ancient Egyptian *Book of the Dead* was carved into it.

Amber

TYPE OF CRYSTAL Not actually a crystal, but still containing healing properties, amber is fossilized resin from prehistoric trees. It sometimes has bubbles, fossilized plants or insects in it. Ranging in colour from golden yellow to honey brown, it is found mostly in Baltic regions such as Latvia and Lithuania, but also in the UK, Germany, Italy, Romania, Poland, Russia and the Dominican Republic.

CHAKRA CONNECTION Throat and solar plexus

ASTRO AFFILIATION Leo, Aquarius

HEALING by purifying mind, body and spirit

Mind This sunny substance is good for combatting depression, relieving stress and improving mood. It is a good stone to heighten the intellect as it enhances memory, clears negative thinking and helps you make better decisions. Amber promotes working patiently through emotional blockages that may be stopping you from living your best life. This gem guides you towards increased peace, trust and stability, even alleviating schizophrenia.

Body A powerful healer and revitalizer, amber can ease pain, alleviate joint problems and draw impurities from the body, helping it rebalance and repair itself. The areas of the body it soothes especially well are the throat, stomach, spleen, kidneys, liver, bladder and gallbladder. An elixir can be drunk to help relieve constipation, for a general detox, or to help with healing and hormone imbalance. Amber is a natural antibiotic and antiseptic, and can be applied to the skin as a gem essence to help fight bacterial infections and acne.

Spirit Amber cleanses the chakras, aura and environment, making it a great addition to any alternative therapist's toolkit. With its strong connection to the Earth, amber is good for grounding the spiritual into everyday reality. It stimulates the solar plexus chakra most, to bring higher energies into the body. It is good for motivating you to achieve your desires with wisdom and generosity.

How to use Use as an elixir for healing or for topical use on wounds. Wear as jewellery at the throat or wrist for long periods of time to feel the effects, or place on the affected area of the body during meditation. Amber can be burned as incense, so is good for cleansing the space in any therapy or treatment room. If treating babies with amber, it helps to have the mother wear or hold the stone first for a time.

Amethyst

TYPE OF CRYSTAL This predominantly purple quartz is commonly found as transparent pointed crystals or masses in Brazil, Uruguay, Mexico, Russia, Sri Lanka, the US, Canada, the UK, India, South Africa and Madagascar. Its colour, from lavender to deep purple, is due to iron and manganese inclusions. Sometimes pieces have white or clear streaks. Buy it as a smooth tumbled stone or a glittery cluster, single point or geode with a beautiful sparkly interior cave.

CHAKRA CONNECTION Crown, third eye and throat

ASTRO AFFILIATION Virgo, Sagittarius, Capricorn, Pisces, Aquarius

HEALING spiritual connection

Mind Amethyst can not only enhance your creativity and inspire new projects, it can also calm anxious internal chatter and boost memory. A powerful healer of the mind, this crystal dispels anger, soothes the nerves and helps overcome sadness and grief after the passing of a loved one or pet. It can also enable you to focus better on negotiating, decision-making or public speaking, improving business success and attracting wealth.

Body Ancient royalty used amethyst to discourage drunkenness, so it supports sobriety, helps with addictions and dampens overindulgence of any kind. It aids detoxing, strengthens the immune system and the liver, and cleanses the blood. It is a good crystal to use to balance hormones, support effective metabolism and ease digestion. It is believed to get rid of gut parasites, increase good stomach bacteria and enable you to rehydrate better. Amethyst can clear up any issues with the lungs and respiratory tract, such as asthma, or skin problems including bruising or swelling. Drink as an elixir to help with arthritis symptoms. It's also a great crystal to alleviate insomnia and stop recurring nightmares by encouraging a deeper, more restful sleep. Amethyst can also ease tension headaches and alleviate hearing problems.

Spirit One of the most spiritual stones, with a very high vibration, amethyst is used to enrich meditation, heighten intuition and develop psychic abilities. As well as tuning you into your inner vision, it will enable you to access your higher consciousness and the spirit world. The ancient Egyptians used to make amulets from amethyst for protection, and it can be used in the same way today to ward off negative energy by creating a protective shield of light around the body.

How to use Use in meditation by holding in your receiving (non-dominant) hand, placing it on your altar or directly on the third eye or crown chakras to open them. Single points can be used in healing by facing them towards the body to attract calming spiritual energy to you, and pointed away from you to take away unwanted energies. Position by the bed or put a piece under your pillow for better sleep. Wear in earrings or a necklace so the gem sits over the throat or the heart, to expand these areas and protect your aura.

Warning: Amethyst fades in sunlight, so don't leave it outside.

Ametrine

TYPE OF CRYSTAL A natural quartz combination of amethyst and citrine, mostly mined in Bolivia. The powerful purple and golden yellow crystals blended together, also known as trystine or by its trade name bolivianite, are created due to differing oxidization states of iron in the crystal. The citrine parts contain oxidized iron, while the amethyst sections are unoxidized, occurring at different temperatures during the formation of the gem. Synthetic ametrine is created through irradiation and may be lower in price – but the real deal is essential for healing purposes.

CHAKRA CONNECTION Crown, third eye and solar plexus

ASTRO AFFILIATION Libra

HEALING by removing blockages to wellbeing

Mind This is a crystal to carry with you to encourage concentration, boost creativity and cope with change. When using ametrine regularly, expect your self-esteem to rise and your innate wisdom to increase as it breaks through negative programming from your upbringing. As your consciousness expands with this gem, prejudices and obstacles to spiritual expansion will disappear and optimism will take over as you realize we are all one. Ametrine guides you to take control of your life, think things through thoroughly and explore all potentials.

Body Good for getting to the root of long-term illnesses, ametrine clears out toxins, strengthens the immune system and is believed to repair DNA, even helping organ transplants succeed. It clears

stress and tension from the head, calming your nervous system. It's a good crystal to use if you have chronic fatigue, general lethargy or depression, as it oxygenates and energizes the body and mind. Gastric upsets and stomach ulcers are eased with ametrine.

Spirit This crystal brings peace, tranquillity and prosperity. It opens the third eye, enabling you to sense future outcomes and heal yourself. It helps you fully understand spirituality from an intellectual perspective, as well as practically helping you connect deeply to your higher consciousness and realize that everything is connected. Ametrine helps your meditation get deeper, quicker, even astral travelling while in the spiritual realms, fully protected from any unwanted energies. It balances your masculine and feminine sides

and puts you in sync with the natural rhythm of yin and yang.

How to use Place ametrine on the solar plexus while lying down comfortably in meditation. Hold it in hands cupped together during a seated meditation, to bring deep-rooted issues into your awareness for examination and healing. Wear all day long as jewellery for the best effect.

Angelite

TYPE OF CRYSTAL Angelite is a highly evolved type of celestine made of calcium and sulphate, compressed under enormous pressure over millions of years. It forms opaque blue-grey nodules with light blue inside and white veins throughout, looking like gossamer angel wings. Mined mainly in Peru, but also found in Mexico, Egypt, Germany, England, Poland and Libya, angelite is usually sold in small, round polished stones.

CHAKRA CONNECTION Throat, third eye and crown

ASTRO AFFILIATION Aquarius

HEALING communication with the angelic realm

Mind Angelite encourages clearer and more compassionate communication with yourself, with others and with spirit. Tuning into this crystal before speaking in public or having an important conversation of any kind helps you talk with awareness and integrity, and fully share your truth. It also dispels anger and is known to comfort anyone grieving, bringing acceptance to any situation that cannot be changed. A good gem to help gain a deeper understanding of astrology as well as mathematics.

Body Incredible for healing mind, body and spirit, this crystal transmutes physical pain and balances it with energies from the etheric realm. It unblocks the body's meridians when placed on the feet. Resonating with the throat chakra, angelite eases inflammation in this area, including balancing the thyroid. It also supports the lungs, assists with weight loss and can act as a diuretic. It helps repair tissues, boosts haemoglobin and clears blood vessels. An elixir can be used on the body as an insect repellent and to soothe sunburn.

Spirit A stone of peace, tranquillity, and acceptance, Angelite is a key crystal for developing your spiritual awareness and psychic skills, assisting understanding of insights as well as dreams. One to add to your meditation altar, it enables clear communication with the angelic realm, your spirit guides or higher consciousness. It increases telepathy and aids astral travel, all while staying connected to reality. For anyone undertaking spiritual healing, clairvoyant or tarot card readings, or rebirthing, use angelite in gem or elixir form to protect your own energy.

How to use Place on the soles of the feet while relaxing face down to clear energy meridians, or position on a particular area of the body or chakra to heal. Position on meditation table or meditate while holding it in your non-dominant hand to receive spiritual communications. Carry in a pocket or wear as jewellery, especially at the throat or neck, or in earrings, to bring about peaceful negotiations or soften speech.

Warning: Make sure not to get angelite wet; water can damage it. An elixir can be made using the indirect method, described on page 39.

Apache tears

TYPE OF CRYSTAL Apache tears are small, round, smooth pieces of black obsidian, sometimes with brown nodules that are translucent when held up to a light. Obsidian is a type of dark volcanic lava turned to glass, most often found in the US but also easily obtained all over the world.

CHAKRA CONNECTION Root

ASTRO AFFILIATION Aries

HEALING negative emotions

Mind These stones work to bust through any self-limiting beliefs, release negative thinking and help make positive changes to your behaviour. Where you might feel stuck in your ways, Apache tears inspire more spontaneity and can help you move forward in times of change, if you tune into them for guidance. They also encourage you to use and expand your analytical skills.

Body A great stone to work with to increase vitamin C and D absorption, Apache tears ease muscle spasms and knee problems. They also support the detox process, clearing out what's not needed by the body.

Spirit Supporting you through funerals and when feeling grief, Apache tears allow you to fully express sadness, shedding tears

of loss and pain, even if long-repressed. Good for grounding your energy, offering spiritual protection, and balancing feelings, these stones absorb negative emotions from yourself and others, and protect you from people's ill will. They guide you towards forgiveness and help your soul recover from abuse.

How to use Position on or next to the root chakra to clear negative energy and ground yourself. Meditate holding one in your dominant hand for protection. Carry them in a pocket, on their own, to occasions where you may feel sad. Position in a room or wherever you need to combat negativity.

Warning: Apache tears are slightly soft and can scratch easily, so keep them wrapped in a cloth or away from other stones. Never use water or salt to cleanse them or make a gem essence.

Did you know?

The name Apache tear comes from a legend of the Native American tribe of the Apache. In the 1870s, about 75 Apaches fought the US cavalry on a mountain overlooking what is now Superior, Arizona. Facing defeat, the outnumbered Apache warriors rode their horses off the mountainside to their deaths rather than be killed by the military. When the wives and families of these warriors heard the news, they cried so much that their tears turned to stone as they hit the ground.

Apatite

TYPE OF CRYSTAL Usually blue and blue-green, but sometimes yellow, white, purple, brown or violet, apatite is glassy-looking, mostly opaque but sometimes translucent. This phosphate hexagonal crystal comes in various sizes and is mostly found in Brazil, Madagascar, Mexico, the US, Russia and Norway.

CHAKRA CONNECTION Throat, third eye, root

ASTRO AFFILIATION Gemini

HEALING manifestations

Mind This stone boosts your intellect and your ability to express yourself fully, communicating new ideas with energy, enthusiasm and clarity. It enhances creative inspiration and gives you the motivation for fulfilling projects. Allow apatite to reduce stress, anxiety and panic attacks. This crystal gives you the strength and courage to carry on after a major setback. It brings about harmony and peace where there is conflict, and encourages openness and sociability.

Body Incredibly, apatite can help heal and strengthen bones, teeth and cartilage, ease joint problems and make new cells grow healthily, as it increases calcium absorption. It can also tackle weight issues, as it's believed to suppress hunger and raise your metabolic rate so you burn fat quicker. It can

also assist with any ailments to do with the throat, eyes, ears and nose, glands, energy meridians and various internal organs. A great all-round healer that gets results for every area of the mental, emotional, physical and spiritual bodies.

Spirit Apatite enables your energy to shine brightly, dispelling your or anyone else's negativity, whether it's anger, sorrow or apathy. By raising your kundalini energy, it releases blockages in the root chakra, which removes frustration and allows guilt-free passion. It's a great stone to help you discover your path in life and take the right steps towards manifesting your dreams, especially if they are in service to others and for the greater good. Holding apatite will deepen your meditation, develop your psychic talents and connect

you to past lives. It also enhances your aura, creating a protective shield around you, especially when dealing with other people.

How to use Place apatite anywhere it is needed to bring inspiration and ideas, such as the office or classroom, as well as in your meditation space to induce better visualization of your manifestations. Hold in either hand while seated in stillness. Position on the appropriate chakra or wherever on the body it feels needed. Wear as jewellery, close to the throat chakra especially, or carry in a pocket to have its energy with you all day.

Warning: Handle apatite with care, as it is brittle and can break if dropped or when in contact with other crystals.

Apophyllite

TYPE OF CRYSTAL This mineral formation, from the zeolite group of crystals, is usually colourless, white, cream, peach or yellowish and rarely green, transparent or opaque. Found in India, Brazil, the Czech Republic, the UK, Italy and Australia, apophyllites grow as small single cubic or pyramidal crystals or large clusters.

CHAKRA CONNECTION Third eye, crown

ASTRO AFFILIATION Gemini, Libra

HEALING by transmitting energy

Mind A stone for introspection, reflection and release of suppressed emotions, apophyllite helps correct any perceived flaws in your character and break through negative beliefs or actions. It calms anxiety, apprehension and fear while bringing your true self into full awareness so you can reveal it with confidence. This crystal reduces stress, boosts brain power and teaches you how to live with uncertainty. It marries universal love with analysis to help you make evolved decisions that fuse mind and spirit.

Body This crystal fully rejuvenates the body, especially the eyes when a piece is placed on each. It is one of the best stones to assist reiki healing, as it enables anyone having a treatment to become deeply relaxed and therefore more receptive to the healing energy being transmitted. Apophyllite supports the respiratory system, helping those with breathing issues. Allergies can be alleviated with this crystal, and the skin and mucus membranes regenerated.

Spirit With its high water content, apophyllite is a powerful energy conductor, enhancing any energies it comes into contact with as well as carrying the information held in the Akashic records. This makes it a good gem for vision quests or shamanic journeys to discover past lives and retrieve wisdom held in the spiritual realms. It connects you clearly to spirit communication, activates your intuition and is effective for scrying - seeing into the future. Meditate with apophyllite and your blissed-out state will stay with you throughout the day.

How to use Place on the area of the body where reiki energy is needed most when undertaking energy healing. Or place over closed eyes or on the chest to treat these areas. Position an apophyllite pyramid next to the crown or on the third eye chakra while lying down meditating to activate the chakras, connect with spirit and receive visions. To scry using apophyllite, look into it from the corner of your eye. Look through a pyramid crystal from the base to the point to open a star gate to travel through in your mind's eye. Make into an elixir to drink so light and energy come into the heart chakra, attracting universal love.

Aquamarine

TYPE OF CRYSTAL For hundreds of years this crystal was prized by the ancients as a stone of courage, to combat dark forces. It was also carried by sailors for centuries as a good luck talisman to protect against drowning. It is a light-blue/green, clear to opaque beryl found mainly in Afghanistan, Pakistan, Namibia, Brazil and the US, and is sold as small tumbled or faceted chunks.

CHAKRA CONNECTION Heart, throat, third eye

ASTRO AFFILIATION Aries, Gemini, Pisces

HEALING through courage

Mind A highly calming stone, aquamarine reduces anxiety, stress, fears and phobias, building tolerance and taking responsibility for yourself and living your truth. Aquamarine clears confusion and stimulates the intellect, helping with study and communication. A stone especially for sensitives and anyone feeling overwhelmed, it can help break old, negative patterns of behaviour and make positive things happen.

Body This is a great crystal for soothing sore throats, swollen glands, thyroid issues and hormone imbalances. With its tonic effect, aquamarine flushes out the kidneys, stomach and other eliminating organs in the body, relieving water retention and swelling. It helps strengthen teeth and jaw and improve eyesight, and can be cooling when used topically as an elixir or drunk to alleviate hay fever symptoms and other autoimmune reactions.

Spirit Aquamarine stills the mind and centres the soul for a deeper meditation and stronger connection with your intuition and higher guides. Heightening spiritual development, it promotes a strong desire to serve humanity. This crystal clears blocks in the chakra system, particularly the throat, allowing for authentic self-expression and the understanding of underlying emotions. Aligning your spiritual body with the physical, it clears and shields the aura, which provides protection against negative energies, including any pollutants in your surroundings.

How to use Wear this stone in earrings and a necklace, or carry it in a pocket to take its energy with you all day. Place on closed eyes or any part of the body to soothe and cool, or use as an elixir to drink or apply topically – to sunburn, for example. In meditation, hold it in your non-dominant hand, place it on a relevant chakra or anywhere it's required. Visualize aquamarine clearing your chakras and cleansing the environment.

Tip Cleanse aquamarine in a blue glass bowl of seawater or salted mineral water on the night of a full moon, rinsing with pure water afterwards.

Aragonite

TYPE OF CRYSTAL Found in small translucent or transparent crystalline calcium carbonite (chalk) formations in coral, limestone or rock, mostly in Spain, the UK, Slovakia, Namibia and China (blue aragonite), aragonite comes in a variety of colours including brown, gold, yellow, white, green and blue. It is often sold as a 'sputnik' cluster with distinct protrusions, but it can come in chalky fan shapes or as coral. This entry covers mostly brown aragonite properties.

CHAKRA CONNECTION Earth, root, solar plexus, crown

ASTRO AFFILIATION Capricorn

HEALING connection with the Earth

Mind This stone encourages patience, discipline and concentrating on the present moment. An effective stress reliever, aragonite stops you pushing yourself too hard and helps develop a more pragmatic attitude to life. It provides strength and support during times of stress and brings sudden, helpful insights, tolerance and flexibility to your mind.

Body This gem generates energy in the body, warming it up and treating chills and Raynaud's disease. A handy pain reliever, aragonite also helps you feel at ease in your body, alleviating stress-related skin flare-ups, such as eczema or psoriasis, and getting rid of wrinkles, bunions or hard skin. It soothes the nervous system, stops muscle spasms and supports the healing of broken bones. A useful stone to boost immunity and combat hair loss, it also helps with vitamins A, D and calcium absorption.

Spirit A good gem to use for grounding energies into the body, as well as healing Mother Earth, this gem stimulates the earth and root chakras, encouraging a deeper connection to our planet. Aragonite raises your vibration to a higher level, ready for a fulfilling meditation. It brings balance back to any spiritual development that seems too fast and unsettling by grounding you firmly in reality while connecting to other realms.

How to use Wear as a pendant for grounding floaty energy. Place underneath your pillow or mattress to combat night twitching and restlessness in mind and body. Hold over or position on any afflicted area, or bathe in an elixir of it to soak up its healing properties. Hold aragonite in the hands to warm them.

Tip To cleanse, bury aragonite in a pot of soil for a full day and night, brushing off the soil afterwards.

Warning: Aragonite is soft, so take care to protect it from damage and never use water or salt to cleanse it. Never burn aragonite, as it releases gases that are toxic to eyes and mucus membranes.

Aventurine - blue/raw

TYPE OF CRYSTAL An opaque stone with a reflective quality from shiny quartz inclusions, found naturally in a royal blue colour, sometimes tinged grey, but also available in other colours, including green (see below), red, peach, orange and brown. They all have similar properties to the raw variety, plus extra, depending on their colour. Sources of aventurine can be found in Nepal, Russia, India, China, Italy and Brazil.

CHAKRA CONNECTION Throat, heart, third eye

ASTRO AFFILIATION Aries

HEALING bad habits that hinder wellbeing

Mind This stone encourages you to live in integrity and helps overcome bad habits of the mind that affect the body and harm the spirit. It stops stammers and neuroses by enabling you to understand how and why they began. Like all blue crystals, raw aventurine improves communication, enhances creativity and eases stress, transforming negative situations for the better. It will bring the intellectual and emotional bodies back into balance, as well as your masculine and feminine sides. This gem also eases anger, quells irritation and promotes empathy, compassion and tenacity, helping to heal the heart of any emotional turbulence.

Body Promoting overall wellbeing, aventurine can take you back to past trauma or upset to find the root of any disease. It is anti-inflammatory, so an elixir alleviates skin flare-ups and allergies. Aventurine can relieve sinus problems and headaches, and refresh the eyes when placed on them while they are closed in meditation. Other areas of the body that benefit from this gem include the nervous system, thymus and adrenal glands, lungs, heart, muscles and connective tissue. It also balances blood pressure, boosts metabolism and lowers cholesterol, making it incredible for staying trim and healthy.

Spirit A powerful heart-chakra protector, aventurine will stop anyone draining your loving energy without reciprocating. It increases psychic awareness and clairvoyant insights, bringing you the self-discipline to stick with a meditation practice or progress with your spiritual development.

How to use Carry in a pocket or hold in either hand when needed. Place or hold near a particular area of the body or chakra location, or use as an elixir. Position in an area in the home where its energy is needed most. Use in a crystal grid to heal areas of geopathic stress. Wear daily to absorb EMFs from technological gadgets, or tape to a mobile phone to protect against radiation.

Aventurine - green

TYPE OF CRYSTAL Opaque quartz with a slight lustre, bright-green aventurine is coloured by fuchsite and sometimes has white or grey banding. It's found in the same places as blue aventurine.

CHAKRA CONNECTION Heart

ASTRO AFFILIATION Aries

HEALING the heart

Mind This light-green gem is great for calming fears and alleviating anxiety, and brings balance back to wildly swinging emotions. Meditate with it before taking exams to reduce stress you may have over doing well. Aventurine's power also encourages decisiveness and good leadership qualities, helping motivate yourself and others.

Body A good all-round healer used to bring the body back into balance and assist with any malignant conditions that might be running out of control. This stone helps speed up your reaction time, thereby improving your sporting ability and reflexes. Great for soothing tired or injured muscles after activity, green aventurine also increases your lung efficiency, keeps your heart healthy and boosts adrenal function. It keeps the urogenital system working well too, especially if a gem is added to your bottle of drinking water and the elixir is drunk regularly throughout the day.

Spirit Green aventurine boosts creativity and aids relaxation, helping you find inspiration easily. It clears the heart chakra and opens you up to the flowing, unconditional love of the universe, attracting love, abundance and new friendships to you while protecting your energy from undue influences. This gem guides you to tune into your spirit guides for wisdom about your life.

How to use Carry a piece with you in a pocket. Wear as a pendant to sit over the heart chakra to clear emotional pain and deep-seated fears, or place over the heart while lying on your back in a relaxing meditation. In a seated meditation, hold in the non-dominant (receiving) hand to receive friendship, and the dominant (giving) hand for giving friendship. Bathe in, or drink, a gem essence to soothe mind, body and spirit.

Azeztulite

TYPE OF CRYSTAL This very high-vibration, colourless or white variety of quartz contains traces of beryllium. Found in one particular mine in North Carolina, in the US, it is very rare and usually expensive.

CHAKRA CONNECTION Third eye, crown

ASTRO AFFILIATION All

HEALING with very high vibrational energy

Mind Always energized, this gem enlivens the mind to prepare for an upshift in consciousness. Ideally, you should have cleared old patterns of thinking and acting, and released any stuck emotions, before working with the high frequency of azeztulite. It brings inspiration and visions of the New Age, if you are ready, and guides you to share its pure vibration with others.

Body This crystal helps channel any kind of energy, making it great for any healing purposes. Its high vibration especially assists with treating cancers and other cell disorders. It also reduces inflammation, which can be a cause of many conditions. Azeztulite supports the chronically ill by revitalizing the will to live and activating the soul's purpose.

Spirit Attuned to the highest frequencies, azeztulite brings down the purest spiritual vibrations for your expansion and evolution. Its powerful energy can be overwhelming for anyone who's not used to it, until it is assimilated, so use with care or combine with aquamarine or ametrine to soften the vibes. It instantly brings the mind to stillness in meditation, and stimulates the rise of kundalini energy up the spine from the root chakra to the crown, activating spiritual awakening. It opens up the third eye to receive insights into the future and help you make decisions that benefit your highest good.

How to use Place on the third eye or crown for activating spiritual ascension. Use in a crystal healing grid placed on the third eye. Position near the part of the body that needs its high-vibrational healing energy.

Warning: Azeztulite is always energized and does not need cleansing.

Azurite

TYPE OF CRYSTAL A deep-blue crystal with gold, green or yellow flecks, often found with malachite in masses and nodules in copper deposits in Australia, Chile, Peru, the US, Russia, China, France, Morocco and Egypt. Sold as a rough or polished stone.

CHAKRA CONNECTION Throat, third eye

ASTRO AFFILIATION Sagittarius

HEALING the mind

Mind Azurite resonates well with the mind and mental processes, facilitating the healing of negative thought patterns, beliefs and grievances that get in the way of wellbeing by helping them come to the surface for full exploration. Giving you clear understanding of past issues, this gem stimulates the memory and brings new perspectives to enable you to move forward into a new reality. It can enhance creativity, compassion and empathy, and encourage you to express emotions and communicate deeper thoughts. It also alleviates sadness, grief or nervousness.

Body A powerful healing stone, azurite brings awareness of the mind-body connection and can help you through any healing crisis by giving you the knowledge that things will get better after reaching rock bottom. It works at an energetic level to clear all chakras and at a cellular level to restore blockages, especially in the brain, joints and spine. This gem helps ease throat ailments, arthritis and any issues with the liver, kidneys, gallbladder, spleen, thyroid, teeth and skin. It assists with a detox, soothes the nervous system and supports the growth of an embryo in the womb.

Spirit Allow azurite to guide your soul towards spiritual enlightenment by clearing and stimulating your third eye chakra and connecting you with divine guidance. It will help you deepen your meditation practice, ensure safe astral travel and tune you into your intuition and psychic talents. Azurite allows more light into your understanding to clear up any fears or phobias around full spiritual expansion so you can tune into spirit without worry.

How to use Azurite is a good crystal to carry at funerals, to ease grief. Wear as necklace or earrings to connect with nearby chakras, or place on or near chakra areas in meditation or healing sessions. Hold in the right hand or place on the third eye area to open up to spiritual awakening. Remove straight away if palpitations occur; they may be induced by this crystal.

Azurite is fairly soft, so keep it separate from other stones and avoid damaging it when you carry it.

Azurite and malachite combined
in a crystal marry the qualities of the gems
(see azurite opposite, and malachite on page 155),
creating a powerful energy conductor in its own right.
Connected to the third eye and heart chakras, azurite with
malachite assists meditation, opens up psychic awareness,
and boosts visualization skills. It also increases rationality
and flexibility.

Mentally, this combination overcomes anxiety, arrogance and
vanity. It busts through ancient mental blocks or patterns of
thinking to bring about deep emotional healing. It teaches that
sometimes it's the simplest changes that can have the most
profound effect towards increased freedom and individuality.

Physically, it supports good skin, teeth, joint and bone
health, aiding flexibility and circulation. It alleviates
stress-related symptoms such as ulcers, and
assists the heart, liver and gallbladder
especially.

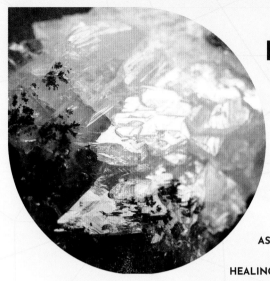

Barite

TYPE OF CRYSTAL This stone is found in white, orange, blue or light-green toned, clear and glass-like layered plates, fibrous masses, and sometimes flowers or angel-wing patterns (especially the blue variety found in Morocco). Most other colours of barite are found all over the world. Blue barite feels heavier than its gossamer wing look would suggest. Also known as baryte or barytine.

CHAKRA CONNECTION Throat

ASTRO AFFILIATION Aquarius

HEALING friendships and motivation levels, helping you go for your dreams

Mind This stone combats shyness, giving you the confidence to communicate your thoughts and ideas freely. A good motivator, it encourages you to take action toward your goals from an independent position while remaining loyal to a particular dream or mentor. Work with this stone to encourage catharsis, releasing old patterns of behaviour to create calm and regulate your emotions, with the help of other crystals and talking therapies.

Body Calming for the stomach and nerves, barite boosts vitality to help overcome chronic fatigue. It's a good crystal to aid detoxification and help with recovery from addictions. It boosts the eyesight, aids memory, and eases sore throats. It's a good gem to carry if you are oversensitive to temperature changes, as it balances your body's reactions to hot and cold. Blue barite especially helps reduce the effects of EMFs and radiation.

Spirit Barite is especially good for building friendships and bringing harmony, intimacy and love into your life. It helps with boundary issues and allows you to stand up for yourself. It fully cleanses and rebalances the chakra system and brain chemistry, promoting overall wellbeing. Expect spiritual insights and intuitive visions when using barite, as it steers you on the right path for the expansion of your consciousness. Blue barite, in particular, connects you to the angels and enhances their messages for you. It fully ignites your spiritual path through deeper awareness. Traditionally, it was a stone used for journeying in your dreams, as it gives you anonymity and protection.

How to use Hold barite in both hands during meditation. Position on the appropriate part of the body for healing. Place at the throat chakra or wear in a necklace at the throat to improve your communication skills and ignite new ideas. Use in a crystal grid for energetic catharsis of yourself or the area gridded. Place next to your bed or on your bedside table to enable journeying in your dreams, fully protected from any unwanted energies while you sleep.

Beryl

TYPE OF CRYSTAL This crystal forms in hexagonal prisms, sometimes with small pyramidal structures, in a wide variety of colours including milky yellow/green and white. Green emerald, blue aquamarine, golden heliodor, red bixbite and pink morganite are all types of beryl with many different healing properties according to their colours. Beryl is found in Brazil, the US, Russia, Pakistan, Australia, France, Norway and the Czech Republic.

CHAKRA CONNECTION Solar plexus, crown

ASTRO AFFILIATION Aries, Gemini, Leo, Pisces

HEALING stress, in all areas of your life

Mind The best stress reliever of all crystals, beryl helps calm the mind, shed baggage and deal with the anxieties and overstimulation of modern life. It filters out the endless distractions and helps you focus on what you need to do. Beryl brings you courage to take new initiatives and adaptability to see you through any setbacks. It also brings wisdom, positivity and vitality.

Body All the elimination organs, such as the liver, kidneys, pancreas and stomach, get a boost with beryl. It's good for the nervous, pulmonary and circulatory systems, and increases your resistance to environmental pollutants and other toxins. Said to reduce belching and aid concussions, it is also used as a sedative stone to relax and calm.

Spirit Beryl can boost amore in jaded married couples, and is good for use in spiritual ceremonies. Crystal balls made of beryl, especially the seer's golden variety, are often used for scrying the future, by looking deeply into them and seeing what images and messages arise. This crystal opens the solar plexus chakra to heighten overall wellbeing, and activates the crown chakra to receive messages from spirit.

How to use Place on the relevant body part or chakra in need of treating. Use beryl in a crystal ball to see the future. Perfect for a bride to wear in a tiara or crown to help her stay calm and focused on her big day.

Pink beryl, aka morganite, connects to the heart chakra, cleaning and opening this energy centre to attract more love, joy and satisfaction of the soul. This calming crystal dissipates resistance to healing and transformation, ridding you of any feelings of victimhood, egotism or closed-mindedness to encourage full emotional expression and spiritual expansion.

Physiologically, morganite treats the symptoms of stressful living and supports the nervous system, the heart and the oxygenation of cells. Lung issues, such as asthma, tuberculosis and emphysema, are apparently assisted with this type of beryl, but not by breathing in the dust, as it is carcinogenic (and generally only happens in beryllium mines). Treat lung problems energetically by placing the gem on the chest area. Morganite also alleviates vertigo and impotence.

Bloodstone

TYPE OF CRYSTAL A popular gem for over 2,000 years, when it was known as heliotrope, bloodstone is made up of green chalcedony, a type of cryptocrystalline quartz, flecked with red or yellow jasper (iron oxide). Stones with more iron oxide are known as 'fancy jaspers'. It is commonly mined in India, but is also found in Russia, the Czech Republic, China, Australia, Madagascar and Brazil.

This powerful healing crystal is sold in tumbled stones, and occasionally cut into reliefs of warriors, dragons or other motifs. These images, including those used in family crests and national symbols, replicate the style of the top of signet rings, which were once used to seal documents. In ancient times, bloodstone was said to be an 'audible oracle', emitting sounds as guidance. It was also believed to banish evil and have the power to control the weather.

CHAKRA CONNECTION Root, heart

ASTRO AFFILIATION Aries, Libra, Pisces

HEALING the blood

Mind This crystal releases fear, enhances courage and helps you act in the present moment. It's a stone to bring strength of mind, discernment and calm decision-making abilities, especially in knowing when to withdraw from potentially dangerous situations – hence being the stone of warriors. It lessens anger and irritability, stress and aggression. Plus, it enables you to realize that after chaos comes transformation.

Body As its name suggests, this gem is a great cleanser for the blood, supporting its flow, healthy circulation and removal of any toxins. It is believed to be helpful in treating leukaemia, and the ancient Egyptians even used it to shrink brain tumours. Bloodstone helps heal blood issues and wounds, such as nosebleeds, anaemia and clotting, plus it regulates women's periods. It gives the immune system a kick, helping stop infections and reduce pus. The heart, kidneys, liver, spleen and bladder are all aided by this powerful healing stone.

Spirit Believed to have countless magical properties, bloodstone increases intuition and boosts creativity. It grounds in spiritual energy, opening the heart chakra and bringing the mystical into everyday actions. It boosts your sense of personal power while encouraging you to be idealistic and selfless. Used as protection from negativity, this stone will keep away bad influences, whether in the waking world, in your dreams (which it activates) or in meditation.

How to use Wear in jewellery continually for optimum physical, mental and spiritual health. Carry with you all day. Meditate regularly holding a piece in cupped hands. Tape over the thymus at night to stimulate the immune system. For a peaceful slumber, place a piece in a bowl of water at the bedside.

Blue John fluorite

TYPE OF CRYSTAL This purplish-blue mixed with creamy white and colourless calcium fluorite is luminous, soft and glassy, and forms in isometric cubes, nodules and clusters, or in masses. Used throughout the 18th and 19th century in jewellery, fireplace surrounds, vases and other decorative items, it is much sought after, as it is only found in the Peak District of Derbyshire in England.

CHAKRA CONNECTION Third eye and crown

ASTRO AFFILIATION Scorpio

HEALING EMF pollution

Mind A crystal to balance the brain, bring calm clarity and help with decision making, blue john gives you the inner strength and focus to cope with change. Work with it to help make intelligent plans for your next steps, especially to get yourself out of negative situations. This stone fosters trust in yourself and others, and encourages you to be more altruistic. Great for anyone studying, Blue John fluorite assists with retaining information and is even believed to raise your IQ.

Body Essential for anyone working with computers and other tech, this crystal helps combat the detrimental effects of EMFs from mobile phones, Wi-Fi and other electronic devices. This can include extreme fatigue, headaches and depression. Blue John fluorite is also beneficial for anyone with emphysema, arthritis, rheumatism and stiff joints, as well as lung issues such as asthma or breathing difficulties.

Spirit Use Blue John fluorite in meditation to bring about deep peace and expand your consciousness, especially through dreams and astral travel. It enables you to tune into the future and develop psychic intuition about what's to come in your life, as well as connect with a power animal for guidance. It's a great stone to boost imagination and creativity, bringing you many possibilities for exciting exploration of your artistic side.

How to use Best positioned next to technological items or carried in a pocket on its own to absorb EMF radiation. Meditate lying down holding a piece in each hand and a piece placed above each eyebrow to balance the hemispheres of the brain and clear mental chatter, or on the throat and third eye areas to increase clairvoyance. Wear as jewellery, but only where it won't get damaged.

Warning: Store Blue John fluorite alone or wrapped in a cloth, as it is soft enough to become scratched.

Boji Stone™

TYPE OF CRYSTAL These peculiar-looking brown, grey or black stones, with their trademarked name, are only found in the Boji Valley in Colorado, in the US. Made from pyrite with palladium, marcasite or other minerals, possibly sulphur, they often come in pairs, with the feminine stones smooth and round and the masculine ones rough with square protrusions.

CHAKRA CONNECTION Root chakra for one stone, while two work on all chakras

ASTRO AFFILIATION Taurus, Leo, Scorpio, Aquarius

HEALING by clearing all blockages to balance

Mind Boji stones clear blockages, such as stuck emotions, replayed trauma and re-lived memories, bringing you back to mental balance. They will help you discover unconscious, self-sabotaging behaviour and habitual negative programming, so you can fully explore your shadow side and release anything that holds you back.

Body These gems unblock stuck energy in your body and stimulate its flow through the meridians. You may feel this as a rush through your whole system that energizes and gives you a much-needed boost when you feel fatigued. Boji stones can speed up recovery from an illness or operation, help with tissue regeneration and reduce pain.

Spirit Good for grounding you back in the present moment after any spiritual-development practice or out-of-body experience, this powerful pair is highly protective. Bojis balance the male-female energies in you, realign the chakras and recharge the aura. The stones help with animal communication and support healthy plant growth. Just make sure not to leave them outside or in the soil cleansing for too long, as they can disintegrate if exposed to harsh elements.

How to use In seated meditation, hold one stone in each hand for 10 minutes or more, or use in a healing grid around you. When lying down, place one above the head and another below the feet. Place on or near painful areas of the body. Wear in a necklace or pendant.

Bornite

TYPE OF CRYSTAL Also known as peacock rock, peacock ore or purple copper, this metallic mineral has copper-coloured flashes that oxidize with air or water to shine a rainbow of blue, green, gold and purple shades - hence the peacock monikers. It is found in masses in Mexico, the US, Canada, Morocco, Chile, Australia, Kazakhstan and various countries in Europe.

CHAKRA CONNECTION All

ASTRO AFFILIATION Cancer

HEALING rebirthing with renewed energy

Mind Bornite gets to the root of negative thinking and self-imposed blocks to happiness so they can be wiped out of the mind, renewing your sense of joy. Helping to regulate emotions, this crystal focuses you on the present moment and balances the right and left sides of the brain. After trauma or during periods of grief, it guides you to see the lessons of the experiences. It generates altruistic feelings towards all life, wanting equality and justice for all.

Body This crystal regulates salt intake, reduces acidity and balances the absorption of potassium. It is believed to ease muscle spasms, help cells regenerate and dissolve calcified deposits such as kidney stones. It also regulates the metabolism and reduces swelling, gout symptoms and fevers. Bornite can be used to treat epilepsy, angina and anaemia. It boosts your energy while calming down adrenaline, and can be programmed to send healing energy from a distance. Taped or worn over the thymus, it helps you receive remote healing.

Spirit Uniting the mind, body and spirit, bornite removes what is no longer needed in your life and encourages you to move on, making it a good stone for rebirthing and releasing old karma. It helps you visualize and create your own reality, aided by inner knowing, intuitive guidance and heightened psychic skills.

How to use Hold in either hand for meditation, intuitive insights or when healing. Place on the area of the body in need of its energy. Use in a crystal grid. Wear bornite set in silver, which stabilizes it, to enhance nurturing of oneself and heighten romantic or platonic love.

Did you know?

Bornite is one of up to 23 other minerals including mainly amethyst and citrine, but also gold, silver, pyrite and epidote in Auralite-23. This newly discovered crystal combination was first found in 2006, sold from 2011 and yet it's over 1.5 billion years old. Mined only in the Auralite-23 mine in Thunder Bay Canada, this gem promotes sharing and group interactions. It enables you to see disagreements from all angles, improve communication skills and break through beliefs that hold you back. It also helps ease headaches, muscle cramps and eye strain.

Bowenite

TYPE OF CRYSTAL Also known as new jade or greenstone (apart from in New Zealand, where greenstone is jade nephrite, an entirely different mineral), this gem is antigorite and is found as granular green masses in Italy, China, New Zealand and the US.

CHAKRA CONNECTION Heart

ASTRO AFFILIATION Aquarius

HEALING by attracting love and friendship

Mind This gem helps you leave the past behind and removes obstacles in your mind that stop you from moving forward with your goals and ambitions. It lifts depression, alleviates grief and helps you get through trauma. It frees you to travel your own path, follow your desires and do what will make you happy, with confidence and success. It is of particular benefit to anyone suffering from fear of heights.

Body Bowenite boosts heart health and helps lower cholesterol. It also balances the hormones, encourages fertility and promotes a healthy pregnancy. Any skin issues can be treated by dabbing bowenite elixir over the area. This gem essence can also be used as a conditioning hair rinse to bring back shine and smoothness, or repair any problems with the head and scalp.

Spirit Called the 'stone of the warrior', this crystal protects you from enemies and connects you to your ancestors for empowerment through adventure and change. Helpful for attracting soul mates and encouraging fidelity in existing relationships, it brings love, friendship and happiness into your life by opening your heart centre through blissful meditation. A good stone to work with for analysing your dreams and trusting in your psychic abilities.

How to use An amulet necklace of bowenite will create a protective shield around you, radiating in all directions. Soak bowenite in water overnight to make an elixir for a hair rinse or skin wash. Place in a child's room to guide them to be more independent and responsible, or in a pet's area to get them to be more active.

Calcite - clear

TYPE OF CRYSTAL Also called calcspar, Iceland crystal and optical calcite, this commonly found crystal comes in many colours of calcium carbonite; many have their own entry in this book, as they heal different things depending on their colour. It is a soft and waxy mineral with a glassy lustre, usually transparent, but sometimes opaque, and often banded. Countries where calcite is found, often along with other crystals, include Brazil, Peru, the US, Iceland, the UK, Belgium, the Czech Republic, Slovakia, Romania and Poland.

CHAKRA CONNECTION All chakras for clear calcite (see each colour for other chakra connections and healing properties)

ASTRO AFFILIATION All

HEALING a cure-all that cleanses, boosts calcium intake and clears the skin

Mind Calcite brings serenity where there is stress, motivation instead of laziness, and renewed trust in yourself when you have experienced setbacks. Stabilizing, calming and positive, it encourages emotional intelligence, discernment and thorough analysis. It helps you know which information is correct and worth retaining, making it a beneficial crystal to carry in a pocket or wear as a pendant if studying or taking exams.

Body Clear calcite is known as a cure-all, as it is a strong detoxifier and antiseptic, especially when drunk as a gem essence in water. It supports the immune system and encourages elimination. This crystal helps boost calcium intake, strengthening the bones and joints, and can help children grow. When a calcite elixir is used on the skin, it is effective at soothing ulcers, warts and hard-to-heal wounds. It can also reduce the tension that causes bad headaches.

Spirit This gem cleanses, realigns and revitalizes all the chakras, bringing you back into balance. It quickly clears negative energies in a room and boosts your own vibration. It also opens up your inner vision, higher consciousness and psychic side, accelerating spiritual growth. Meditating with calcite can enable channelling and facilitate astral travel in the spiritual and interdimensional realms. It will also help you remember everything you experienced when you come back to Earth, and use those insights to move forward with renewed purpose.

How to use Hold on or next to the relevant area for 10 minutes or more for healing. Use as an elixir internally or externally. Place in a healing grid around your bed. Wear as a pendant or carry in a pocket, but make sure it is not with any other stones, as it is easily damaged.

Warning: Never use salt or water to cleanse this crystal, as these will harm it.

Calcite - blue

TYPE OF CRYSTAL This grey-blue crystal is one of the many colours of calcium carbonate found in the same countries as clear calcite, but most commonly in Mexico.

CHAKRA CONNECTION Throat, third eye

ASTRO AFFILIATION Cancer

HEALING... communication

Mind This particular calcite stills the mind of constant chatter and alleviates anxiety, so your brain can relax, your emotions come into balance and your body feel fully rested. Place in the bedroom to aid deep relaxation while you sleep.

Body This gem can relieve throat infections and any issues to with the voice (such as laryngitis), the neck or head. Its calming effect helps bring focus and tranquillity - in particular to those with ADHD. Blue calcite is a lovely, gentle stone to help with recuperation after injury, operation or severe illness. It soothes frayed nerves, reduces pain, especially in the back, and lowers blood pressure, restoring you to full health.

Spirit Blue calcite is good for enabling harmonious conversations with friends or relatives, especially where there has been animosity or an argument. It also aids clear communication with spirit and enhances intuition.

How to use Position on or near the right chakras or areas for pain relief. Hold in either hand. Carry in a pocket or purse. Place in any area, such as the living room or a business meeting room to assist with calm, centred communication.

Healing the planet

Blue calcite is a great gem to use to perform some distant healing on the oceans, all sea creatures and the birds. Sit quietly in meditation and send your awareness to the seas and all the fish, mammals and crustaceans that live in them, along with all the birds that fly above. Send the light blue healing ray of this crystal out to all the beautiful beings you are seeing in your mind's eye. Say a quiet prayer to grant healing for all life in the waters and air of our world.

Calcite - green

TYPE OF CRYSTAL This pale-green to dark-emerald shade of calcite, sometimes with white veins inside, is waxy with a slight lustre in its raw form, shinier when tumbled and polished. It is found in the same countries as clear calcite. Sometimes green and other coloured calcites are acid treated to enhance their natural shading and texture, but this doesn't affect their healing properties.

CHAKRA CONNECTION Heart

ASTRO AFFILIATION Cancer

HEALING the mind

Mind A fantastic healer of the mind, this crystal removes anxieties and eases panic attacks. It takes away habitual harmful thinking, including old beliefs and stale familial programming, to bring balance back to your thoughts and emotions. This creates the chance for new manifestations to come to you, including increased prosperity and abundance on all levels.

Body This is a powerful stone to use in a healing grid to help boost your immune system, clear up bacterial infections and get rid of diseases in the body. Arthritis inflammation, ligament or muscle tightness or bone adjustments can be helped with this gem. Its cool green colour takes the heat out of burns and fever, calms the adrenal glands and quells any anger issues manifesting in the body.

Spirit Green calcite grounds and centres your spirit, enhances intuition and increases your psychic skills when used in meditation. It works well to support children in standing their ground and putting their point of view across calmly. If anyone is laughing at you, green calcite helps you cope.

How to use Carry in a pocket. Use in a healing grid. Put a piece in the garden or garden shed to increase your horticultural skills. Place on the body, especially over the heart chakra, while lying down and it will absorb any negativity or disease from the body. Make sure you cleanse it well after use, as green calcite takes on the extracted energy.

Calcite - orange

TYPE OF CRYSTAL Found in masses in Mexico, as well as in many of the same places as clear calcite, this variety comes in orange shades ranging from pale to bright.

CHAKRA CONNECTION Sacral, solar plexus

ASTRO AFFILIATION Cancer, Leo

HEALING reproductive system, sexual expression and self-esteem

Mind Orange calcite helps you feel calm and balanced, lessening aggression or belligerence. It releases fear and alleviates depression. Any problems in your thinking will be dissolved with orange calcite so you can reach your maximum potential without a negative mindset holding you back.

Body Expect this crystal to energize you and cleanse the lower chakras in particular, bringing you more vitality and increased sexual energy. Orange calcite helps heal the reproductive system, so anyone trying for a baby should carry a piece with them to balance their hormones and increase fertility. A circle of orange calcite crystals surrounding your bed can also boost the chances of having a baby, as well as removing stress and aiding a calm, restful sleep. Orange calcite is also beneficial for

the gallbladder and soothes kidney, bladder and intestinal issues, including irritable bowel syndrome. It removes mucus from your body, clearing the airways, sinuses and throat.

Spirit Radiating positive energy, orange calcite enhances self-esteem, boosts inspiration and heightens creativity. Meditating with a piece of it will help integrate spiritual expansion into your physical body, so your soul is fully embodied in everything you do.

How to use Place on or near relevant chakras. Carry with you in a pocket for renewed positivity and increased fertility. Keep in the area where you need to be creative, or in the bedroom for healthy sexual expression. Grid around your bed for full relaxation. Drink an elixir of calcite to increase

calcium absorption, boost the immune system and stimulate healthy tissue growth. This can also be applied to the skin to treat warts, ulcers and wounds.

Orange calcite meditation

Meditate lying down with a piece of orange calcite above your groin area and visualize its vitality boosting your sexual energy and circulating it around your whole body to radiate out into the world. It will help you and others embrace your sexuality.

Calcite - pink (mangano)

TYPE OF CRYSTAL This calcite ranges from light to more peachy pink, with white banding and veins running through it. It is found in masses in Brazil, Peru, Russia, the Czech Republic, Iceland, the UK and the US.

CHAKRA CONNECTION Heart

ASTRO AFFILIATION Cancer

HEALING with reiki energy and universal love

Mind Mangano calcite alleviates anxiety, dispels fears and helps combat resistance in the mind. It's a helpful stone to support your healing from abuse, assault or trauma, as it imparts self-worth and acceptance to anyone wearing or working with it. Used to encourage forgiveness, mangano calcite enables you to let go of grief from past events and replace that sorrow with empowering, unconditional self-love.

Body This crystal helps you rest well, fall into a deep sleep and stay asleep all night, free from nightmares, so you wake calm, peaceful and fully restored. Any nervous-system dysfunction and tension can be relieved with gentle, soothing pink calcite.

Spirit By opening the heart chakra, this pretty gem promotes a deep love of all. It heightens awareness of everything being united as part of the one consciousness that creates the universe. It helps you connect with the angelic realm and beings in other dimensions, and is a lovely crystal to use when doing reiki, as it amplifies the healing energy.

How to use While lying down in meditation, place pink calcite on the heart chakra. When seated, hold it in the dominant hand to share reiki energy or love, or the non-dominant hand for receiving love or universal energy. Keep in the meditation area, bedroom or any healing space for it to exude its gentle energy. Carry it in a pocket or wear it as a pendant over the heart.

Calcite - white

TYPE OF CRYSTAL Found in all the same places as the other calcites, but often looking distinctly different in 'dogtooth' formations, tiny slices or leaves of white crystal.

CHAKRA CONNECTION Crown

ASTRO AFFILIATION Cancer

HEALING... through connection with higher realms

Mind Allow this crystal to bring clarity of mind, especially when you sit with it in meditation. Sit with it long enough and it will bring all the answers you need.

Body This is a great gem to use for a detox, as it supports the healthy functioning of the liver, kidneys and lymphatic system.

Spirit Meditating with white calcite opens up the crown chakra and assists with connection to the higher dimensions of awareness, helping you receive a response to any questions you may have about your path and purpose. It also cleanses your aura and the energy fields of others, as well as magnifying the life force and raising your frequency to attract all the good experiences you desire.

How to use It can be placed on any chakra for energy clearings. Carry in a pocket. Position on a meditation altar or hold in either hand to encourage connection with higher dimensions during meditation. Put a piece of white calcite under your pillow for the same spiritual connection during sleep.

Calcite cleansing tip

Recharge calcite as well as yourself by adding it to your bath and soaking by candlelight. When it crumbles, its work is done, so bury it in the soil with gratitude for its healing help.

Calcite - yellow (lemon) or golden

TYPE OF CRYSTAL Found as above in a golden honey tone or light lemon colour, this crystal is sometimes referred to as lemon calcite or golden-ray calcite. It is found all over the world.

CHAKRA CONNECTION Solar plexus, crown

ASTRO AFFILIATION Cancer (lemon), Leo (golden)

HEALING through joy

Mind This sunny stone eases tension and makes you feel better overall by increasing confidence, self-worth and empathy. It encourages joy, optimism and the nourishing relaxation of mind, body and spirit. Allow it to stimulate your higher mind, sharpen your intellect and enable you to see the bigger picture of any situation. Golden calcite stimulates willpower, giving you the strength to avoid addictive substances.

Body Another good eliminator of toxins, yellow calcite supports the pancreas, spleen and kidneys, while golden calcite boosts circulation, the endocrine glands, gallbladder and liver. The lighter yellow stone helps minimize bone growths and regulate calcium deficiency. The golden variety can help drive infections from the body when they begin.

Spirit An elixir of this gemstone is uplifting for the spirit and is highly expansive for your energy field. It will deepen your meditations, enabling you to reach the highest source of guidance and astral travel, and channel messages from spirit. Golden calcite promotes past-life remembrance, supports healing visualizations and helps with divination exercises such as reading Tarot cards or runes.

How to use Wear as any kind of jewellery or carry in a pocket. Place on or near the solar plexus or crown area when lying down relaxing. Hold in the non-dominant hand in meditation to receive its benefits. Drink as an elixir.

Carnelian

TYPE OF CRYSTAL This translucent, brightly coloured crystal is a type of chalcedony quartz, with iron oxide making it red, orangish-red, orange and pink, sometimes with brown, white or yellow bands or inclusions. Found in Brazil, Peru, Uruguay, India, the UK, the Czech Republic, Slovakia, Romania and Iceland, carnelian was used by bygone cultures to smooth the dead's passage to the afterlife. Its name comes from the Latin word for flesh. Ancient warriors wore it around their necks to make them bold in battle, and it's long been believed to bring shy people out of their shells. A high-energy crystal symbolizing life, it was known by the Ancient Egyptians as the 'sunset stone', as they believed it channelled the heat of the sun into anyone who wore it.

CHAKRA CONNECTION Root, sacral

ASTRO AFFILIATION Taurus, Cancer, Leo

HEALING mental and physical lethargy

Mind Carnelian can give you a mental boost, kicking your mind out of lethargy and improving clarity, concentration and analytical skills. Use it to feel better all over and stimulate mind, body and spirit. It's great for anyone studying, creating or performing as it helps with inspiration, memory and speech, and brings courage, vitality and personal power. A stone to attract positivity into your life, it's worth carrying to help overcome abuse, as it teaches you to trust yourself again. Explore your deeper issues with this gem and say goodbye to detrimental conditioning once and for all.

Body A good stone to help raise your metabolism and help with digestion and eating disorders, carnelian increases the absorption of vitamins and minerals for improved tissue regeneration and blood nourishment. Activating the root and sacral chakras, it increases sex drive, relieves impotence and boosts fertility. Plus, it can be good for people with ME, lower back pain and neuralgia. Working on all bodily fluids, carnelian stimulates the kidneys, spleen, liver, pancreas and thyroid. It can also combat breathing issues such as hay fever, asthma and bronchitis.

Spirit This powerful crystal grounds and anchors you in the present, clears chattering thoughts in meditation, and protects against your and others' anger, envy and resentment. Carnelian helps you accept the natural cycle of life and death, fearing nothing, and replacing the blues with joy and love for life. The gem strengthens your connection to spirit guidance and can smooth the parent-child connection after upset or trauma.

How to use Carnelian can cleanse other stones just by being placed next to them, protect the home from the front door, and bring abundance. Carry in a pocket, or wear in a belt buckle or belt pouch to stimulate the lower chakras, boosting life force. Position next to the bed to increase sexual energy. Place on or near appropriate chakras. Put a piece of carnelian in the fridge or food cupboards to increase your willpower and avoid overeating.

Celestite

TYPE OF CRYSTAL Also known as celestine, this gem is usually translucent blue, ranging from a delicate, ethereal light shade to much deeper hues. Sometimes it contains shades of green, grey or violet, and occasionally can be found in yellow, white or tones of red and orange. Its tabular crystal masses or nodules consist of strontium sulphate, and are commonly found in India, where it has been mined for thousands of years, but also the US, Mexico, Peru, Egypt, Madagascar, Indonesia, Germany and Gloucestershire in the UK.

CHAKRA CONNECTION Throat, third eye, crown

ASTRO AFFILIATION Gemini

HEALING through angelic connection

Mind Clarity of thought will be yours with this crystal, as well as the release of stress, anxiety and despair. Mental disorders can be alleviated with this gem, which brings calmness, better communication skills and sharpened analytical abilities. In a conflict, it can bring resolution and harmony, improving fraught relationships through peaceful dialogue and respectful compassion, and cooling fiery tempers.

Body As with all light-blue stones, celestite opens and heals the throat and any ailments connection to this area. It improves eyesight and helps hearing issues, as well as providing general pain relief by bringing love energy to the area of affliction. It flushes out toxins and relaxes muscles.

Spirit The crystal for the New Age, celestite is a high-vibration stone that supports divine communication and connects you strongly with the angelic realm, higher beings and your deepest self. Expect insight and intuition to increase using this crystal placed on the third eye chakra in meditation, as well as better dream recall, out-of-body experiences and increased clairvoyant skills. Natural abilities in music and art are enhanced with celestite. It truly uplifts the soul, ignites spiritual development and guides you on the road to enlightenment.

How to use Position a large piece of celestite in a room to raise the energetic frequency. Hold in cupped hands during meditation, keep on an altar or use in a crystal ball for scrying. Place on or near relevant chakras to stimulate, or an area of the body to heal. Wear as earrings or a necklace. Put a piece in a creative space, music area or on your desk for added interdimensional inspiration.

Warning: Never place celestite in direct sunlight, or it will lose its colour.

Chalcedony

TYPE OF CRYSTAL Light, ethereal blue, white or greyish chalcedony is a silica crystal made from quartz and morganite. It comes from South Africa, Morocco, Turkey, the UK, the US, New Zealand, Brazil, Mexico, Russia, Iceland, Austria and the Czech Republic. Hard, with a lustrous surface, it makes a beautiful gem for jewellery. It also comes in pink, purple and red chalcedony, all of which have the following generic qualities, as well as different ones for each colour (see opposite).

CHAKRA CONNECTION Throat, third eye

ASTRO AFFILIATION Cancer, Sagittarius

HEALING by lessening the effects of ageing and calming communication

Mind The gem helps heal childhood issues and assists with emotional expression, reducing negative feelings and bringing balance to mind, body and spirit. It transforms melancholy into happiness, self-doubt into self-reflection, and guides you toward being more open, joyful and enthusiastic.

Body A powerful cleanser of the body, blue chalcedony clears mineral buildup in the veins, cleans out open wounds and lessens brain plaque in dementia patients, reducing the effects of senility. It can help combat alcoholism and heighten the mothering instinct, also increasing lactation. Improving your physical energy generally, it boosts the functioning of the eyes, spleen, gallbladder, blood and circulatory system. It can even assist the healing of bones and increase the body's absorption of important minerals.

Spirit Chalcedony encourages goodwill, positive connection and cooperation with others. Add to this enhanced telepathy and intuition, and chalcedony is a must for any group activity or meet-up. It can absorb negative energy and low-vibration emotions, and quell the effects of bad dreams. It also improves communication with spirit through meditation.

How to use Wear in jewellery, especially a ring or choker-style necklace. Position on or near relevant chakras or areas of the body for healing. Hold in non-dominant/receiving hand when meditating. Put a piece in a room that needs to be calm or where considered communication is to take place. A piece of chalcedony under the pillow or on the bedside table will bring better dreams.

Other colours of chalcedony and their healing properties:

Pink: A supremely spiritual stone, pink chalcedony promotes empathy, trust and deep inner peace. It strengthens the heart, boosts immunity and regulates lymphatic flow. Problems with breastfeeding can be helped with this gem.

Purple: Also called Aztec chalcedony, this crystal encourages connection through kindness, generosity and receptivity, which brings a strong sense of belonging. It helps you release issues from childhood, and stabilizes your mental state, even to the point of reducing the symptoms of dementia. This gem helps the nerve endings when pain, pressure and extremes of temperature are too much.

Grape chalcedony: Also purple, and sometimes grey or green, this variety has tiny grape-like nodules all over it. It is particularly effective at combatting ageing issues such as hair loss and wrinkles as well as arthritis and rheumatism. Opening the heart chakra, it dispels anger, fear and depression, and can even aid bipolar disorder. It assists your spiritual development, increasing prophetic dreams, deepening meditation and giving you confidence in your intuition.

Red: This chalcedony assists in manifesting your desires by helping you create a plan of action to fulfilment. With its red colour, it links to the blood, helping with clotting and circulation without raising blood pressure.

Charoite

TYPE OF CRYSTAL This predominantly purple stone is found only in Russia, in large violet masses, occasionally with inclusions of white quartz or black manganese.

CHAKRA CONNECTION Crown, heart

ASTRO AFFILIATION Scorpio, Sagittarius

HEALING the heart-mind connection

Mind Charoite can improve analytical skills. It puts things into perspective and lengthens the attention span, making it a beneficial crystal for anyone with ADHD. It enables you to accept others as they are, as well as the present moment, and take advantage of opportunities when they arise in order to move forward effectively. Removing resistance, stress and obsession, charoite helps you follow your own ideas rather than those of others.

Body Physically, this gem re-energizes the body and helps with general aches and pains, such as headaches or cramps. It can improve the health of the eyes and the heart, and regulate blood pressure. Any liver or pancreas damage can be rectified with this crystal. It helps overcome insomnia and encourages deep sleep and a

sense of calm in children. A highly beneficial stone to bring balance and calm in body and mind for anyone with autism or bipolar disorder.

Spirit This crystal helps you cope with spiritual transformation by opening, balancing and aligning the crown and heart chakras, raising your vibration and cleansing your aura. It connects you to the unconditional love of the universe, as well as spiritual guidance and your inner wisdom and insights. Use charoite to enhance your clairvoyant skills and ability to live fully in the present moment. Grounding the esoteric into the everyday, it ignites past-life memories to redress karma and steers you on a path of service for humanity.

How to use Very effective when used in a healing grid of crystals. Drink as an elixir for a full-body

cleanse and to stabilize after emotional upset. Place or wear over your heart in a pendant, or wherever it is most needed, touching the skin for best effect.

Chiastolite

TYPE OF CRYSTAL Alternatively called cross stone or andalusite, this gem is found in Spain, Chile, Russia and China. It is a variety of andalusite that forms in chunky crystals, most often in brown shades, grey or olive green, with a black graphite cross pattern. Ancient cultures used it to ward off ill intent and curses, and it is still used today for spiritual protection. Its name comes from the Greek word *chiastos* meaning 'cross marked'.

CHAKRA CONNECTION Sacral

ASTRO AFFILIATION Libra

HEALING the flow of life and ability to set clear boundaries

Mind This stone boosts brain power, dissolves fears and illusions, and encourages you to face reality with increased problem-solving ability, practicality and creativity. It helps get rid of guilt and transforms disharmony into ease, enabling you to overcome habitual thought patterns and behaviours that no longer serve you. It also encourages devotion, whether to a partner or spiritual practice.

Body This crystal balances the immune system, repairs chromosome damage and can ease paralysis. To help reduce a fever, heal rheumatism and gout, and fortify your nerves, try working with chiastolite. It also stimulates lactation in new mothers and stanches blood flow where needed.

Spirit Chiastolite is a crystal for protection and to help you stay strong in challenging situations. Good for anyone making the transition to the afterlife, it enables understanding of death and the dying process, and gives answers to the deeper mysteries of life. A stone to bring about change and rebirth, it can also help with astral travel and attuning to your soul purpose.

How to use Wear around the neck on jewellery or position on the body wherever it is needed.

Ritual to release negativity

- After cleansing your chiastolite stone, start carrying it in your pocket daily, especially whenever you are likely to come across any conflict or negativity.
- When anything hostile happens, grasp the stone in your hand and squeeze it as hard as you can. Feel the discordant energy from the negative situation going through you and into the stone, being trapped safely inside it.
- When you next have the chance, submerge the crystal in running water. Ideally, this should be held by you as you dive into a river or stream, but holding it under water in the sink as the tap runs will work just as well.
- Take the deepest breath possible as you do this, and, keeping the gem under water, slowly release your breath, visualizing all the negative energy from the stone (and the event earlier) getting carried away by the running water.

Chrysanthemum stone

TYPE OF CRYSTAL This gem features a flower-like pattern made of celestite or calcite, bursting outwards inside black dolomite, limestone, gypsum-bearing clay or porphyry. It is found in China, Japan, Canada and the US.

CHAKRA CONNECTION Root, crown

ASTRO AFFILIATION Taurus, Aquarius

HEALING equilibrium

Mind The gentle presence of this stone calms the mind and strengthens the character, overcoming jealousy, bigotry, ignorance, superficiality and self-righteousness. It encourages you to live more from a place of love and harmony with the world. This attracts the same qualities back to you, inspiring you to begin exciting new endeavours and relationships with confidence. Thinking more deeply and trusting in yourself and others, assisted by this crystal, will reduce animosity or resentment.

Body Chrysanthemum stone helps the body through any life transition, maturing and developing in a healthy way. It boosts fertility and supports the female reproductive system, dissolves fibroids and alleviates cystitis. Another good gem for getting rid of toxins, it helps the eyes, skin and skeleton.

Spirit Helping to generate a child-like, playful and innocent curiosity while on your spiritual path, this crystal encourages your authentic self to bloom and awakens your true purpose. Chrysanthemum stone keeps you grounded while you follow your dreams, without distractions. It enables you to see the bigger picture of your life, and realize that you can have stability, more connection with the present moment and a deeper sense of fulfilment.

How to use Wear as jewellery. Carry with you in a pocket all day. Position a piece in a room to enhance the energy in that area. This crystal can be used as an elixir, but it needs to be made in an indirect way - by placing the stone in a glass bowl inside a bowl of water. The delicate flower part may be affected if it comes into contact with water.

Chrysoberyl

TYPE OF CRYSTAL This very hard crystal forms in hexagonal, tabular, translucent shades of yellow and green. Some show a different colour when under artificial light. It is found in Brazil, the US, Sri Lanka, Tanzania and Russia. Its name comes from the Greek word *chrysos*, meaning 'gold white spar', and *beryllos*, which refers to its beryllium content. In Asia especially, Chrysoberyl has been a prized stone for thousands of years, believed to provide whoever wears it with protection from the evil eye. It amplifies the effects of other crystals.

CHAKRA CONNECTION Sacral, solar plexus and crown

ASTRO AFFILIATION Leo

HEALING self-esteem

Mind This is a good stone to help you break negative cycles of thinking or behaviour, bringing peace of mind to you through any meditations with it. Use chrysoberyl to set personal goals by imbuing the crystal with your deepest thoughts and intentions and harnessing its power of motivation to follow them through. This gem can also help you see both sides of an argument, bringing understanding and forgiveness to your relationships. It can help ease anxiety and other symptoms of depression, encouraging you to release emotions such as anger, sadness and grief. This gem can also improve your memory and bring a clear sense of inner peace, the more you meditate with it.

Body Chrysoberyl boosts the health of the liver, kidneys and pancreas. It supports good eye health, delaying any macular degeneration, and is effective at reducing insomnia. It can clear up coughs and reduce congestion. Digestion issues, such as irritable bowel syndrome, can be eased with chrysoberyl, which also helps with stomach ulcers and other intestinal problems. This crystal is believed to lower blood pressure, which may prevent strokes, and balance cholesterol. Wear this stone to help you accept and gain more knowledge of any illness or affliction you have.

Spirit Heightening your sense of self-esteem, chrysoberyl encourages you to be kind to yourself and develop your spirituality in your own way. It will bring a deep peace to all meditations you do while holding it. Chrysoberyl connects you deeply to the universal flow of energy, bringing you good luck and prosperity. Working with it can enhance your psychic skills while protecting you from negative energies.

How to use Wear in a ring or bracelet, or carry in a pocket. It can be put with other crystals, as it won't damage them. When lying down in meditation or relaxation, position on the sacral or solar plexus chakra, or hold in either hand. For a powerful crown chakra-opening meditation, hold the stone in your non-dominant hand and focus on your breathing. When you inhale, imagine white light entering through the crown of your head and filling your entire body. Then, as you exhale, visualize any negative energy or emotions flowing out of your body and being released.

Chrysocolla

TYPE OF CRYSTAL This blue-green mineral consists of hydrated copper silicate, and forms as opaline crusts, masses and layers in Peru, Chile, Mexico, Zaire, Russia, the UK and the US. It often contains inclusions or bands of other minerals, and is usually sold as polished or tumbled stones.

CHAKRA CONNECTION Solar plexus, heart, throat and third eye

ASTRO AFFILIATION Taurus, Gemini, Virgo

HEALING by supporting most internal organs

Mind A stone to help with writing and teaching, chrysocolla boosts communication skills and truth-telling, and allows you to keep a cool head in any situation. It brings confidence, self-awareness and sensitivity when you speak, and inspires motivation and ideas for artistic endeavours. This crystal can help you stay impartial in an argument, release feelings of guilt and bring about joy. Monks and hermits used this crystal in ancient times as it can alleviate the anxiety and depression often associated with having to stay in one place.

Body This incredible heal-all stone aids afflictions of the hips and other joints, improving symptoms of arthritis and rheumatism as well as supporting the workings of the intestines, liver, kidneys, pancreas, thyroid, muscles and blood. Ulcers, leukaemia and restless-leg syndrome can all benefit from using this gem. Chrysocolla increases lung capacity, helping with breathing issues such as asthma, bronchitis and emphysema. It's also useful for anyone with diabetes, as it encourages healthy metabolism, insulin production and glucose levels in the blood. One for easing PMS and period pains, it also assists a healthy pregnancy. It has a cooling action to soothe burns, sore throats and tonsil infections.

Spirit Use this tranquil stone to heighten female sexuality and connection with the Goddess, and to encourage men to show their vulnerable emotions. It can revitalize stale or stabilize fraught relationships, and heal heartache after a breakup. Chrysocolla cleanses all the chakras and aligns them with divine energy. Positioned at the third eye, it can activate your psychic vision; at the throat chakra, it helps you know when to speak up and when it's best to stay quiet. It brings you peace, compassion and great inner strength, taking away any negative energies from yourself, others and your environment.

How to use Place directly on the skin or body area where there is discomfort, pain or disease. Hold on or over the relevant chakra while seated or lying down resting.

Chrysoprase

TYPE OF CRYSTAL This opaque chalcedony comes in various green shades, from deep green to bright apple green, often with white, black or brown banding. It is found in the US, Brazil, Australia, Tanzania, Poland and Russia.

CHAKRA CONNECTION Sacral, heart

ASTRO AFFILIATION Libra

HEALING the heart

Mind A useful stone for clearing brain fog and bringing back mental dexterity, chrysoprase assists those with anxiety, depression, schizophrenia and any neurotic patterns of thinking. It calms compulsive thinking and actions, and helps overcome judgmental attitudes, arrogance or inferiority, guiding you toward accepting yourself, others and everything in life with an open mind.

Body A good gem for boosting fertility and balancing the hormones, chrysoprase also guards against sexually transmitted diseases. It is all for improving the health of the heart and spleen, as well as rectifying eye problems, skin issues and gout. It helps increase vitamin C absorption, ease digestion problems and soothe upset stomach due to stress. It can help with a detox as it removes heavy metals in the body and boosts liver function. A stone to bring about a relaxed, peaceful sleep, free from nightmares.

Spirit To deepen your meditation practice and increase intuitive insights, use chrysoprase. It opens the heart chakra, attracting love and commitment, encouraging hope, healing heartache and supporting independence. Working to heal the wounded inner child and trauma from childhood, chrysoprase also energizes the sacral chakra, anchoring divine energy into the body and giving you a sense of being part of the great oneness.

How to use Wear in a pendant over the heart chakra, or place on this area while lying down in a relaxing meditation. Hold in either hand for a while to feel its benefits. Chrysoprase can be drunk as an elixir for acute cases of illness. Carry it with you to attract prosperity.

Cinnabar

TYPE OF CRYSTAL Found abundantly in tabular and needle-like crystals and masses in China and the US, this expensive stone is made of mercury sulphide and most likely vermilion. Usually brick red and sometimes containing gold or grey, it can be lustrous or dull. Its name comes from a Persian or Indian word for 'dragon's blood'.

CHAKRA CONNECTION Root

ASTRO AFFILIATION Leo

HEALING assertiveness

Mind This is a good stone to help boost your financial know-how, improve your organizational skills and attract success in business. It increases your powers of persuasion and assertiveness without it heading into aggression. Cinnabar is great for improving the fluency of your speech, and helps with group cohesion and community cooperation.

Body Bringing strength, vitality and flexibility to your body, this gem helps combat weight gain and allows your outer appearance to sparkle. It's also great for cleansing the blood and boosting fertility.

Spirit Cinnabar helps bring about a personal transformation for the better. It aligns all the energy centres, releasing any blockages to spiritual awakening. Allow it to assist your connection to the great consciousness behind all of existence, and know that you are where you are meant to be and everything is as it's supposed to be.

How to use Position next to the root chakra while sitting or lying down in meditation. Hold in your receiving/non-dominant hand to attract its qualities into your life. Keep in your wallet or on your work desk for increased abundance. Carry it with you.

Note: Do not make cinnabar into an elixir, as ingesting it is toxic. It is where mercury comes from, which is poisonous.

Citrine

TYPE OF CRYSTAL A golden or sometimes lemon-coloured quartz coloured by volcanic activity, mostly found in Brazil, the US, Russia, Madagascar, France and the UK. Natural citrine is fairly rare, so shops often sell amethyst that's been heat-treated until it turns a vivid yellow. They share similar properties, but crystal healers prefer to work with natural citrine because its energy is more consistent.

CHAKRA CONNECTION Solar plexus, crown

ASTRO AFFILIATION Aries, Gemini, Leo, Libra

HEALING with positive, invigorating energy

Mind Citrine is a highly positive, energizing stone, good for lifting any negative mindset, acting on constructive criticism and helping you move forward optimistically. It helps you make the right decision and smooths out upsets you may have with others. This joyful gem stops you dwelling on the past so you can go with the flow of whatever new experiences come your way, exploring potential paths with enjoyment. If you're working on manifesting your dream life, imbue citrine with your intentions as it attracts wealth, success and happiness. If studying, learning or teaching, carry citrine with you for extra brain power, concentration and creative self-expression.

Body Warming and energizing, citrine invigorates the body, boosting its process of elimination, from easing constipation to getting rid of cellulite. It helps anything related to the digestive system, improving its healthy functioning and alleviating nausea and vomiting. The liver, spleen, kidneys and pancreas also get a boost with citrine, combating infections, jaundice or anaemia. It improves eyesight, thymus function and tissue regeneration, and balances the thyroid. An elixir can relieve any menstrual issues and soothe the hot flushes of menopause.

Spirit A powerful protector of the aura, citrine is one to always carry with you as it enables you to sense impending danger. It transforms negative energy into positive, and can rectify relationship discord and dispel anger. This crystal cleanses all the chakras, but especially the sacral and solar plexus, boosting self-esteem, confidence and joy. It also opens up the crown chakra to higher guidance, intuition and a deeper spiritual awareness.

How to use Wear as a ring, earrings or choker-style necklace, with the point of it facing downwards to bring the golden ray of spirit down into the physical realm. Meditate with it by holding a piece in the receiving/non-dominant hand or by looking into a citrine sphere. Place on relevant chakra or area of the body for healing. On your work desk or creative space, it will bring new ideas and motivation. Carry it to attract prosperity.

Warning: Citrine never needs cleansing, as it transmutes, dissipates and grounds energy. But it does fade in sunlight, so never leave it outside or near a sunny window.

Creedite

TYPE OF CRYSTAL A clear to opaque white, orange, yellow, brown, blue and sometimes purple crystal that grows in 'drusy' form, small needle-like crystals attached to a host stone, or in radiating prismatic clusters. Obtained in parts of Mexico and the US, it is a calcium aluminium sulphate fluoro hydroxide mineral.

CHAKRA CONNECTION All chakras, but especially crown, third eye, throat and etheric chakras above the head

ASTRO AFFILIATION Virgo

HEALING by removing obstacles and delays on your spiritual journey

Mind This crystal encourages a deeper understanding of why things happen, so you can see life experiences as gifts. Creedite promotes detached observation and helps you drop worn-out, self-pitying narratives and unnecessary dramas. With this gem, you can become more centred in peace instead of overwhelmed by emotions; get over a love that rationally could not work; and ensure you follow through confidently with previously postponed plans. This gem is good for overcoming depression as well as discovering and removing the mental blocks to happiness and fulfilment.

Body Creedite is helpful for torn muscles and ligaments, fractured bones and for improving nerve issues due to degeneration or malfunction. Another good blood detoxifier, it is believed to help stabilize the pulse rate. It can also assist the body in its absorption of vitamins A, B and E, boosting the immune system a great deal.

Spirit Strongly connecting you to divine energy, creedite clears, realigns and recharges all the chakras and takes you instantly to a clear meditative state. It has the potential to quickly raise your frequency, bringing expanded awareness and cleansing euphoria. This crystal facilitates and helps remember the insights from lucid dreaming, out-of-body experiences and past-life recollection. It also enables you to understand the wisdom communicated in ancient texts and the Akashic records, the etheric library where everything is recorded, past, present and future. A good gem for channelling, it brings clear messages from higher spiritual planes, including the angels and your spirit guides.

How to use Hold in meditation or place on or near the appropriate chakras while lying down, breathing deeply, with eyes closed. Use in a crystal grid and leave in place for maximum effect. Creedite purifies the energy of other stones but needs to be cleaned afterwards.

Dalmatian stone

TYPE OF CRYSTAL Sometimes called Dalmatian jasper, this pale grey, cream or beige-brown jasper with black or brown spots of iron oxide is patterned like a Dalmatian dog. A mixture of quartz, tourmaline and microcline, it is found in Mexico.

CHAKRA CONNECTION Root, sacral and the earth chakra beneath the feet

ASTRO AFFILIATION Gemini

HEALING animals, especially dogs

Mind With its potent combination of crystals, this stone assists with any learning, reflection and planning, all of which help with setting and achieving your life goals. Containing tourmaline, this stone can quickly transform outworn and negative thought patterns and beliefs, diminishing excessive thinking and overanalysis, and even depression, so you can move out of your head, into your body and enjoy life to the full. Families and friends find it good for harmony, fidelity and cooperation.

Body A stone to ease muscle cramps, sprains and fraught nerves, Dalmatian stone boosts cartilage strength and physical stamina, making it excellent for athletes. It can give you the determination to quit smoking as well as extra energy, improved mood and a better balance of emotions. This crystal helps with bowel issues, such as IBS and constipation, as well as skin reactions and allergies. Dalmatian stone invokes calm, especially in children, encouraging a restful sleep, free from nightmares. It also promotes animal training and healing, especially with dogs, helping you make this a profession.

Spirit This crystal reminds you that you are a spiritual being having a human experience, and to joyfully live every day of your incarnation. It protects you from physical danger and helps you let go of any trauma in the past. Dalmatian stone brings happiness, devotion and composure to relationships, releasing any negativity from previous issues. It also balances the yin/yang, feminine/masculine energy within.

How to use Place a grid around the person or pet being treated. Meditate while holding the stone or place it on or near the chakra or area where it is most needed.

Danburite

TYPE OF CRYSTAL This fairly hard translucent crystal comes in many colours including yellow, white, pink and light purple, with white or grey banding. It is found in Japan, Mexico, the US, Russia, Switzerland, the Czech Republic and Myanmar, and is sold as polished gems, clusters or points.

CHAKRA CONNECTION Heart, throat, third eye, crown; the specific colours relate to the corresponding chakras

ASTRO AFFILIATION Leo

HEALING karma

Mind Danburite is a crystal for new beginnings, helping you leave the past behind, clear old karma and release the mind from the patterns holding you back. It can help with psychological recovery after an operation, when you might be feeling down and frustrated, as it brings patience and peace.

Body This powerful healing gem aids a good a detox, treating and improving the workings of the gallbladder and liver. It can clear long-term allergies such as hay fever. If you need to gain a bit of weight, danburite will assist. It also helps with motor function and eases muscle stiffness.

Spirit A spiritual stone with a high vibration, Danburite opens you up to pure heart energy, unconditional love, and connection to higher consciousness and the angelic realms. In meditation, it will bring an elevated level of awareness, infinite wisdom and intuition. Sometimes this crystal contains a formation that looks like the Buddha, so it is believed to exude spiritual light and guide you on a smooth path toward enlightenment.

How to use Wear as jewellery, especially in a necklace or earrings. Carry in a pocket. Keep in your meditation area or on your altar. Place on the relevant chakras, but especially over the heart. A piece under your pillow at night can encourage lucid dreaming.

Desert rose selenite

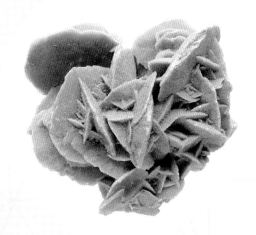

TYPE OF CRYSTAL Also known as gypsum rose, Sahara rose, sand rose or rose rock, this unique gem resembles a rosette, with sand-coloured 'petals' of gypsum, baryte and sand particles, sometimes brown, tan, cream or white. The radiating clusters of fanning petals form when the crystals are created in arid, sandy conditions, and range from pea-sized to 10cm in diameter. It is found in Germany, Austria, France, the UK, Greece, Poland, Russia and the US.

CHAKRA CONNECTION Third eye, crown

ASTRO AFFILIATION Taurus, Capricorn

HEALING sex drive and motivation

Mind A good gem to focus the mind and clear confusion, desert rose calms racing thoughts and encourages acceptance of your true self, promoting self-worth and confidence. It can help get to the root of subconscious thought patterns that lead to addictions, and release them. Desert rose boosts your motivation and initiative to pursue your goals. With this crystal as your talisman, expect synchronistic opportunities to come your way.

Body The healing benefits of desert rose include keeping the muscles flexible, the skin supple and soft tissue regenerating healthily, clearing up psoriasis and other skin issues. It also supports bone strength and brings special relief for backaches. This stone works wonders for your sex drive, increasing fertility and improving prostate health in men. It soothes ulcers, reduces travel sickness and nausea, and helps fight off viral infections.

Spirit Delicate desert rose helps cleanse your energy from the inside out, enabling you to meditate more deeply and raise your energetic vibration. It offers plenty of comfort for the soul as you awaken, and helps you connect with your higher self and your guardian angels, open your third eye and heighten your intuition. It also promotes prophetic dreaming and clairvoyant skills, and will enable you to see white light and feel loving energy from the angelic realm.

How to use Hold gently in either hand in meditation or sit in front of a piece on your altar. Place the gem on or next to the appropriate chakras or areas of need on the body. Handle with care, as it is very fragile. Make sure you keep this stone dry, as it disintegrates easily. Cleanse it only under full moonlight (no rain) or by smudging with sage.

Diamond

TYPE OF CRYSTAL Found in Australia, South Africa, Angola, Botswana, Brazil, Venezuela, the US, Russia and India, diamonds are usually small octahedral, dodecahedral and trapezohedral crystals. Rough, uncut and unpolished diamonds are translucent and come in many colours including white, yellow, blue, brown, pink, red, orange, green, black and grey. Coloured gems are usually treated or enhanced in some way, but all diamonds are a symbols of purity, commitment and wealth. They are the only gem made of one element - carbon - and are formed around 100 miles under the earth's crust, carried to the surface by volcanic activity.

CHAKRA CONNECTION All chakras, especially the crown

ASTRO AFFILIATION Aries, Taurus, Leo

HEALING by boosting the effect of all other crystals

Mind This famous precious gemstone clears mental anguish and emotional pain, linking the intellect with the higher mind to give you the clarity, positivity and invincibility needed to get over any hurt. It will point to any negative thinking or childhood issues and encourage transformation. A good stone for new beginnings, diamond eliminates fear, boosts the imagination and increases inventive ideas for new paths.

Body Traditionally used to counteract poisons, diamond is still good for detoxifying and cleansing, benefitting the brain in particular. It also rebalances the metabolism and treats chronic conditions and allergies. Its sparkly nature is said to improve eyesight and clear glaucoma. It is effective at blocking the harmful effects of EMFs from mobile phones and Wi-Fi routers.

Spirit Amplifiers of energy, diamonds are powerful manifesters of abundance and love, enhancing the bond between a married couple. They will clear your aura of anything clouding your bright inner light, so your true self can shine with a revitalized energy body and you can learn to love yourself more. Activating the crown chakra, diamonds will connect you to divine wisdom, your higher self and your soul's yearning for enlightenment.

How to use Place directly on the crown chakra in meditation. Hold next to any area in need of purification or healing. Wear in a necklace or as earrings to block EMFs from phones. Carry it with you to attract abundance. Position on your meditation altar to elevate your practice.

Diamond - Himalayan

TYPE OF CRYSTAL Also called pakimer diamonds, these are small and perfect, clear, bright, double-terminated quartz crystals found only in the Himalayan mountains of India and Pakistan.

CHAKRA CONNECTION Crown

ASTRO AFFILIATION Cancer, Scorpio, Sagittarius

HEALING long-distance relationships

Mind These gems enable you to live more in the present moment. They help you release fears or stresses, and open your mind to being more spontaneous. They also improve your memory.

Body Another good gem to use for a detox of the body, Himalayan diamonds alleviate headaches, boost metabolism and help combat infectious illnesses. They also promote longevity and help reduce the signs and symptoms of ageing.

Spirit Bringing a sense of relaxation and a good cleanse of the spirit, this crystal helps you stay in energetic connection with long-distance friends or lovers. Clearing any blockages in your crown chakra, Himalayan diamonds attune you to a higher power, which can enhance your psychic skills and enable you to perform healing from a distance.

How to use Place on the crown chakra in meditation or on the area of the body you want to help. Put a piece of Himalayan diamond on a photo of someone far away with whom you want to connect or heal. Carry it in a pocket or wear as jewellery.

Did you know?

• Diamonds are the hardest natural substance on earth, measuring a ten on the Mohs Hardness Scale and at least 58 times harder than anything else in nature. This makes them extremely effective at cutting, polishing and drilling, which is why many industries, including automotive, mining, and military, use diamond saws and drills.

• In 2011, a chemistry professor discovered that a candle flame contains millions of tiny diamonds. About 1.5 million diamond nanoparticles are created in a candle flame every second it burns.

• You can have the ashes of your deceased loved one turned into a little man-made diamond.

Diopside

TYPE OF CRYSTAL The chromium-rich type of chrome diopside, one of many varieties, forms in prisms, often with rhomboid terminations. It is usually a dull green colour but sometimes black, and is found in crystalline inclusions and masses in Afghanistan, Canada, Russia, Brazil, South Africa, Italy, Germany and the US.

CHAKRA CONNECTION Third eye and crown

ASTRO AFFILIATION Virgo

HEALING by bringing wellbeing through service

Mind This calming crystal brings a sense of overall contentment and ease, as it clears the mind of stagnant negative emotions, helps trapped tears flow, and promotes peace and wellbeing. It also bolsters the intellect and encourages learning, particularly supporting analysis and the study of mathematics. Work with dioptase to reduce feelings of victimhood stemming from past events, by learning forgiveness and trust. Regularly using dioptase gives you a renewed joy in life and appreciation of your talents.

Body Green diopside helps with recovery after any surgery, trauma or bad illness. It can improve the health of the heart, lungs and kidneys, and relieve stress, soothe ulcers and regulate blood pressure. It also boosts circulation, balances hormones and the acid/alkaline makeup of your body, alleviating the symptoms of an upset stomach. This gem is also good for reducing inflammation and helping with muscle spasms and aches.

Spirit Black dioptase especially expands your sense of compassion and connection with the Earth, guiding you into service for the good of others, in harmony with the planet. Both colours bring benefits to a regular meditation practice, by heightening psychic ability, raising consciousness and giving your spiritual development a nudge. Green diopside can be used for successful Earth healing as well as calming distressed animals.

How to use Grid on the spot or on a photo of an area of the Earth to be healed. Position near animals or in their bed. Place on third eye chakra while lying down in relaxation, or on the crown chakra when seated. Hold next to the place on the body to be helped.

Dioptase

TYPE OF CRYSTAL This rare, expensive stone is found in small clusters or points in parts of Russia, Iran, Peru, Chile, Congo, Namibia and North Africa. Its rich green colour, coming from copper in its mineral makeup, ranges from a deep blue-green to bright emerald.

CHAKRA CONNECTION Heart and third eye

ASTRO AFFILIATION Scorpio, Sagittarius

HEALING the heart and raising vibration

Mind Focusing the mind on the present moment and releasing the need to control outcomes are the main mental health benefits of this crystal. Dioptase detoxifies your thinking, dissolving the anguish and pain associated with grief, betrayal or abandonment. Its rich green colour enters the heart to resolve any inner-child wounds and heal deep sadness, bringing in a new vibration of love and pointing you toward fulfilment. It also promotes understanding of the causes of your dis-ease.

Body A powerful heart healer, dioptase can heal long-term conditions and prevent heart attacks, bringing down high blood pressure and helping overcome any shocks. An elixir can be drunk to relieve headaches and migraines, soothing pain of any kind as well as reducing fatigue, nausea and stomach upsets. It is believed to regenerate the liver, especially after addiction to alcohol, which it can help you overcome. Dioptase can also boost thymus function, activate T-cells to combat viruses, and relieve Ménière's disease symptoms.

Spirit This gem can have a dramatic effect on the whole of your energy field as it shifts all the chakras up to a higher level of functioning, expanding your consciousness to new heights as a result. This process assists you in your awakening, helping you realize what inner riches you possess. Positioned on the third eye in meditation, dioptase can bring psychic visions, past-life recollection and attunement to spirit.

How to use Position on the heart chakra to heal. Wear in a pendant hanging over this area to bring yourself into the now. Hold in your non-dominant hand to receive love. Position in the bedroom to promote loving relationships. Carry in a pocket or purse to attract abundance. Drink sparingly as a gem essence to relieve pain and other bodily symptoms of dis-ease. Dioptase contains copper, so you do not want to ingest too much of it.

Dolomite

TYPE OF CRYSTAL First discovered in the Dolomite Alps in northern Italy but now also found in Spain, Brazil, Mexico, the US, Canada and Switzerland, this crystal is made up of calcium magnesium carbonate. It comes in prismatic columns or rhombohedral tabular masses, often with curved faces, and makes up around two per cent of the Earth's crust. Its colours range from white, grey, pink, brownish-white and colourless, sometimes fluorescing white to pink under ultra-violet light.

CHAKRA CONNECTION Heart, crown

ASTRO AFFILIATION Aries

HEALING calcium deficiencies

Mind A crystal to promote original thought and abstract ideas, dolomite brings powerful inspiration for writers, inventors and entrepreneurs. Its uplifting nature helps alleviate grief, sorrow and loneliness, and enables you to face fears and phobias with courage and confidence. It helps you drop attachments to drama in your life, and removes blockages in your mind, such as resistance or victimhood, that might be stopping you from living your best life.

Body This stone helps the body metabolize calcium, thereby strengthening teeth and bones, nourishing skin, hair and nails, and aiding the full function of muscles, cells and the nervous system. Dolomite also helps with insomnia, stopping nightmares and sorting out irregular sleep patterns. It supports a good detox,

boosts metabolism and balances appetite while increasing your stamina and endurance during exercise, making it a good gem for weight management. It relieves PMS symptoms, evens out hormone imbalance, and heals any issues with the reproductive system and genitals. This powerful crystal can also realkalize your body if it's too acidic, and even help prevent cancer.

Spirit Dolomite is another very protective stone, balancing and grounding erratic or chaotic energy in a room if positioned there. It opens and elevates the heart chakra, encouraging self-love, which attracts more love into your life and helps you cherish the wonderful life you have. This stone can guide you to new ways of enhancing your connection with the divine, such as through tai chi,

a walking meditation or shamanic journeying.

How to use Carry it with you when walking. Hold in your non-dominant hand while meditating. Position on the area of the body or the chakra required for healing. Place under your pillow or by the bedside to help with sleep, calming nerves and bringing love into your life.

Emerald

TYPE OF CRYSTAL Emerald is a much-prized bright-green, translucent and transparent type of beryl found in India, Egypt, Zimbabwe, Tanzania, Austria, Brazil and Colombia. Rough-cut, large chunks of emerald are cloudy and readily available, but once polished to smaller precious gems it becomes stunningly clear and highly attractive.

CHAKRA CONNECTION Heart

ASTRO AFFILIATION Aries, Taurus, Gemini

HEALING by cleansing and bringing clarity and balanced connection

Mind This life-affirming gem releases negative thinking and replaces it with a positive mindset, focusing on inspired intentions and uplifting actions to help you overcome challenges. Emerald brings mental clarity, enhanced memory, honesty and discernment. Expect increased patience, mutual understanding and the ability to eloquently express your truth when working with this crystal.

Body Emerald has antiseptic properties, so it helps with bacterial and viral infections and supports the immune system to speed recovery. It was once used as an antidote to poisons; hence it bolsters the bile ducts, clears out the kidneys and detoxifies the liver, ridding it of jaundice. It is also thought to reduce plaque on the teeth and soothe insect bites. Blocked sinuses, asthma symptoms and tired, itchy eyes, as well as the symptoms of diabetes and rheumatism can be eased with this crystal. The heart, muscles and spine all get support from vitality-enhancing emerald.

Spirit In days of old, this gem was used to protect the wearer from enchantment and wizardry, and to be able to tell the future. It is said that if emerald changes colour, it signifies the unfaithfulness of a lover. Today its powers include kick-starting your clairvoyance and receiving wisdom from higher planes of existence. Emerald opens the heart chakra to bring success in love, including feelings of unity, loyalty and domestic bliss in all relationships. Alleviating a bad mood, this precious gem ensures mind, body and spirit are in balance, giving you a deep inner knowledge of unconscious issues and desires. It's another powerful consciousness elevator, helping broaden your spiritual outlook and abilities.

How to use Wear emerald in jewellery, especially necklaces, bracelets or an engagement ring to balance and strengthen the relationship, or on the little finger to lift your awareness and increase abundance. Try not to wear it all the time, though, as it can trigger negative feelings. Position on the heart chakra in meditation or next to any area of the body for healing.

Eilat stone

TYPE OF CRYSTAL Also known as King Solomon stone, this turquoise, blue or green mottled and opaque gem is named after the Israeli city of Eilat, where it was once mined. Still found in Israel and Jordan, it's a beautiful and powerful mix of several copper minerals, including malachite, turquoise, azurite and chrysocolla. The unique patterning is caused by the oxidization of iron, copper and manganese. This stone is usually cut into cabochons for jewellery, to show off its superior lustre and brightly coloured patterns.

CHAKRA CONNECTION Heart and throat chakras especially - but all chakras get a boost

ASTRO AFFILIATION Taurus, Leo

HEALING through regeneration - of cells, Mother Earth, love and light

Mind Known as the 'sage stone' due to its mind-enhancing combination of minerals, this crystal promotes wisdom and creative inspiration, to help you cope with challenges. Alleviating depression and ridding you of fears and memories from troubling events, this gem helps you express yourself and own your power.

Body A good physical cleanser, this stone flushes out toxins, stimulates the lymphatic and immune systems, and helps cell and tissue regeneration. It is thought that this stone even helps with tumours and issues with the liver or bones. Allow Eilat stone to take away pain, fever or problems with your sinuses. It can also ease menstrual symptoms.

Spirit Eilat stone encourages emotional healing after traumatic events such as rape, incest or violence, as well as any kind of sexual control or misogyny. It reunites a fragmented soul and reintegrates the self, even clearing the Akashic records of past-life trauma. Helping you radiate a lightness of being, Eilat stone heightens your awareness of how beautiful Mother Earth is, harnessing the power of creation available from Source energy.

How to use Hold Eilat stone next to the area in need of healing, or place on the relevant chakra. Use in a healing grid. Wear in a pendant over the thymus, at heart level, or in any other type of jewellery.

Warning: Eilat stone contains iron, copper and manganese; all are beneficial to our bodies in trace amounts, but not in excess. Do not make Eilat stone into an elixir to drink. If the malachite part of this stone causes palpitations, which it sometimes can, remove the Eilat stone and replace it with calming rhodochrosite or smoky quartz.

Epidote

TYPE OF CRYSTAL This translucent crystal, made of a silicate mineral that forms rocks, is generally found as elongated shapes, often inside quartz. It is obtained in many countries around the world, including Europe, Russia, Mexico, Brazil, and parts of Africa and the Middle East. Also known as pistacite because of its pistachio shade, its colours range from yellowish-green to occasionally brownish-green to almost black, and it can be lustrous and transparent or nearly opaque.

CHAKRA CONNECTION Heart and third eye

ASTRO AFFILIATION Gemini

HEALING by serving as a catalyst for change

Mind Epidote is another powerful stone to help bring negative thought patterns or memories of past trauma to the surface in order to transform. It helps you let go of resistance to change and awakening. Some can find it a super-strong catharsis, so you may wish to get professional therapy to help you process it. Ultimately, epidote wants you to live life to the max and manifest all you dream of. It will stop you from slipping back into feeling sorry for yourself or being too critical with harsh self-talk. It helps you see your and others' strengths and weaknesses, relieves stress and anxiety, and encourages you to set realistic goals.

Body Highly supportive of the body's natural ability to heal and be in balance, this gem is good to use while recovering from a long illness or operation. It boosts the immune and nervous systems, functions, and brain power. An elixir of this crystal is said to improve skin softness and help with dehydration. The liver, gallbladder and adrenal glands all get a helping hand with the energy from epidote.

Spirit A gem for good relationships, epidote brings prosperity and abundance. It helps attune you strongly to spirit and gives you the nudge you need if you are resistant to your spiritual path. It will widen your perception of life and bring you a richer sense of identity and personal power to make the best of your time on Earth.

How to use Place on or next to the heart centre, hold in either hand, or keep on an altar for meditation. Position near or on areas of the body in need of assistance. Grid around you in seated or supine relaxation.

Eudialyte

TYPE OF CRYSTAL This variety of dark pink, black and green garnet, often mixed with other minerals, is becoming more readily found in Russia, Greenland, Canada, the US and Madagascar. It is usually mottled and can be opaque or transparent.

CHAKRA CONNECTION Heart, root and earth chakras

ASTRO AFFILIATION Aries

HEALING previous choices and past-life loves

Mind If you've made the wrong choices in the past, eudialyte can help you rectify them by clearing away guilt or regret and bringing more joy, creativity and fulfilment. If you have tough decisions to make or need to end a relationship, this crystal can help you do it with calm consideration and dignity instead of arguments and discord. Any depression can be lifted and negative emotions such as anger, resentment or jealousy transformed with this gem. Instead, you will learn self-forgiveness and confidence.

Body This is a highly beneficial crystal to help with any eye disorders, as it is believed to stabilize the optic nerve. Another good gem for soothing the nervous system, it boosts energy and brings your brainwaves into harmony, leaving you feeling an alert state of equilibrium. Eudialyte is thought to lessen some of the symptoms of multiple sclerosis, lupus, Alzheimer's and Parkinson's by stimulating the body's innate healing ability.

Spirit Energizing the root and heart chakras, this crystal activates kundalini, or life-force energy, aligning you to your personal power, life purpose and the divine within you. If you've had any issues with God or Source, this gem gets to the reason why, even taking you back to past lives in meditations to explore old karma. It can guide you to the perfect soul mate for you, and if there is resistance on their part, eudialyte will reveal any unexpected issues for resolution.

How to use You can hold this gem in either hand while sitting or lying down in meditation. Place on or near the relevant chakra or area of the body in need of assistance. Leave in a healing grid of crystals, especially with metamorphosis quartz to ease the discomfort of change. Sleep with eudialyte under your pillow or next to your bed for answers to questions regarding your love life. It is mildly radioactive, so use sparingly.

Flint

TYPE OF CRYSTAL Solid, glassy and often covered in white chalk, this type of chalcedony is found all over the world and has been considered sacred since ancient times. Originally black, it weathers to other colours including grey, brown and white, blue, orange and yellow. It was used in burials by cultures of antiquity to help smooth the path of the dead to the afterlife.

CHAKRA CONNECTION Crown

ASTRO AFFILIATION Aries, Scorpio

HEALING stabilizing inner realms with outer experience

Mind This stone rids the mind of outdated and unhelpful thinking habits as well as psychological blockages regarding your connection to other people. It reduces shyness, combats negativity and decreases arguments. Helping you become more aware of body language, it increases intimacy between partners and heightens telepathic skills. Black or brown flint in particular can assist in finding the root causes of depression and help you accept your shadow side. Orange flint will eliminate obsessiveness, while blue flint can bring you focus and concentration after clearing mental blocks.

Body Flint is a good cleanser of the body, helping clear out the liver, lungs and digestive system. It will dissolve kidney stones and disperse pain, especially in the back or jaw. With its link to wise femininity

and ancient use in rites of passage to womanhood, flint can benefit the reproductive system, boost skin suppleness and smooth wrinkles. Any skin growths, warts, moles and cuts can be healed with flint.

Spirit A powerfully protective stone, flint not only shields you from ill will and negative energy but also effectively conducts harmful EMFs away from you. It will bring in your guides and other spirit help when you need it, and can be used as an anchor to the Earth in a shamanic journey to reconnect with your soul. A flint shard can be used for chakra healing and psychic surgery, clearing the etheric blueprint of past-life wounds as well as healing the Earth.

How to use Wear as a pendant, hold in meditation or position as

appropriate. In a healing crystal grid, combine with selenite to ground any spiritual downloads you may receive.

Fluorite - clear

TYPE OF CRYSTAL Fluorite is a soft, transparent mineral that comes in many colours, including clear, blue, green, purple, brown, yellow and rainbow, some with their own entry below. Its cubic or octahedral formations can be found in Australia, the US, Brazil, Peru, Mexico, China, Germany, Norway and the UK.

CHAKRA CONNECTION Crown for clear fluorite; other colours connect with different chakras (see below)

ASTRO AFFILIATION Capricorn, Pisces

HEALING disorganization

Mind Fluorite helps you get organized with any learning you have to do, aiding your ability to structure your studies and daily to-do lists in a less chaotic way. It assists with information processing and retention, and enables quick-thinking objectivity, focusing your mind on the bigger picture and a higher purpose. Fluorite also gently brings subconscious patterns of behaviour to the surface to be examined and resolved. This crystal can break you out of narrow-mindedness and increase self-confidence.

Body The clear variety of fluorite puts up a powerful barrier against EMFs from computers or mobile phones, as well as geopathic stress from the Earth. It can cleanse, purify and balance anything out of alignment in the body, including repairing DNA damage, mobilizing joints and alleviating inflammatory ailments such as arthritis and rheumatism. The cells, bones, teeth, spine, nerves and skin are all nourished by this mineral, which can remove pain from all these areas, heal ulcers, shingles and other skin afflictions, and decrease signs of ageing. A gem essence of fluorite is a powerful tonic to fight viruses and infections, and can even give your libido a boost.

Spirit Good for psychic protection, fluorite helps you know when you're being influenced by energies that are not your own. It stops external manipulation and cleanses your aura of unwanted negativity. By grounding spiritual energies in the body, it can speed up your spiritual awakening, make you more aware of different spiritual realms and increase your intuition. Clear fluorite aligns all the chakras, attracting the universal flow of energy into your practical reality.

How to use Wear in earrings or place on top of the head in meditation to activate the crown chakra and decrease stress. Stroke fluorite across the body toward the heart to alleviate pain. Hold in the hand to soothe frayed nerves. Make into an elixir using the indirect method (see page 39) as fluorite is so soft it might disintegrate if immersed in water. Drink gem essences occasionally to heal many physical issues. Place a piece of fluorite between you and your computer or other EMF emitter to take in the negative frequency, or spray a gem essence into the environment.

Fluorite - blue

TYPE OF CRYSTAL This soft, clear mineral comes in colours ranging from blue-green to light blue and is found in the same places as clear fluorite (see opposite). It can scratch fairly easily, so don't carry it with other stones, and wrap it individually to store.

CHAKRA CONNECTION Throat, third eye

ASTRO AFFILIATION Capricorn, Pisces

HEALING calming communication

Mind This shade of fluorite boosts your creative mind and rational thinking. It can help stabilize mental or emotional turmoil by bringing order to your thoughts. A gem to encourage calm, clear communication, it facilitates kind honesty. It also focuses the mind on the most important issues in your life.

Body Blue fluorite is a dual-action stone, either revitalizing or calming your energy, depending on what's needed. It is especially beneficial for any ear, nose, throat or tear-duct issues.

Spirit Another brilliant crystal to support your spiritual transformation, especially when meditated with regularly. Use it to increase communication with the spirit world and angelic realm.

How to use Wear in a necklace or earrings to activate the upper chakras. Place on or next to the relevant chakras or areas of the body that need healing. Hold in your non-dominant hand during meditation or keep on your meditation altar to receive its benefits. Position in any room that needs calm communication to happen there.

Cleansing tips

As fluorite absorbs negativity, it needs regular cleansing after every use, but never with water or salt, as it may get damaged. Instead, smudge it with sage smoke or leave it under a full moon. It can also be cleaned by burying it in soil for a few days or leaving it submerged overnight in a bowl of uncooked brown rice. Throw away the rice after cleaning the crystal and dust off any remaining particles with a clean cloth.

Fluorite - green

TYPE OF CRYSTAL As previous entries, but in shades of green from dark to light aqua.

CHAKRA CONNECTION Heart

ASTRO AFFILIATION Capricorn, Pisces

HEALING emotional and stomach upset

Mind Effective at clearing negativity from an environment, green fluorite helps diffuse emotional upsets, heal heartbreak and aid recovery from trauma, bringing your being back into balance. It enables you to access information buried deep in your subconscious that might be keeping you stuck in old, conditioned thinking and behaviour, clearing the path to freedom and happiness.

Body This colour of fluorite clears infections, particularly in the digestive system, giving you an energy boost. It can improve the health of the stomach, colon and intestines, clearing out constipation, alleviating colitis and stopping cramps. It also gets rid of nausea. Heartburn and sore throats can be soothed with an elixir of this gem.

Spirit Green fluorite is a good gem for clearing negative energy from the aura and the chakras, from the heart outwards. It can aid your ability to tune into your inner voice and the wisdom of your heart, guiding you on the path of unconditional love from Source.

How to use Wear as a pendant over the heart area. Hold in either hand during meditation or place on the heart chakra when lying down. Put a piece of green fluorite in an area with dense EMFs, such as in front of a Wi-Fi router or cordless phone, to block harmful radiation.

Fluorite - purple

TYPE OF CRYSTAL This supremely clear crystal can be found in the same places as all fluorite, in shades from dark to light purple and bright violet. Usually tumbled and polished smooth, it also has a very soft surface, so take care when mixing or carrying with other crystals to ensure it doesn't scratch or mark. Again, never cleanse with salt or water.

CHAKRA CONNECTION Third eye, crown

ASTRO AFFILIATION Capricorn, Pisces

HEALING through high vibrations

Mind The purple variety of fluorite encourages peace of mind and calm, aiding rational decision-making and communication in the process. It also brings sharper focus and enhances your overall mental ability.

Body Purple fluorite can assist in the healing of bone or bone-marrow disorders. Through meditative enquiry, it can get to the deeper spiritual reasons for any dis-ease, enhancing the body's healing ability once the light of awareness is shone on the root causes of your problems.

Spirit This high-vibrational stone is a must-have for your meditation practice as it stimulates the third eye, opening you up to psychic visions and spiritual guidance, to be mixed with common sense and grounded reality. Expect your intuition to be heightened when working with this crystal.

How to use Always keep fluorite in your meditation space. Hold in your non-dominant hand, or position on the third eye or crown chakra when sitting or lying down meditating. Wear as earrings or in a necklace to activate the connected chakras, or place in an area of your home or workplace that requires enhanced focus.

Fluorite - rainbow

TYPE OF CRYSTAL This unusually beautiful crystal carries bands of clear colours including blue, purple, violet, pink, green and aqua. Rainbow fluorite can be found in the same places as all colours of fluorite.

CHAKRA CONNECTION Solar plexus, heart, throat, third eye, crown

ASTRO AFFILIATION Capricorn, Pisces

HEALING by balancing mind, body and spirit

Mind Rainbow fluorite is great for concentrating the mind on a certain issue and coming up with a creative solution; it's especially helpful if you've been wrangling with a highly complex problem. It can also bring the emotions into harmony after they've been up and down for a while.

Body This gem is good for maintaining the health of the eyes, ears, nose and throat, clearing the sinuses and any infections in these areas. Rainbow fluorite makes a powerful talisman to carry to protect body and mind against disease. Rainbow fluorite is a gentle gem to use for healing animals, by using it to send energy through in a Reiki treatment or meditation, or by placing near their beds (but out of their way in case they play with it or eat it).

Spirit A brilliant chakra balancer, rainbow fluorite ignites divine inspiration and communication with Source energy and beings in higher dimensions, facilitating spiritual awakening and enlightenment.

How to use Position on the relevant chakra or hold in the non-dominant hand in meditation. Place on an altar or wear in a pendant over the heart area to heighten intuition. Put a piece wherever you need to be more creative. Rainbow fluorite needs cleansing and charging after every use to keep its energy pure. Run it through sage smoke or place it outside on the night of a full moon, but never in water or salt.

Fuchsite

TYPE OF CRYSTAL Also called chrome mica or green muscovite, this variety of mica, which sparkles in the light, is mixed with chromium inclusions, giving it a very dark to light green colour when polished. It forms in layers, masses and sometimes tabular rough crystals in Brazil, India and Russia.

CHAKRA CONNECTION Heart

ASTRO AFFILIATION Aquarius

HEALING physical and emotional recovery

Mind Fuchsite contributes to your understanding of how you interact with others, easing relationship difficulties and power struggles. It encourages self-worth and stops any sense of martyrdom, saviour complex or victimhood, fostering resilience and freedom instead. If you are helping someone else but it's actually holding them back, this stone will encourage you to step aside and let them learn their own lessons.

Body Commonly known as a healer's stone, this gem aids general physical recovery and can bring guidance on health and wellbeing matters. Fuchsite helps any practitioner intuitively pick up information about what needs attention and how to heal it. It guides you to the most beneficial holistic and herbal remedies. Fuchsite can improve the health

of the heart, realign the spine and increase flexibility in the muscles and skeleton. Red and white blood-cell ratio can be balanced and skin conditions such as eczema relieved with this crystal. Repetitive strain injury and carpal tunnel syndrome may improve after using fuchsite.

Spirit This is a powerful emotional healer, aiding your recovery from trauma, illness or blackmail. It clears the heart chakra of blockages, releasing you from any hurt to do with unrequited love. It helps you access and clear karma from past lives where servitude was a theme.

How to use Place on the heart chakra when lying down resting. Always position in meditation area or healing space when treating others. Hold in non-dominant (receiving) hand to get intuitive insights about medical conditions.

Place on any area of the body in need of healing. Put a piece under your mattress or pillow for healing. Carry in a pocket or wear as jewellery.

Warning: Do not make fuchsite into an elixir, as it will dissolve.

Garnet

TYPE OF CRYSTAL Found all over the world, this vibrantly coloured silicate mineral family comes in different types according to chemical composition, including almandine, hessonite and uvarovite. Either transparent or translucent, this semiprecious stone can be found in green tones, yellow or gold, orange, pink, purplish and black, but the most highly prized is a vibrant red. Garnet has been used since the Bronze Age, when it was often carried as a talisman to warn against danger and used decoratively on swords and jewellery, as found at the Anglo-Saxon burial site at Sutton Hoo. Its name comes from the Middle English word *gernet*, meaning 'dark red', and it was widely traded around the world from Sri Lanka and South India, where such gemstones were initially produced.

CHAKRA CONNECTION Root chakra for red, sacral for orange, solar plexus for yellow or gold, heart chakra for green

ASTRO AFFILIATION Leo, Virgo, Capricorn, Aquarius

HEALING sex appeal and commitment

Mind Good to use in a crisis or a time of great change, garnet brings courage and hope even when the outlook is bleak. It helps you re-frame your perception of yourself and others, bringing past-life lessons to the fore. It will also enable you to release outdated ideas and self-sabotaging behaviour patterns, filling you with increased self-confidence.

Body Garnet is great to use in any healing session with other gems, as it amplifies their energy. On its own, it can boost metabolism and thyroid function, and help the vitamins and minerals from the food you eat be fully taken into the body, boosting bone health, iodine intake and calcium absorption. A powerful regenerator of DNA, it also purifies and re-energizes the blood, heart and lungs. Any issues with your cells or spine can also be rectified with this crystal, while rheumatism and arthritis symptoms can be relieved.

Spirit A stone of commitment, garnet inspires infinite love and deep devotion. Plus it balances your sex drive, removes inhibitions and enhances your sexual prowess. It can bring passion or serenity into your life – whichever is needed. It clears negative energy from your aura and cleanses the chakras, opening the heart especially and enabling your kundalini, or life-force energy, to rise while you stay grounded.

How to use Garnet amplifies all other crystals, so include in a crystal grid to maximize the combined effect, or place near the root chakra in a powerful full-body crystal healing with other stones positioned on their relevant chakras (see page 37). Hold in either hand during meditation or place on the third eye area for past-life recall. Keep on an altar. Wear as earrings or a ring, or in a pendant over the heart.

Gem silica

TYPE OF CRYSTAL This rare and valuable variety of chalcedony and quartz is translucent, and a bluish-green to greenish-blue colour from being found near copper in rock crevices and fractures in Arizona and New Mexico in the US, Mexico, Peru, China, and the Philippines. Also known as chrysocolla chalcedony or gem silica chrysocolla, it may be found in the centre of a rock, making a stunning, sparkling geode.

CHAKRA CONNECTION Throat, third eye, crown

ASTRO AFFILIATION Taurus, Gemini, Virgo

HEALING your voice

Mind Gem silica brings peace of mind, tranquillity and acceptance. It keeps anger and sarcasm at bay in yourself and others, and helps you process and balance emotions. It gives eloquence and clarity to anyone speaking in public, or if you need to have a difficult conversation with someone about a sensitive subject.

Body Enhancing all the properties of chrysocolla, the gem silica variety speeds up healing. It is especially beneficial for the throat, voice and vocal cords, ridding the area of nodules or infections such as laryngitis, and heightening your speaking and singing abilities.

Spirit This crystal can improve your chanting in meditation, raising your frequency to greater levels and making your aura radiate more positively. Work with gem silica to bring clairvoyant visions and a strong sense of intuition, especially about things you need to say to others. With this stone, you will be able to clearly explain the insights your higher self has given you.

How to use Carry a piece with you if you need to express yourself honestly. Wear as a choker-style necklace close to the throat to boost this chakra and heal this area. Meditate while holding in either hand while sitting in front of a piece on your altar, or with a stone positioned on a certain chakra.

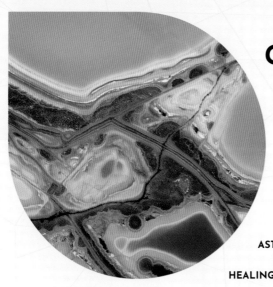

Gaspéite

TYPE OF CRYSTAL Found in just about every shade of green imaginable, this opaque, marbled and veined mineral is a rare carbonite, rich in nickel, iron and magnesium. Once found only in Quebec, Canada, it is now mined in Australia and small amounts have been found in Germany, Italy, South Africa and Japan.

CHAKRA CONNECTION Heart and earth star chakra (a few feet underground beneath your feet)

ASTRO AFFILIATION Virgo, Sagittarius

HEALING the deeper wounds of the heart

Mind Meditate with this stone and your mind may bring up past memories to explore, reflect on and resolve. If you feel bitter, angry or resentful over something someone did or said, gaspéite will dissolve rigid thinking around the hurtful events. This gem also gives you the ability to ask for help. Simply sit on the ground with a piece, think of the difficulties you'd like answers about, and trust that the information will come to you.

Body Highly beneficial for the liver, gallbladder and intestines, gaspéite can disperse gallstones, help with cirrhosis and ease nausea and travel sickness.

Spirit Gaspéite grounds spiritual energy into your body, strengthens your soul for tough times ahead and gives your aura a protective shield. Through the vibrations of this stone, your heart will unlock, enabling you to go deeper into past hurts, release stubborn blockages and let in light to heal. A good stone to hold when doing a shamanic journey or soul-retrieval work, it helps make you invisible to negative entities and gives you the courage to face your fears.

How to use Wear as jewellery. Use in a crystal healing grid. Hold in meditation or position on the relevant chakra or area of the body for healing. Keep a piece in your pocket when travelling to relieve sickness.

Goethite

TYPE OF CRYSTAL Usually brown, black or silvery, but sometimes orange, yellow or red, this iron hydroxide mineral makes the tiny starbursts in star hollandite quartz found in Madagascar and South Africa. It's also sometimes seen inside amethyst in Brazil. Ribbed and opaque, goethite alone forms in a variety of shapes including prismatic crystals, scales, masses, stalactites and structures that resemble pipe organs and radiating needles. Goethite was used as pigment in the famous cave paintings of Lascaux, France, which are over 16,000 years old. It is found abundantly in Germany, the UK, France, the US and Canada. Large deposits of this mineral have also been found on the surface of Mars by NASA expeditions.

CHAKRA CONNECTION Root, sacral, third eye

ASTRO AFFILIATION Aries

HEALING by tuning into nature

Mind Another good gem to increase your communication skills, goethite brings inspiration for change along with a practical, can-do attitude. It releases your mind from past-life stories and any beliefs about yourself that no longer serve you. It will fill you with compassion for yourself and all you've been through, making you aware of the gifts in the challenges, renewing your confidence and creative self-expression.

Body Goethite gives you an energy boost so you can enjoy life to the full. Increasing the flow of oxygen around the body, it can help you work out, lift weights and get into better physical shape. It combats epilepsy and assists with the functioning of the veins, alimentary canal and digestive system. It also clears any ailments or infections from the ears, nose and throat. A good gem to use if you are anaemic, it is also believed to ease heavy menstrual flow. It can promote the whole body's recovery after a trauma, as it aligns with the innate healing power of nature. Expect an enlivened sex drive when using goethite.

Spirit This crystal helps you have more fun, which raises your vibration and leads to spiritual transformation. Meditating with goethite will quickly bring you to a simple state of being as well as align all your chakras with the core of the Earth and a higher consciousness. Useful for any kind of divination, it can boost your psychic abilities, enabling you to hear messages from Spirit and the angelic realm. Connecting strongly to the planet, this crystal can help you work with the Earth spirits, or devas, and tune into and heal the meridians and ley lines around the globe.

How to use Hold or place on the appropriate chakra or area of the body to be treated. Meditate outside with this crystal, holding it in either hand, to fully tune into all of Mother Nature's energies. Sit in a crystal grid with this and other supportive stones to contact Earth spirits and align with your natural healing ability.

Halite

TYPE OF CRYSTAL Known as a natural form of salt, this fragile, transparent crystal is commonly found beside salt lakes or the ocean in parts of the US, India, North Africa, France and Germany. It is usually clear, but also comes in pink or, very rarely, blue, and forms in large masses, columns or cubic formations.

CHAKRA CONNECTION All chakras

ASTRO AFFILIATION Cancer, Pisces

HEALING emotional wellbeing

Mind This crystal works to cleanse your emotions of negativity, diffusing anger and ridding you of old patterns of thinking and behaving. It gives you the chance to move past problems, reducing anxiety and ameliorating abandonment issues or rejection fears so you can feel at ease once again. Use to increase your general sense of wellbeing and vitality.

Body Stimulating the body's meridians, halite gives extra *oomph* to any acupuncture and acupressure treatments. It supports the respiratory system, enabling you to breathe freely again after illness. It's a good gem to use for a thorough detox, as it benefits the liver, kidneys and bladder, reducing water retention and revitalizing the skin. It boosts metabolism and assists with intestinal issues, helping the

colon function better. Bipolar disorder and other mood imbalances can also be helped with this crystal. Blue halite can increase iodine absorption and help the thyroid and thymus glands function better.

Spirit A stone of purification, halite pulls out and protects your soul and aura from unwanted entities or psychic attack, especially if you have been drinking or using drugs and are unguarded to attachments. It creates an energetic barrier to another's undesired attention and lust. Pink halite, in particular, gives a full etheric cleanse and energy boost, enabling you to fully love yourself. Halite encourages spiritual discernment, helping you tune into your intuition to determine the right path for your evolution. Blue halite especially cleanses the third eye, heightens your mystical

awareness and connects you to the divine realms.

How to use Try using pink halite as a bath bomb: have a relaxing soak in hot, steamy water mixed with this dissolved mineral for a full energy cleanse. Halite works well with other crystals, grounding their healing properties in the body, so use it in a healing grid. To absorb negative energy or damp, place in a pouch or pocket, or in the room that requires the cleanse. Rejuvenate this gem by placing it in a bowl and covering it with brown rice overnight.

Warning: Do not make halite into an elixir; it is water soluble, and will dissolve. Halite is not for drinking.

Hawk's eye

TYPE OF CRYSTAL This is a dark-blue variety of tiger's eye, which is quartz embedded in crocidolite. Used for centuries to heal mind, body and spirit, it is commonly found in South Africa, Korea, Myanmar, China, Australia, Spain, Canada and Brazil.

CHAKRA CONNECTION Throat and third eye

ASTRO AFFILIATION Capricorn

HEALING physical and spiritual vision

Mind This crystal relieves stress and anxiety and brings mental clarity. It can help you see the big picture in times of chaos and confusion, enabling you to face issues calmly instead of spiralling into worst-case scenarios. For this reason, it helps bring balance and peace of mind to anyone suffering from post-traumatic stress, hypochondria or insomnia. ADD and ADHD can be assisted with the focus, concentration and relaxation hawk's eye brings. Grief and depression are also alleviated with this stone, which encourages a more positive outlook.

Body One of the main physical areas hawk's eye helps with is the eyes, improving their overall health, combatting diseases and assisting with vision. Coughs and any issues with the throat, such as laryngitis, can be eased with this crystal. It's also a good gem for boosting metabolism, assisting digestion and peristalsis, and relieving heartburn, bloating, nausea or sickness. Believed to be a diuretic, it assists the smooth functioning of the kidneys and bladder. Joint problems created by arthritis can also be alleviated.

Spirit Another highly protective stone for shielding against negative energy and ill will, hawk's eye is good for grounding and connecting you with the Earth. It powerfully clears and realigns your chakras, stabilizing your whole being. As well as cleansing and balancing your aura, hawk's eye can help you see and read the energy fields around others. Meditate with this crystal for deeper insights, heightened intuition and connection with other realms, enabling you to divine the future. It can also assist with astral travel, shamanic healing or past-life journeys, giving you access to deeper wisdom.

How to use Hold or place hawk's eye on the relevant chakra or area of the body in need of its energy. Meditate with this crystal by holding it in either hand or sitting in front of it placed on your altar.

With your eyes closed, allow the powerful energy of this stone to fill your body and mind, releasing any worries. Now visualize yourself soaring through the sky like a hawk, seeing the world below you. Feel its courage and strength fill your being, and know that you can handle anything life throws at you. When finished, thank the hawk's eye stone for its guidance and let its energy go, bringing your awareness back to your own energy. Journal about any feelings or insights you experienced.

Hematite

TYPE OF CRYSTAL Made of iron oxide, hematite is usually deep red, brown or grey with a slight lustre when raw, changing to smooth, shiny silver when polished. Some hematite has reddish-brown streaks and marks in red when rough-cut and rubbed against another stone. Its name comes from *hemo*, the Greek word for blood, due to its colour when ground into a powder, and also because it supports anything to do with blood in the body. It occurs in rosettes, masses, layered plates and other shapes in the UK, Italy, Switzerland, Sweden, Morocco, Brazil and Canada. Only synthetic hematite is magnetic; it's better to use natural non-magnetic hematite.

CHAKRA CONNECTION Root

ASTRO AFFILIATION Aries, Aquarius

HEALING the blood

Mind This crystal calms stress, balances emotions and helps develop self-control and confidence. Hematite is one to carry with you for extra strength and resilience when going through tough times, trying to kick a bad habit, or combat overindulgence or addiction. This gem highlights any unfulfilled dreams or inspirational ideas you need to work on, and gives you the focus and concentration to go for them. Studying mathematics or any technical subject? This crystal can help.

Body Backache, broken bones or vertebrae issues can be rectified with hematite. This crystal detoxifies the spleen and supports the kidneys in cleansing the blood supply. Strongly connected to the blood, hematite restores and regulates flow, and helps the absorption of iron and the formation of red blood cells, thereby assisting with anaemia and clotting. It also treats leg cramps and circulatory conditions such as Raynaud's disease. An elixir can be used to reduce a fever.

Spirit Another good grounding stone, it absorbs negative energy and protects you from anything harmful entering your aura, even when journeying out of the body in soul retrieval or astral travel. Bringing the mind, body and spirit back into balance, hematite restores harmony and helps you surmount any obstacles to your wellbeing.

How to use To realign the spine, place one piece of hematite at the top and one piece at the base while lying down. Place on or hold next to the root chakra or relevant area of the body when in supine meditation. Wear it as a ring, but not for long periods of time. Carry it with you. Position in any room to transform negative vibes.

Warning: Do not use where inflammation is present, or for long durations.

Hemimorphite

TYPE OF CRYSTAL Easily obtained from the US, Mexico, China, Zambia and the UK, this unusual crystal forms tiny, needle-like pyramidal or striated protrusions, sometimes in fan shapes, on a matrix. Alternatively, it is found as a crust with many little rounded segments looking like a bunch of grapes and known as a botryoidal formation. It can be colourless, blue, green, grey, white or brown and is best used tumbled smooth for any healing endeavours.

CHAKRA CONNECTION Throat

ASTRO AFFILIATION Libra

HEALING by setting realistic goals to manifest your highest potential

Mind Inspiring creative projects and a sense of social responsibility, hemimorphite removes selfishness and attachment to the ego, enabling you to maintain enthusiasm and motivation for your ideas and plans for the good of all. It shows that you create your life with your thoughts, so you must take responsibility for your own happiness by having realistic goals. Anger and angst are both dissolved with this gem, which encourages an optimistic outlook and honest communication of your emotions.

Body Once an antidote to poisoning, this crystal still brings relief from pain and vomiting, and helps with blood disorders and heart issues. It's a good gem for improving your overall health. It assists in losing weight, balances hormones, soothes burns and stops restless-leg syndrome. Skin ailments such as ulcers, herpes and warts can be treated with hemimorphite.

Spirit This stone protects against manipulation and maliciousness. It raises your frequency, both physically and energetically, connecting you to wisdom from the most elevated spiritual sources as well as other dimensions. Expect super-fast self-development with hemimorphite, as it synchronizes your soul with your higher self, releasing any outside influences that don't support the highest potential of your soul plan.

How to use Hold tumbled hemimorphite in your receiving hand while meditating. Place in your creative workspace to bring tenacity to your artistic endeavours. Use in a healing grid. Position on the throat chakra, on or next to the area of the body in need of its revitalizing energy.

Hiddenite

TYPE OF CRYSTAL A green variety of kunzite from Pakistan, hiddenite comes in shades ranging from emerald green to a much lighter yellowish-green.

CHAKRA CONNECTION Third eye, heart

ASTRO AFFILIATION Scorpio

HEALING by diagnosing disease in the body

Mind Another stone to support new beginnings, hiddenite attracts more intellectual and emotional experiences into your life, linking the mind with the heart to birth a rich, fulfilling and inspiring future. It fosters success with any studies. Any sense of failure from past endeavours is released with this crystal, which brings support and reassurance from others and the universe, especially to anyone who normally soldiers on independently.

Body Hiddenite detects illness and ailments in the body in need of healing. Use it to pinpoint areas that are weak, cold or have disease that can be treated with other crystals or methods. It is beneficial to the chest and boosts the thymus gland.

Spirit Meditate with hiddenite to connect with other worlds

and open yourself up to spiritual support, insight and understanding. It grounds love from Source into physical reality. This gem can be used to brush away blockages in the aura.

How to use Place on the third eye chakra while lying down in meditation, for spiritual wisdom. Or meditate with it held in either hand. Carry daily for support. Wear as a pendant over the chest. Position on the thymus area at the top of the chest to support this gland. Sweep a piece of hiddenite over the body to discover problem areas. They may be detected by a change in the crystal, such as an energetic pulse or pull, or sensed strongly in you as you move the gem over the body.

Howlite

TYPE OF CRYSTAL This white or sometimes light-green stone with black marbling is often dyed vivid blue to look like lapis lazuli or turquoise, but howlite is an effective healing stone in its own right. It is found in abundant masses and nodules in the US.

CHAKRA CONNECTION Crown

ASTRO AFFILIATION Gemini

HEALING poor sleep

Mind A highly calming stone, howlite stills an overactive mind and encourages patience and dignified, reasoned communication. If you are quick to anger, a piece of this crystal in your pocket will absorb your aggression as well as rage from others directed at you. It also stops self-criticism and self-centredness, and pushes your positive personality traits to the fore. Howlite improves the memory and inspires a thirst for knowledge. It can help you realize your goals, whether intellectual, material or spiritual.

Body Howlite promotes good sleep, which lowers stress levels and boosts the immune system in the process. It helps the body balance calcium absorption, improving the health of teeth, bones and soft tissue. The circulation is also given a kick-start with this gem.

Spirit Fully balancing the chakras and opening up the crown, howlite connects you strongly to a higher consciousness, filling your mind with deep wisdom and insights. Meditating with this crystal can facilitate out-of-body experiences or journeys in your mind to past lives, to help you release ancient contracts or emotional triggers that still destabilize you. Letting your gaze rest on howlite may transport you to another dimension in your mind's eye. Placing a piece on your third eye can attune you to the life between lives and other spiritual realms to assist with your awakening.

How to use Keep in your meditation area. When seated, hold in either hand or place on the crown chakra. Put under a pillow, on a bedside table, or in a grid around your bed to relieve insomnia. A gem essence can be made with howlite and sipped an hour before bedtime to aid calm, restful sleep.

Idocrase

TYPE OF CRYSTAL This flecked, transparent, lustrous or resinous silicate mineral is also called vesuvianite, as some of the best specimens of this crystal come from Mount Vesuvius, in Italy. Also found in the US in masses and short prismatic crystals, it comes in various colours including green, yellow, brown, pale blue and white.

CHAKRA CONNECTION Heart

ASTRO AFFILIATION Sagittarius, Capricorn

HEALING your sense of danger

Mind Idocrase invigorates and purifies the mind, clearing negative beliefs to facilitate clearer, more supportive thinking. Any fears around imprisonment or constraint, likely connected to past-life experiences, are released smoothly with this stone. It gently dissolves anxieties, diffuses anger and builds inner security and confidence, which then increases creativity, inventiveness and curiosity from a place of safety, freedom and joy.

Body This stone helps the body absorb nutrients from food, bringing you back into balance physically and emotionally, alleviating intestinal issues and helping overcome depression. A lost sense of smell can return with this gem, which also strengthens tooth enamel and boosts bone health. It soothes any skin ruptures from external conditions such as eczema or acne, or internal ones, including diverticulosis.

Spirit Another good gem for protection, idocrase brings awareness of danger along with the courage to deal with it. It provides abundant empathy for the plight of others, encouraging cooperation and a heightened sense of clairsentience. This crystal naturally resonates with your higher self, revealing all the information you need to nourish your soul and find your purpose.

How to use Meditate with this crystal by holding it in either hand, or sitting in front of it on your altar. Wear in a pendant over your heart. Place on or near the chakra or body area in need of treating.

Iolite

TYPE OF CRYSTAL Coloured from indigo to violet, sometimes with a hint of grey, green, brown or yellow, this clear crystal changes colour according to the angle of light shining on it. Also known as water sapphire, cordierite and dichroite, it is found in specialist shops in the US and India.

CHAKRA CONNECTION Third eye, crown

ASTRO AFFILIATION Taurus, Libra, Sagittarius

HEALING psychic vision

Mind A stone to spark inspiration and help you express your true self, regardless of what others expect, iolite clears unhelpful repetitive thinking and increases focus. It can help you take responsibility for your relationships, working on improving them if there is discord or letting them go if they are not for your highest good.

Body Of great support if you have issues with alcohol, iolite helps ease addictions, supports detoxification and regenerates the liver, reducing fatty deposits. It can assist with weight loss, reduce a fever and even treat malaria. Iolite is highly beneficial to the respiratory system, sinuses and pituitary gland. It can alleviate migraines and is believed to kill bacteria. Work with this crystal to build a strong constitution.

Spirit Iolite aligns the chakras and activates the third eye, bringing insight and heightened psychic intuition. It helps you tune into deep inner guidance and messages from spirit. Helpful to uncover hidden realms and truths during shamanic journeying or astral travel, it gets to the root of addictions to assist in healing. This gem gives off an electrical charge to re-energize your auric field. It will help you live more in the moment and increase spiritual visualizations during meditation.

How to use Wear as jewellery, especially earrings, so it is near the chakras it activates. Carry on its own in a pocket. Keep on your meditation altar. Sit holding it in your non-dominant hand to receive its benefits. Position on the relevant chakras or areas of the body in need of healing.

Warning: This moderately hard gem might need extra protection, to keep it from being damaged if it is being used with other stones.

Jade

TYPE OF CRYSTAL Usually watery green with a creamy yet translucent quality, jade is found in many other colours including blue, blue-green, cream, white, purple, red, orange, brown and black. Jade is in fact a combination of two silicate minerals - jadeite (the clear variety) and nephrite (creamier) - both of which are sold alone and have their own entries in this book. This crystal is found in masses in Italy, Russia, the US, the Middle East, Myanmar and China, where the symbol for jade is one of the oldest in written Chinese, dating back to 2950BC.

CHAKRA CONNECTION Heart and third eye - but all the chakras, depending on colour

ASTRO AFFILIATION Aries, Taurus, Gemini, Libra, Pisces

HEALING through good fortune and good health

Mind This crystal brings peace and serenity as well as the wisdom and good fortune those states attract. It helps you solve problems, muster up courage and have more confidence in who you are and what you want to do. Jade encourages you to go for your goals, taking each step toward your dreams with ease, balance and positivity. It also gives the ability to be self-sufficient.

Body A stone for longevity, jade nurtures many parts of the body, especially helping with fertility, childbirth and menstrual issues. It also helps detoxify and balance fluids in all the elimination organs such as the bladder, kidneys, spleen and gallbladder, as well as the lymphatic and immune systems. It improves heart health, calms the nervous system and nourishes the skeleton, especially joints. Jade can aid the healing of stitches, acne, and eye irritations, ridding the body of bacterial or viral infections.

Spirit Jade brings love, luck and emotional balance, protecting you from harm and creating harmony, even in dysfunctional relationships. Working with it will increase spiritual insight and guidance while keeping you grounded. Known as the 'dream stone', jade increases dreaming and dream recall, especially when placed under your pillow before sleep, or on your third eye. This gem generates the knowledge that you are a spiritual being having a human experience. Through meditation, it connects you to ancient civilizations and information to help you on your journey, as well as giving you access to the spirit worlds for guidance.

How to use Wear as a pendant, especially over the heart. Carry in a pocket to attract good luck. Hold in either hand to transfer its energy into the body, as the ancient Chinese believed. Place on an altar for meditation insights when you sit in front of it. Position on or near the relevant chakra for healing.

Do not use water or salt to cleanse this crystal.

Other colours of jade:

With all the same properties as green jade, different colours of jade have other, extra connections and purposes. All can be used in the same way as green jade.

Blue or blue-green jade gives you the gift of reflection to bring about inner peace and serenity, transforming worry and positive action. It encourages patience, especially if life seems overwhelming or you're going through a divorce or lawsuit. A good crystal to inspire creativity, blue jade mends broken relationships and attracts lifelong friends.

As well as helping with all the ailments and areas of the body as green jade, the blue variety especially brings pain relief from chronic illness and afflictions. It improves lung health, helping with breathing issues such as asthma and bronchitis.

Brown jade will help you adjust to any new environment, grounding you in the present moment to bring deep comfort. Allow it to connect you to the Earth, enabling you to trust in the reliability of others.

Lavender jade will help you set clear boundaries and expectations of behaviour from others to help bring about inner peace. It can assist in coming to terms with emotional upset and trauma.

Orange jade brings happiness and renewed awareness of the fact that everything is connected. Gently invigorating, it will give you a boost of energy to pursue your dreams.

Red jade is obviously connected with love and passion. It helps stimulate endorphins and release tension and energy from anger, enabling you to be constructive rather than destructive with any fierce emotions.

White jade is a great help when making decisions as it attracts the most relevant information to you to assess. It helps remove any distractions to your purpose and pushes you toward the best possible outcome.

Black jade - see Lemurian black jade.

Jadeite

TYPE OF CRYSTAL Part of the mineral that forms jade, jadeite is also found separately, although rarely, and in many of the same colours as jade. Colours sometimes mix, making a swirling pattern or veins in the waxy stone that is found in masses or occasionally small, elongated prismatic crystals, in the US, Guatemala, China and Myanmar. The most prized, translucent emerald-green variety, created by chromium, is also known as imperial jade. What is called new jade is actually bowenite, not jade.

CHAKRA CONNECTION Heart

ASTRO AFFILIATION Aries, Taurus

HEALING relationships

Mind Jadeite helps anyone wearing it to see the beauty in all things, boosting your mood and alleviating depression.

Body The Mayans and Aztecs believed jade could ease pains inside the body, so it can be used for that purpose. It also helps balance high blood pressure and assists with healing after an operation. Restless-leg syndrome and cramps of any kind can be alleviated with jadeite. It is also a good gem for improving the health of the testicles.

Spirit A stone of purity, jadeite helps smooth relationships, encouraging compassion, love and group cohesion. It will open your heart in readiness for romance. It's also believed to help anyone performing magic spells to ensure they work out well.

How to use See previous entry; also wear as a bangle to deflect negativity. Rest with some jadeite on any area of your body where there is pain.

Protect jadeite from damage from other crystals, if stored together, by wrapping it in a soft cloth.

Jasper

TYPE OF CRYSTAL Jasper is found all over the world in many colours, often red or brown, but also yellow, green, blue and purple. All coloured crystals are opaque with spots or banding running through, often water-worn or small and tumbled.

CHAKRA CONNECTION All chakras, depending on colour

ASTRO AFFILIATION Depends on colour; see other entries

HEALING all, to bring wholeness

Mind Unifying mind, body and spirit, jasper is known as the 'supreme nurturer', as it supports all systems during stressful times, providing grounding and stability. It will help you get a handle on any problems with honesty and assertiveness. This stone enables you to think quickly and imaginatively, transforming your ideas into practical action. Add to this the boost to organizational skills and tenacity that jasper brings, and you'll be a powerhouse of productivity and service to others.

Body Jasper cleanses and aligns the chakras for complete wellbeing. Different colours of jasper can activate certain chakras (see page 37). It is a good gem to support healing through a long illness or hospitalization. It supports the digestive and circulation systems and gives the sexual organs and libido a boost. Drink as an elixir to re-energize but not overstimulate the whole body.

Spirit This protective gem absorbs negative energy, revitalizes the aura and clears EMF pollution from your surroundings. It will guide you through shamanic journeys and aid your recall of the messages revealed in them as well as in your dreams. Highly effective in pendulum dowsing, jasper brings balance to your yin and yang energies and supports you with answers during unavoidable conflict.

How to use Place on the skin next to relevant chakras or areas of the body in need of support or healing. All colours of jasper can be placed on the chakra that corresponds to their colour (see section on chakras, page 37). Hold in either hand while meditating. Jasper works best over the long term, so carry in a pocket or wear every day as jewellery. Place a large piece of brown jasper in a room to absorb negative vibes.

Other shades of Jasper

Blue

CHAKRA CONNECTION Throat

ASTRO AFFILIATION Gemini, Pisces

HEALING by connecting deeply to the spirit world

Mind Blue jasper opens up the throat chakra, to enable better communication and creative self-expression.

Body A good gem to balance any mineral deficiency in the body, blue jasper can help sustain you during fasting. It also heals degenerative diseases over time.

Spirit This variety of jasper connects you deeply to the spirit world, stabilizes your auric field and assists astral travel when placed on the navel or heart chakra when lying down.

Brown

CHAKRA CONNECTION Root, third eye

ASTRO AFFILIATION Taurus, Capricorn

HEALING by detoxing

Mind Strongly connected to the Earth, brown jasper encourages ecological awareness and alleviates ill health due to geopathic stress or other environmental factors. It brings balance and stability to your thoughts, and gives you the strength of mind to give up harmful addictions such as smoking or doing drugs.

Body A good stone for cleansing the body of pollutants and toxins, brown jasper boosts the actions of all elimination organs and clears the skin of problems. It also stimulates the immune system, improving overall health.

Spirit Brown jasper helps you quickly centre yourself in your meditation practice. If placed on the third eye chakra while lying down, it can facilitate astral travel and memorable past-life regression sessions, where the deep karmic causes of issues in your present life are revealed to you for healing.

Green

CHAKRA CONNECTION Heart

ASTRO AFFILIATION Aries, Libra, Pisces

HEALING opening you up to universal love

Mind Obsessions are examined and released with green jasper, which calms anxieties, alleviates distress and gives you the courage to cope with change.

Body Another beneficial crystal for a detox, green jasper clears skin issues, nourishes the blood and stimulates the kidneys, liver, bladder and intestines. It alleviates bloating, indigestion and acidity in the digestive tract. Ailments of the upper torso, including inflammation and even cancer, are relieved with green jasper.

Spirit This jasper, like all green gems, activates the heart chakra, opening you up to receiving unconditional love from the universe, including attracting diverse friends and renewing fraught relationships. It brings harmony back to your life if anything is out of kilter.

Red

CHAKRA CONNECTION Root

ASTRO AFFILIATION Aries, Taurus

HEALING by grounding energy

Mind Coloured by iron oxide inclusions, red jasper makes an excellent worry bead or palm stone as it calms the mind and emotions when touched regularly. Red jasper brings any issues to light before they expand into bigger problems and stimulates insights and ideas to help move forward. Unfair situations can be brought to a head for resolution with red jasper.

Body This variety of jasper is said to prevent illness, bringing good health. It allegedly purifies and strengthens the blood, liver and circulation system. Any bile duct or liver blockages can also be cleared up with this stone.

Spirit Great for grounding your energy, this crystal activates the root chakra, highlighting your survival instinct as well as aiding rebirth. Place a piece under your pillow at night to help you remember your dreams and assist with astral travel. It can deepen your meditations, cleanse and balance the aura and firm up boundaries, bringing greater awareness and protection from negative influences.

Yellow

CHAKRA CONNECTION Solar plexus

ASTRO AFFILIATION Leo

HEALING physical pain relief

Mind A stone to help with intellectual endeavours, yellow jasper brings confidence in your abilities and a positive outlook on life.

Body Yellow jasper energizes your whole body, making you generally feel much better. It especially stimulates digestion, the stomach and the endocrine system. For pain relief, place yellow jasper on the forehead, chest, throat, wrist or wherever your body needs relief.

Spirit This crystal is said to protect you when travelling and when doing any spiritual practice or healing. It activates the solar plexus chakra, which brings positive energy into your life.

See also picture jasper, mookaite and tiger's iron for other varieties of jasper.

Jet

TYPE OF CRYSTAL Opaque dark brown or black, and looking a lot like coal, jet is actually fossilized wood from the UK, US and Canada and, therefore, not strictly a crystal.

CHAKRA CONNECTION Root

ASTRO AFFILIATION Capricorn

HEALING via protection

Mind Any fears, depression or feelings of grief are relinquished with jet, which can help bring erratic moods into balance. It encourages you to take full responsibility for your life, via your thinking and attitude, overcoming dark emotions and moving forward with renewed optimistic vigour.

Body Jet activates kundalini energy stored in the root chakra by fully clearing this area of the light body of blockages and sending the life force rising through each chakra, promoting wellbeing. Traditionally, this gem was used to relieve menstrual cramps, and it is still known to ease stomach aches as well as migraines and epilepsy symptoms. Swollen glands anywhere in the body can be reduced with jet, and the common cold kicked out of the system.

Spirit Expect your sex drive to increase with jet, while you remain grounded and balanced emotionally. This crystal is effective at shielding you from illness, violence and witchcraft, especially when combined with red jasper. Worn as a talisman around the neck, it was used by ancient cultures to ward off dark entities. It will protect you during shamanic journeys or any spiritual expansion, while opening you up to psychic experiences and enlightenment.

How to use Position anywhere on the body, but especially at the root chakra or chest area to assist with kundalini rising all the way to the crown. Wear as jewellery, especially set in silver in a pendant at your heart for protection from harm.

Kambamba stone

TYPE OF CRYSTAL This stone is made of fossilized algae containing black, swirling circular patterns of quartz with green feldspar centres. It can be found in mottled green ground mass, with larger crystals embedded, in South Africa and Madagascar. It is also known as kumbamba stone, khambab stone, crocodile rock and kambamba jasper (although it's not jasper), and is sometimes mistaken for nebula stone.

CHAKRA CONNECTION Third eye

ASTRO AFFILIATION Libra, Pisces

HEALING through intervention

Mind Beneficial for the mind in many ways, kambamba stone helps with learning, especially languages, investigating or examining the past. It is also good for design work, aiding your ergonomic understanding and visualization of ideas, enabling you to see your creations or inventions in actuality. This gem also alleviates anxiety, giving you patience, courage and confidence.

Body Kambamba stone helps with pregnancy, water retention and dehydration as it governs the fluids in the body. It encourages you to get enough liquids if you need more or release fluids if you have too much. It also gives you plenty of endurance when exercising.

Spirit This stone enhances creativity, helping you commit to a daily practice of art, sculpture, painting or music. It lets you find the calm centre of stillness inside yourself, even when you are busy and surrounded by commotion. Meditation will be enhanced when holding this crystal, as well as your connection with the environment, garden and the land your ancestors came from.

How to use Hold in either hand during meditation. Place on the third eye if lying down. Carry in a pocket to find calm in chaos.

Kunzite

TYPE OF CRYSTAL This variety of spodumene is usually light pink, but it can also be lilac, yellow or blue. Sometimes two or three colours are found together in one flattened prismatic crystal with striations. Green kunzite is called hiddenite (see page 130). Afghanistan is a common source of kunzite, as are Brazil, Madagascar, Myanmar and the US.

CHAKRA CONNECTION Heart, throat, third eye and crown

ASTRO AFFILIATION Aries, Taurus, Leo, Libra, Scorpio

HEALING through loving self-expression of emotions

Mind Kunzite allows you to freely express emotions, with an emphasis on developing calm, loving communication. It brings peace of mind instead of panic, soothes feelings of stress and removes obstacles from your path. Overblown desires, compulsions and control issues can be balanced with this gem, which develops mature thinking and alleviates low mood. It can assist in the recovery of memories, helping you reflect, look inside yourself and take the advice of others. It links the intellect with intuition for optimum mental wellbeing.

Body Kunzite removes blockages in your body that might lead to disease. It helps release addictions, assists recovery after stressful situations, and strengthens the nervous system. This mineral contains lithium so, especially when drunk as an elixir, it can help alleviate psychiatric disorders and depression. Your immune system, heart muscles and circulation will all get a boost with kunzite, which can also ease joint pain, reduce epileptic fits and quell the after-effects of anaesthetic. Women's issues to do with sexuality and menstruation can also be relieved with this crystal.

Spirit This high-vibration spiritual stone exudes a deep peace, helping even those who find it hard to meditate reach a centred stillness. Kunzite heals past hurts in relationships, even if from past lives, enabling you to trust and let love in again. It opens up the heart centre, aligning it with the higher chakras, which helps you accept the unconditional love of the universe. It also protects you from negative energy, shielding and strengthening the aura.

How to use Drink as an elixir to help lift depression. Wear as jewellery, especially as a pendant, to open the heart chakra, as well as shield you from EMF stress. Sticking a piece onto your mobile phone or computer can also help block radiation from these devices. Keep on your altar or hold in either hand to deepen meditation practice. Place on or next to the appropriate chakras or areas of the body in need of healing. Hold at the solar plexus to stop panic attacks. Position in a room to support a loving discussion that needs to be held.

Warning: Do not place kunzite in sunlight, as it will fade.

Kyanite

TYPE OF CRYSTAL This silicate mineral often comes in shades of blue with striations of white or grey going through it, although sometimes its base colour can be green, yellow, pink, white, black or grey. Only found in Brazil, it forms in long opaque or transparent slabs of wand-like crystals, or as blades embedded in larger pieces of another stone. When polished, it has a lovely, soft lustre.

CHAKRA CONNECTION Throat, third eye

ASTRO AFFILIATION Aries, Taurus, Libra, Pisces

HEALING by amplifying high-frequency energy

Mind A natural tranquillizer, kyanite brings calm and serenity where there is anger and stress. It improves memory and stimulates the higher mind, linking it to logical thinking. This gem cuts through ignorance and illusion, dispels fears and relieves frustrations. By activating the throat chakra, kyanite enhances communication and self-expression while encouraging fairness and speaking one's truth.

Body By instantly aligning the chakras in the light body to bring overall wellbeing, kyanite revitalizes muscles, helps with weight loss and is an effective pain reliever. It can soothe throat or voice issues, heal infections and reduce fevers and blood pressure. Brain health will get a boost with kyanite, as it supports the cerebellum and treats neurological problems. If you need help with your thyroid or parathyroid, adrenal glands or urogenital system, have a regular treatment with kyanite.

Spirit Use this crystal to aid meditation, attune to spirit guides and connect deeply to your intuition and psychic side. This gem will assist with your ascension by bringing the light of spirit into the body, raising your consciousness and amplifying your vibration. This leads to positive manifestations, greater compassion and increased integrity. Kyanite can be of great comfort for anyone passing over into the spirit realm through death, as it opens one up to spiritual truths. It also guides you to have healing dreams and remember any messages in them that might help you.

How to use Position on or near relevant chakras or areas of the body in need of healing. Wear as a pendant, ideally hanging low between solar plexus and heart, or in a choker-style necklace around the throat to open up this chakra. Carry in a shirt pocket. Place in any room where good communication is needed, or where you need to be focused on work or study.

Tip Kyanite does not absorb negative energy, so it never needs to be cleansed. But you can rejuvenate it by leaving it near plants first thing in the morning.

Warning: Kyanite should never go near water or salt. Do not make into an elixir, as it contains aluminium.

Labradorite

TYPE OF CRYSTAL Shimmering like the Aurora Borealis - which the Inuit people believe is inside this crystal - labradorite flashes a rainbow of colours. This effect, known as labradorescence, is due to layers of different minerals reflecting light inside the often grey, murky green, greyish-blue or black stone. It forms in crystalline masses of feldspar, a mixture of silicate and aluminium, in Canada, Norway, Italy, Finland, Greenland and Russia. Its name comes from the place where it was discovered by missionaries in 1770 - Labrador, Canada - although the indigenous people there are believed to have already used it for over a thousand years before the missionaries 'found' it.

CHAKRA CONNECTION Third eye, crown

ASTRO AFFILIATION Leo, Scorpio, Sagittarius

HEALING through transformation

Mind Helping rid the mind of fears, insecurities and anxieties, labradorite removes mental attachment to past disappointments, bolstering faith in oneself and in a benevolent universe. It can calm overactive thoughts and light up your imagination. Sitting with labradorite enables deep introspection and reflection. It balances the light and dark within you as well as matching your intuitive wisdom with rational thinking and solid analysis of situations. It can also help important but suppressed past memories surface for contemplation and healing.

Body Labradorite clears up colds, helps with eye issues and can remove warts by rubbing or tapping the affected area with the gem. It also aids digestion, regulates the metabolism and reduces blood pressure. Brain health gets a boost with labradorite, and the symptoms of gout and rheumatism can be alleviated. Hormones become balanced and pre-menstrual tension eased by using this special stone.

Spirit Wearing a piece of labradorite enables one's natural magical and intuitive abilities to come to the fore, bringing psychic messages from the divine into your mind for understanding. It is a stone of transformation, assisting you through changes. Its reflective luminescence symbolizes the spiritual expansion possible when meditating with this stone, aligning you with right timing and synchronicities. This crystal cleanses and heals the aura, protecting it from unwanted energies and projections from others. Helping raise your consciousness, it will keep your vibration high as you journey to other worlds, past lives or the Akashic records to reveal the deep mysteries of life.

How to use Place on the body or chakra area where and when it is needed. Wear as earrings or a necklace. Put under your pillow for dreams full of insight and wisdom. Hold in either hand or keep on your altar. During meditation, ask labradorite to fill your body with its shimmering rainbow of colours to open up all your chakras and keep your vibration high.

Sit looking deeply into labradorite at dawn or dusk, when its power is most potent. Imagine all of humanity as one being of light, free from the limitations of the past and fears of the future, activating infinite possibilities in the present moment. As part of this pure light of oneness, allow yourself just to be for as long as you wish.

Lapis lazuli

TYPE OF CRYSTAL This rich, deep-blue opaque crystal, with veins or flecks of gold or white in it, was crushed and used as ultramarine, a pigment for dyeing the robes of ancient royalty, as well as for oil paints in the Middle Ages. Kings and queens of ancient Egypt lined their burial chambers with it, and wore it on eyelids to improve eyesight. Its expensive mixture of calcite, lazurite, sodalite, sulphur and pyrite is easily obtained in Chile, Italy, the US, Russia, Afghanistan, Egypt and the Middle East.

CHAKRA CONNECTION Throat, third eye

ASTRO AFFILIATION Sagittarius

HEALING by opening up your inner vision

Mind Lapis lazuli quickly relieves stress, bringing about deep peace and serenity. It allows anger to be released and compassion to take its place. It will help you know and communicate your deep truths with honesty, grace and integrity. Plus, it enables you to actively listen to others, hearing their side without judgment, allowing harmony to enter a conflict and smooth out relationship issues. This gem stimulates the higher mind, encouraging clarity, objectivity and organization, as well as creativity through connection to the divine.

Body By balancing the mind, body, spirit and emotions, lapis lazuli helps you feel better and overcome depression. It boosts the immune, lymphatic, nervous and respiratory systems. Headaches, migraines, earaches and any kind of pain can be relieved with lapis

lazuli. The throat, larynx and thyroid are all helped by this gem, which also purifies the blood and lowers blood pressure. Insomnia, vertigo, dizziness and hearing loss can also be alleviated by lapis.

Spirit Looking like the night sky, lapis lazuli gives you expansive inner vision by opening the third eye chakra, stimulating your psychic powers and connecting you with your spirit guides. Intuitive guidance and visionary, prophetic dreams will be yours if you meditate with lapis regularly. Gaze into it with relaxed eyes and you may travel in your mind to past lives you experienced in ancient cultures, such as Atlantis or Sumeria. Lapis lazuli encourages deep inner knowledge and enlightenment while protecting you from psychic attack and returning negative energy to its source.

How to use Position on the third eye or throat chakra while lying down in meditation, or hold in either hand while seated, sending its royal-blue light to any area of the body for healing. Wear as jewellery, especially as earrings, in a pendant or at the throat. Place in the workplace to stay organized, inspire trust and maintain integrity.

Larimar

TYPE OF CRYSTAL Also known as dolphin stone or blue pectolite, this sea-green, blue, grey or red stone, often veined with white, comes from the Dominican Republic and the Bahamas. Once thought to be from the zeolite family of crystals, larimar is often found in the cavities in basalt rocks.

CHAKRA CONNECTION Heart, throat, third eye and crown

ASTRO AFFILIATION Leo

HEALING the Earth through connection with the goddess

Mind Of great benefit in times of change and stress, larimar radiates peace and love, calming emotions and helping you go with the flow. It stops self-sabotage and takes away restrictions in your mind to all you desire. It can bring balance to bipolar disorders. This crystal alleviates guilt, removes fear and quells aggression while giving you the ability to take control of your life with playfulness and positivity. Creativity, clarity and constructive thought can all be yours with this stone.

Body Stimulating all of the above chakras, larimar encourages self-healing. It dissolves energy blockages in the head, neck and chest, soothing throat complaints and removing pain when placed on the site of an injury. Issues with cartilage, constricted joints or blocked arteries can be rectified with larimar. It can be used on the feet to help soothe aching muscles or as a reflexology tool to pinpoint disease and clear the energy meridians in the body.

Spirit This crystal brings a soft, gentle spiritual healing, enabling you to see who you are deep inside, detached from the encumbrances of the material world. It helps you release former heartache and blockages to true love from past-life contracts. A gem to open you up to other dimensions, larimar easily takes you into a deep meditative state, connects you with the angelic realm and guides the soul on its highest path. Use it to help with the healing and evolution of the Earth by aligning with the goddess energy, boosting your innate femininity and restoring your connection with nature.

How to use Hold a piece in either hand while meditating. Carry in a pocket or wear as jewellery for a long period of time. Use on the feet for reflexology. Gently stroke over the body or put on the relevant chakras to remove unwanted energy or entities. Place on the Earth to balance energy and heal geopathic stress.

Lazulite

TYPE OF CRYSTAL This azure-indigo gem is a crystallized aluminium magnesium iron phosphate mineral that forms in grainy, dense masses or little pyramidal patterns. Discovered in Austria in 1795, it was named after the German word for blue stone, *lazurstein*. It is found in Canada, the US, Brazil, Australia, Sweden, Switzerland and Madagascar.

CHAKRA CONNECTION Third eye

ASTRO AFFILIATION Gemini, Sagittarius

HEALING by bringing divine energy into your daily life

Mind Lazulite boosts self-esteem and confidence. It also promotes deep insight into psychological issues, including the root cause of addictions, and guides you to solutions via your intuition and elevated thinking. It rids the mind of obsessions, the need to control or to have more of something you don't need, heightening your strength of mind and determination to heal. Use lazurite to harness higher wisdom to help you pursue practical goals.

Body Migraines can be relieved with lazulite, which also assists anyone with sun sensitivity, however that manifests. It helps mend fractures and many issues to do with the liver, lymphatic system, pituitary gland and thyroid. The whole immune system is given a boost by this crystal.

Spirit Much like quartz, lazulite connects strongly to the spiritual realms and brings the divine down to Earth in you, heightening your intuition and raising your vibration. Meditate with it placed on your third eye and expect to reach a profoundly blissful, serene state, fully sensing your connection to Source. Lazurite supports astral projection by almost disconnecting you from the physical so you can explore the spiritual realms even further.

How to use Carry with you daily to heighten intuition, raise your frequency and bring the spiritual into everyday life. Hold in either hand while meditating or treating bodily ailments. Place on the third eye while lying down. Position on any area of the body in need of its energy. Use in a crystal healing grid.

Lemurian (black) jade

TYPE OF CRYSTAL This rare, mottled black or greyish blue-green stone contains a mixture of jade, quartz, iron pyrite and other minerals, and is found in only one mine in Peru. It can also be known as black Inca jade or midnight Lemurian jade.

CHAKRA CONNECTION Root, heart and earth star

ASTRO AFFILIATION Taurus, Libra

HEALING the dark times

Mind This transformational crystal brings courage and determination to get through blocks to a better life. It heals memories of abuse and stabilizes emotions. Lemurian jade encourages you to have a sense of gratitude for what you have, rather than focusing on what's lacking.

Body Lemurian jade gives the immune system a boost, relieving chronic disease. It strengthens the heart and helps with the recovery process after a long illness or operation. This gem is also good for the health of both male and female reproductive systems. It is a wonderful support for anyone going through or helping with palliative care.

Spirit This highly protective stone keeps you safe from predatory people and helps you traverse dark times with confidence that the light will return and gifts will arise out of these experiences. It attracts to you anyone meant for your soul's transformation and aids spiritual transition, especially when passing over. Use this gem for shamanic healing, to connect to Earth spirits, power animals and nature at its most wild. Lemurian jade attunes you to the divine feminine, allowing this energy to rise in both men and women, balancing the equilibrium between humanity and the planet. It facilitates endings and new beginnings, giving you the strength to delve deeper into your true inner self throughout all life's changes.

How to use Place on the earth star chakra beneath your feet to help heal the planet by sending healing energy through you and into the Earth, visualizing it working its magic. Position or hold on areas of the body for healing. Hold in either hand during meditation or shamanic work to deepen the connection to Mother Earth.

Lepidocrocite

TYPE OF CRYSTAL This red or reddish-brown fibrous or even crusty-textured crystal is often found as an inclusion in other crystals, such as quartz, in countries including Spain, India, Brazil and the US.

CHAKRA CONNECTION Heart, third eye, crown

ASTRO AFFILIATION Sagittarius

HEALING by grounding spiritual energy into the body

Mind Lepidocrocite calms the mind and emotions, balancing the brain of anyone with ADHD, hyperactivity or bipolar disorder. It helps synchronize rational, practical thinking with spiritual insights and intuition, grounding the soul in day-to-day reality. Any negative thoughts, confusion, anxiety or aloofness are replaced with unconditional love and harmony with this crystal, which helps you see all your strengths and the signposts on your path.

Body Use this crystal to enhance the healing effects of other stones. On its own, it benefits the liver, heart and lungs, easing breathing difficulties and suppressing the appetite. It also balances hormones and aids the workings of the reproductive organs, increasing fertility. Said to help the iris in particular, it can also improve eyesight and general eye health. This powerful gem can even be used to dissolve tumours and assist with cell regeneration.

Spirit Bringing spiritual energy down through the crown and grounding it into the body, this gem aligns and activates all the chakras. It helps you recognize and commit to your soul path and purpose, manifesting it to the best of your abilities and empowering others along the way. Working with lepidocrocite will enable you to connect to your spirit guides and angels, teach truth instead of dogma, and observe without judgment, making you an excellent spiritual leader.

How to use Hold in either hand during meditation. Place on or near the relevant chakras, especially pointing towards the crown while lying on the floor. Use in a healing grid to amplify the other crystals' energy.

Lepidolite

TYPE OF CRYSTAL Lepidolite can be colourless, lilac (greyish-purple to pink), yellow or grey with white or brown striations. Usually opaque, with a lustre, it is sold in raw mica form or as polished stones. It is easily found in short prismatic and tabular crystals, in larger masses or layered plates known as 'books' in Brazil, the Dominican Republic, the US, Madagascar and the Czech Republic.

CHAKRA CONNECTION Throat, heart, third eye and crown

ASTRO AFFILIATION Libra

HEALING negativity of any kind, and stress-related health issues

Mind This supportive stone takes away stress and replaces it with calm trust that all will be well. It lifts depression, negativity and despondency, and puts a stop to obsessive thinking, enabling clear analysis and focused decision-making. Lepidolite provides objectivity, concentration and the ability to achieve important goals independently and without distraction. Helpful to bring confidence and ease to childbirth, it is good for all transitions in life, including passing over. It is also beneficial for anyone studying or learning.

Body Stress-related digestion issues, such as cramps and constipation, and nerve problems, including sciatica and neuralgia, are relieved by this crystal. It can ease allergic reactions, tendonitis and joint problems. Addictions, anorexia and epilepsy can be sorted out using this stone, which also alleviates sleep disturbances and brings about deep emotional healing. Use this stone to clear sick-building syndrome and stop EMF pollution from technological gadgets. Your entire immune system will get a boost with this gem, which detoxifies the skin and relieves exhaustion. Drink an elixir of lepidolite to soothe menopause symptoms.

Spirit Lepidolite works for the highest good, improving meditation, awakening insights, and helping you connect deeply with the divine. It helps facilitate astral travel, shamanic or spiritual journeying, and accessing the Akashic records. It highlights experiences from past lives that are blocking your progress in this life, projecting you onto your future path without undue influence from others.

How to use Place a piece of lepidolite on a problem area of the body and it will vibrate gently, getting to the root of the disease. Place on the relevant chakra or area of the body in need of its energy. Put a piece under your pillow to alleviate sleep disturbances. Position a raw mica chunk of lepidolite near to any EMF-emitting device. Wear as a necklace or earrings. Carry in a pocket. Hold in either hand during meditation or keep on your altar.

Limonite

TYPE OF CRYSTAL The iron hydroxide inclusion in red and yellow phantom quartz is a crystal in its own right, forming yellow, orange and brown, dense, glassy masses or cubic or bladed shapes that can look rusty, metallic or dull on the surface. Limonite is abundant in Brazil, the US, Cuba, Russia, India, Zaire, Namibia and Europe. It is thought to have been used over 4,000 years ago as the red, yellow and brown pigment for paint in Neolithic cave paintings.

CHAKRA CONNECTION Earth star, root and sacral

ASTRO AFFILIATION Virgo

HEALING with inner strength in a crisis

Mind In the face of urgent or difficult situations, limonite activates inner strength to either help you find the courage and endurance to stand your ground without the need to fight, or, if necessary, remove yourself from the situation. This stone stops you from feeling overwhelmed or confused by external events. It sharpens the mind to help you rise above challenges and brings increased self-love and acceptance.

Body Traditionally, limonite was used to treat dehydration and reinvigorate a youthful appearance. It aids digestion and helps with the absorption of calcium and iron from food. This crystal is believed to be able to reduce a fever and remove jaundice, purifying the body from toxins that are causing these issues. It supports the health of the liver and the musculoskeletal system.

Spirit Limonite heightens your telepathic skills, tuning you into the thoughts and feelings of others while remaining stable in your own being. It protects from other people's mind games or manipulation, and shields against psychic attack. This gem grounds and keeps the physical body safe while undertaking spiritual journeys or deep transcendental meditations.

How to use Hold on or next to the root chakra to ground. Place next to area of the body in need of treatment. Make into an elixir to sip for dehydration. Use in a crystal grid for yourself to sit in, or the Earth underneath to be healed. Hold in either hand during meditation. Try the following visualization:

Sit comfortably with a piece of limonite in cupped hands. Close your eyes and imagine a tree in front of you, with its roots lightly folding around your body. As the tendrils embrace your physical being, see them nurturing your cells, organs, limbs and head with restorative and rejuvenating energy. As your physical body revitalizes, your emotional and etheric body will also purify. Sit in this frequency of restoration from the Earth as long as you wish before opening your eyes and having a drink of water to ground and replenish.

Lingam

TYPE OF CRYSTAL Also called Shiva lingam, this red-brown and beige or grey, small, smooth, rugby ball-shaped variety of opaque jasper is occasionally found in India, in the River Ganges and its tributaries. Seen as sacred for thousands of years, it symbolizes the Hindu god Shiva's union with his consort Kali, and represents potent sexuality as well as the marriage of opposites, such as male and female energies, body and soul, the spiritual and the physical.

CHAKRA CONNECTION All, especially the root and sacral

ASTRO AFFILIATION Scorpio

HEALING sexual issues

Mind Lingam stone encourages looking within to let go of outdated thinking around sexual expression. It's especially good for releasing lingering emotions connected to early childhood, particularly sexual abuse, as it helps trust in male energy again (where the abuser was a man).

Body This gem boosts fertility, supports the prostate gland and can ease menstrual and menopause symptoms. Any issues to do with sex, such as impotence and inability to orgasm, can be alleviated with this crystal. Back pain and conditions of the spine can also be helped with lingam. This stone stimulates the subtle meridians of energy and electrical flow in the body to bring balance.

Spirit By activating the root and sacral chakras, the lingam stone raises and controls kundalini energy rising, increasing sexual dynamism and expanding erotic awareness. It connects you to your higher self, enabling you to reach peak experiences in your meditation. Good for a spiritual detox, lingam cuts etheric ties from a past sexual connection, re-energizing the root chakra in readiness for a new relationship. Use this smooth stone to create a ritual for self-love to harness your feminine powers and attract a sexual partner.

How to use Include in a healing crystal grid. Hold in either hand in meditation. Programme it by holding in cupped hands and stating your intention for it, such as to release etheric hooks from a past lover and clear residual energy in your sacred area in readiness for a new person to come into your life. Sit or lie down with it placed close to your root chakra to clear it and activate kundalini energy.

Lodestone

TYPE OF CRYSTAL Heavy for its size, lodestone is a naturally magnetic, black or brownish-grey, iron oxide sold in a grainy cluster, often with small, fuzzy pieces of magnetic matter on its exterior. Also often known as Magnetite (although this is the non-magnetic version of it), it is found in masses and octahedral crystals in the US, Canada, Mexico, Italy, Austria, Finland and Romania.

CHAKRA CONNECTION Root

ASTRO AFFILIATION Gemini, Virgo

HEALING through its ability to attract or repel, stimulate or sedate

Mind Lodestone rids the mind of fear, anger and grief, bringing a more objective and positive perspective along with the tenacity to get through anything, free from attachment to any outcome. However, it will guide you out of harmful situations and help you avoid confusion. It encourages inner stability by balancing the emotions with the intellect.

Body Highly beneficial for sports injuries, lodestone relieves muscle aches and pains, strains and cramps. It sustains life force in the body, bringing vitality and stimulation where needed, or calming overactive organs if necessary, using its powerful positive-negative polarity. Anti-inflammatory and helpful for the blood, it can stop nosebleeds. It is beneficial for those with asthma, arthritis, and skin or hair issues.

Spirit Amplifying the law of attraction, lodestone magnetizes love, loyalty and commitment toward you in the hope of fulfilling your desires. It aligns all the chakras and energy meridians of the body, and connects the root chakra with the earth chakra to encourage grounding and promote planetary healing. It can boost telepathy and visualization, aid deep meditation and enable you to trust your intuition. Lodestone helps you be fully in the present moment.

How to use Hold in either hand for grounding in meditation or any time you need to feel stabilized and secure. Place on or next to the root chakra when lying or sitting down meditating. Position on an achy joint or on the back of the neck and base of the spine while lying down for a full treatment. Carry in a pocket to attract what you want.

Put a piece at the end of the bed to stop leg cramps at night.

Warning: Keep lodestone in a separate container to stop other metals from being magnetized to it.

Magnesite

TYPE OF CRYSTAL This usually white, but also grey, brown or yellow crystal is found in many different forms and sizes in the US and Brazil. Sometimes it looks a bit brain-like; other times it's marbled and chalky or crystalline (although this is rare).

CHAKRA CONNECTION Heart, third eye and crown

ASTRO AFFILIATION Aries

HEALING magnesium intake

Mind This crystal stimulates the mind, bringing intellectual ideas into practical application. It harmonizes the left and right hemispheres of the brain, bringing equilibrium between creativity and logic, sensitive spirituality and the factual, scientific side, which induces a positive outlook on life. Emotions are calmed with this crystal, which alleviates fears and nervousness, and overcomes intolerance and irritability. If you are deceiving yourself, magnesite will take your awareness to it and the reasons behind unconscious thoughts and feelings holding you back. It can help egocentric types listen and focus more on others.

Body With its high magnesium content, magnesite assists with the absorption of the mineral, which aids cellular detox, helps muscles relax and eases menstrual or stomach cramps. It relieves the pain of gallstones or kidney stones as well as headaches or migraines. Teeth and bones get a boost from this gem, which also balances body temperature and neutralizes body odour. It is said to prevent epilepsy and heart disease, increase fat metabolism and disperse cholesterol, preventing angina, heart disease and strokes by keeping arteries clear of plaque build-up.

Spirit Magnesite deepens meditation and centres your soul, bringing a heavenly peace into your life. Placing this crystal on the third eye area is said to increase visualizations. Positioned on the chest area, magnesite will open the heart chakra, encouraging unconditional self-love and deep affection for others, even where there is damaging behaviour or addiction. With magnesite, you can be fully supportive yet unaffected by another person, by allowing them to truly be themselves.

How to use Meditate holding a piece, or place it on your third eye or chest area while supine. Position on the relevant areas of the body and chakras as above. To help with magnesium absorption and ease cramps and afflictions, this gem can be drunk as an elixir or applied topically to the skin. Carry with you when dealing with another person.

Malachite

TYPE OF CRYSTAL This opaque, bright-green copper carbonate hydroxide mineral has dark and light green, white and sometimes black concentric bands and striations in it, making marble-like patterns. Found in the Democratic Republic of the Congo, Russia, the Middle East, Zambia, Romania, Mexico, Israel, Australia and the US, it comes in all sizes and is often tumbled and polished to a high gloss, which makes it safe to touch. In its raw form, malachite is toxic. It should be handled with extreme care; avoid breathing in its dust and use only polished stones as an elixir. Only apply it externally; never ingest it.

CHAKRA CONNECTION Heart

ASTRO AFFILIATION Scorpio, Capricorn

HEALING everything – sometimes intensely

Mind A stone of psychological transformation, malachite encourages you to live life to the full by overcoming phobias, taking more risks and sharing your truth with others. It calms erratic emotions, boosts your mood and alleviates depression by showing you the blockages to positive change and growth. Old beliefs, shyness and inhibitions can all be released with this crystal, which also aids in letting go of past traumatic experiences for deep emotional healing. It helps you develop empathy and supports good friendships. This gem can also heighten your ability to process new or difficult concepts and help you become more observant.

Body Malachite increases endurance and balance. It stops muscle cramps, including from PMS and childbirth (for this reason, it has been called 'the midwife stone'). With the help of conventional treatments, this crystal can alleviate all manner of ailments, including asthma, arthritis, diabetes and epilepsy. It is said to improve eyesight, lower blood pressure and assist the pancreas, spleen and parathyroid to function better. It also aids cellular detox, encourages the liver to release toxins and gives the immune system a massive boost. Bone fractures, swollen joints, vertigo, travel sickness and any sexual diseases can be helped with it.

Spirit With its strong connection to nature spirits and the natural world, malachite heals the Earth, protecting against radiation, clearing plutonium and absorbing EMF pollution from the environment. Helping you breath more deeply, it grounds spiritual energies into everyday reality. It can amplify both positive and negative vibrations to aid transformation. Malachite clears and stimulates all the chakras, helping you attune to guidance from other realms and your own intuition, while at the same time offering energetic protection.

How to use Place on or next to the heart chakra or third eye, or on the solar plexus to absorb negative feelings. Gaze deeply into a piece while meditating with soft focus. Hold in either hand while meditating with eyes closed. Wear in rings or bracelets on the left hand or wrist. Carry a small, smooth stone with you when on a plane to counteract radiation from flying. Place on areas of the body in need of healing. Only use elixir externally, and make it with polished stones only or via the indirect method (see page 39).

Marcasite

TYPE OF CRYSTAL This iron sulphide gem has the same chemical makeup as pyrite, but their crystalline structures differ, giving them different healing properties. Found in the US, Mexico, France and Germany, marcasite comes in metallic masses of yellow or white on black, or as small, rough crystals.

CHAKRA CONNECTION Solar plexus

ASTRO AFFILIATION Leo

HEALING lack to bring abundance

Mind If your thoughts roam or you suffer from confusion, use marcasite to bring concentration and clarity. It relieves mental and emotional exhaustion, encourages patience and improves memory. This is a great gem for looking inside yourself objectively, dispelling any thoughts of lack, martyrdom or victimhood, enabling you to shine your inner light and attract your rightful abundance.

Body Good for any skin complaints, marcasite helps moles, freckles and warts reduce in size, colour and frequency. A warmed elixir of marcasite can be used to treat corns on the feet, either by dabbing the liquid on the affected area or using as a soothing foot bath. This crystal also cleanses the blood and stimulates the spleen. It balances energies in the body, boosting vitality and overall wellbeing.

Spirit This crystal creates a psychic shield around you, especially if involved in any spiritual clearing or entity removal from others. It heightens clairvoyance and awareness of other dimensions and etheric beings. Plus, it helps ground you in reality, supporting practical action backed by expanding spirituality.

How to use If you are fatigued, wear marcasite as jewellery to increase energy. Hold in either hand while meditating, sitting or lying down. Use in a healing grid. Make into an elixir anddab on skin complaints.

Menalite

TYPE OF CRYSTAL Also known as goddess stone or fairy stone, this chalky white, light grey or brownish mineraloid opal forms naturally bulbous shapes that look like prehistoric goddess figures. It is rare, but found mostly in Morocco and other parts of Africa, the US and Australia.

CHAKRA CONNECTION Crown

ASTRO AFFILIATION Cancer

HEALING the sacred feminine

Mind This crystal removes fear of the unknown and replaces it with confidence and inner strength in your hidden talents and your ability to cope with life's changes. It removes fear of death and reassures one of eternal life. Use menalite when starting new projects, to help manifest all you desire and attract abundance.

Body This stone supports fertility, lactation and the female reproductive system. It assists with menstruation issues and helps anyone going through the menopause, alleviating night sweats and other symptoms. Menalite smooths major transitions in life, especially involving hormonal changes such as puberty or childbirth.

Spirit Connecting you to wise feminine energy and ancient

priestess power, menalite guides you through the transitions of womanhood, allowing femininity to flourish and innate female sexuality to awaken. It helps remind you of life's constant cycles, making it an excellent stone if you're going through a rebirth of any kind or are in need of spiritual rejuvenation. This sacred stone has been used since ancient times to assist shamanic journeying to other realms and connect with spirit guides in the form of creatures of the Earth, as well as Mother Earth herself. Use it to enhance divination, discover your power animal and heighten intuition.

How to use Place in a healing grid or on appropriate chakras or areas of the body in need of healing. Hold during meditation as an anchor while journeying to other spiritual realms or call on

your power animal. Keep under your pillow during menopause to alleviate night sweats or hold during hot flushes at any time of day.

Merlinite

TYPE OF CRYSTAL This combination of quartz and psilomelane is usually white and translucent with black tendril-like inclusions and maybe a slight opalescence. It is found in New Mexico in the US, and in India.

CHAKRA CONNECTION Root, third eye

ASTRO AFFILIATION Pisces

HEALING by bringing balance and magic into your life

Mind Encouraging calm and harmony, merlinite helps you see both sides of an argument and releases mental blockages to a better life, so you can move forward with optimism. It helps turn negative experiences into positive teaching moments, and reprogrammes detrimental beliefs and behaviours to encourage beneficial change. It creates equilibrium between the intellect and intuition.

Body Instigating survival instincts, this crystal supports the heart and gives your sexual energy and natural vitality a boost. It aids the respiratory system, encouraging oxygen to flow freely around the body. Merlinite encourages good circulation and stimulates or soothes the intestines – whichever is needed. It can help assimilate higher vibrations of spiritual energy into the body, along the spine and to the brain, harmonizing the whole nervous system.

Spirit As its name suggests, merlinite brings magic into your life as it contains the wisdom of ancient magician-priests, alchemists and shamans. It's a good gem to use to access other dimensions, journey between worlds and visit the Akashic records, to retrieve memories from past lives or see glimpses of the future. Any spell work or spiritual ritual is greatly improved with this stone, as it is attuned to all the elements and symbolizes the unity of Earth, fire, air and water. It also brings balance between the spiritual realms and Earth plane, yin and yang, feminine and masculine.

How to use Position on the third eye chakra while lying down to travel in the mind's eye during meditation. Place next to the root chakra to stimulate sexual energy. Use in a healing grid or medicine wheel to unify the elements. Wear over the heart in a pendant or in earrings.

Meteorite

TYPE OF CRYSTAL Created in the vacuum of space, hard, heavy meteorites come from the moon, Mars, asteroids, the heads of comets and possibly even the big bang. Thought to be between 4.5 billion and 13 billion years old, these ancient space rocks come in different classes depending on their mineral composition: chondrites, made of silicate minerals; achondrites; and irons containing ferronickel. They are brown, black, metallic grey and sometimes silver when polished, and are found mostly in China, Russia, Argentina, Antarctica, Northwest Africa and the Sahara.

CHAKRA CONNECTION Root, third eye, crown

ASTRO AFFILIATION All

HEALING homesickness, connection to others and to nature

Mind Feelings of melancholy and homesickness can be soothed with this space crystal, which fosters connection between distant friends and relatives, making it beneficial if you are moving to a new home or emigrating to another country. Meteorite helps with spatial awareness and organizes your thoughts into a more coherent argument, if needed. It can also help you have a stronger mental and emotional connection to nature.

Body The iron variety of meteorites can be made into an elixir to help with anaemia, bolstering the blood and bringing vitality back to you after suffering from fatigue or post-viral syndrome. They also bring endurance, so are great to use for long-distance running or any challenging sporting event.

Spirit Carrying high-frequency energy from the sun and space, meteorites bring great change, not always good. However, they also enhance your spiritual energy and energize your aura, raising your vibration and helping attract all you want to manifest. They can ignite your metaphysical capabilities, enhancing meditation, clairvoyance, telepathy and communication with other dimensions.

How to use Hold in either hand to receive a boost of energy, or meditate with it to raise your frequency and increase intuitive skills. Place on your meditation altar. Carry it with you. Place on the appropriate chakras. Cleanse with salt or sage smoke before use, as this slightly porous stone picks up energy from its surroundings.

Warning: Make iron meteorite only into an elixir; do not make a gem essence from chondrites or achondrites. Use the elixir sparingly; too much iron is bad for the liver.

Microcline

TYPE OF CRYSTAL One of the most common feldspar minerals, microcline is unique due to its 'plaid' formation of lines. It forms some of the largest crystals on the planet, and is found in granite, along with quartz and mica, in Russia and the US. Microcline comes in a variety of colours, from colourless, white, cream and light yellow to brighter salmon-pink and red, green and blue-green. It is used industrially in the production of porcelain, ceramic and glass products.

CHAKRA CONNECTION Third eye

ASTRO AFFILIATION Libra

HEALING through touch and cooperation

Mind This common crystal brings comfort and calm, soothing troubled minds and creating peace and stability in your life. Meditating with it creates space between your thoughts, allowing clarity to arise and your ideas to be clearly expressed.

Body Microcline boosts brain function. It helps the hands, fingers, toes and feet and enhances your sense of touch. Have a massage and let your mind and body relax, or try treating someone else to the same with this stone present, emanating its energy. A smooth piece of microcline works wonders on tired, achy muscles.

Spirit A crystal to encourage cooperation, microcline assists with any team-building, family or group cohesion. It encourages deep meditation and enhances symbolic dreaming, recall and interpretation of the messages in the imagery.

How to use Hold in either hand while meditating. Rub fingers and hands, toes, feet and sore muscles with a smoothed stone. Place in the centre of a group activity for better cooperation.

Moldavite

TYPE OF CRYSTAL Found only in the Czech Republic, Germany and Moldova, along the banks of the river Moldau, moldavite has extraterrestrial origins. It was created when a meteor crash-landed into Earth nearly 15 million years ago in the Bohemian Plateau. It comes in round or flat drop-like or disc shapes, spheres, ovals or spirals – all common liquid splash patterns. This rare, reformed green tektite is glassy, with carved, etched or wrinkled patterns in raw, unpolished stones in green shades, including deep forest green, olive and greenish-brown. Once as prized as emerald, it was discovered in the archaeological site of the Venus of Willendorf, the oldest known goddess statue. It was used by the Neolithic people of eastern Europe, in 25000BC, for arrowheads, cutting tools, and as amulets for protection.

CHAKRA CONNECTION Heart, third eye, throat and crown

ASTRO AFFILIATION All signs, but especially Aquarius

HEALING through powerful transformation

Mind This gem brings mental balance, easing doubts and worries, particularly about money, giving you fresh insights and solutions to problems, and helping you tap into the unlimited power of the universe. Working with moldavite regularly opens the mind to new possibilities, which it guides you to via magical synchronicities. Unconventional and inspiring, it encourages the cathartic release of outdated beliefs and ideas that no longer serve you. This crystal supports empathy and compassion, and helps the mind and heart work together to improve your life.

Body This otherworldly crystal has an intense vibration that is often felt quickly and dramatically. The first time you hold moldavite, it can feel warm to the touch in the hand, then moving through the body. It activates the heart chakra, which can be felt as a pounding pulse, sweating or flushing of the face, acting as a general tonic to rejuvenate and bring anti-ageing benefits and physical equilibrium. It can be useful as a diagnostic tool, making one aware of the root cause of disease, then aiding with releasing and healing.

Spirit Moldavite is an energy amplifier that opens up all the chakras, assisting spiritual ascension and expansion, especially when placed on the crown while seated. A 'stone of connectivity' linking universal and earthly energies, it increases connection to the higher self, Ascended Masters and clairsentient guidance from those in the spiritual realms as well as extraterrestrials. It's a good gem to help facilitate altered states, such as through astral travel, lucid dreaming and hypnosis, as well as to journey into past, future and other lives, to discover what path of action is needed right now. Hold a pair of Boji Stones after a spiritual experience with moldavite to ground your energy.

How to use Use in a crystal grid to heighten other crystals' vibrations. Carry a piece of moldavite or wear it as jewellery to rejuvenate – but slowly get used to wearing it, as it can lead to light-headedness. Hold it up to the light and look into it for a shift in consciousness. Lie down with a piece on your heart area to find out why you are incarnated here at this time. Placed at the throat, it will communicate how to heal the planet. On the third eye, it will take you to the future, to know how to act in the present for the best possible outcome for humanity.

Warning: Do not clean with salt or saltwater, as they will scratch its surface.

Mookaite

TYPE OF CRYSTAL Difficult to extract where it forms underneath the bedrock clay of creeks in Western Australia, mookaite is a patterned red and cream type of jasper, also found in beige, brown, grey and even purple, sometimes containing tiny fossils. It varies in hardness from crumbly to carvable and polishable, and is believed to have formed during the Cretaceous Period 145–66 million years ago.

CHAKRA CONNECTION Root

ASTRO AFFILIATION Leo

HEALING through flexibility and forward movement

Mind This flexible crystal encourages versatility when presented with new situations and brings a calm disposition with which to face life. Meditate with mookaite when you have to make an important decision or want new stimulation for creative ideas or work endeavours. It enhances communication and self-esteem, and combats loneliness and depression.

Body This stone creates optimum physical stability by fortifying the immune system, purifying the blood and easing water retention. It is said to heal wounds, especially hernias, and boost the health of the thyroid gland and stomach. Mookaite also aids weight loss.

Spirit Mookaite points out all possibilities on your path and helps you choose the best one,

enabling you to move forward with joy and confidence. It brings balance between internal and external experiences so neither one dominates. Benefitting your meditation practice and dream analysis, this crystal helps ground the spiritual into practical reality.

How to use Meditate with mookaite held in either hand, or placed next to the root chakra while seated or lying down. Place on meditation altar. Position on or near any area or wound in need of healing.

Moonstone

TYPE OF CRYSTAL This variety of feldspar is a sodium potassium aluminium silicate. It looks translucent milky white, but can also be dusky pink, grey, pale yellow and sometimes blue or black; it always has an opalescence, shimmering like the moon. Found in India, Sri Lanka and Australia, it is said to lose its sheen if the person using it holds too much anger inside them, and its colour can sometimes change according to the cycles of the moon.

CHAKRA CONNECTION Sacral, third eye, crown

ASTRO AFFILIATION Cancer, Libra, Scorpio

HEALING by calming and balancing emotions

Mind This 'stone of new beginnings' reminds us that, just as the moon goes through phases, we live in a constant cycle of change and can be optimistic rather than fearful of things ending. In fact, this gem helps you let go of relationships and situations that are not for your highest good, and aligns you with synchronicity. Support for emotional triggers and irrational overreactions comes with this crystal, which soothes stressful feelings and reduces aggressive, macho energies. Bringing gifts of receptivity and emotional intelligence, it helps men and masculine women tap into and express their more feminine side.

Body Moonstone boosts fertility, balances hormones and helps with pregnancy and childbirth. It aids any issues with menstruation and menopause, including PMT, water retention and hot flushes. This gem aligns the body with natural biorhythms and stimulates kundalini energy, increasing sex drive and overall vitality. An elixir used topically can encourage a youthful, bright appearance for skin, hair and eyes, as well as alleviate pain from insect bites and reduce swelling. Drinking a moonstone essence was traditionally used to stop insomnia, and it can also stop sleepwalking and calm hyperactive children. It eases the effects of shock and stress, especially on the digestive tract.

Spirit As its name suggests, moonstone is strongly connected to the moon, teaching you to go with the ebb and flow of life, and tune into your natural intuition and psychic skills. Meditating with this crystal assists communication with the divine and brings connection with spiritual beings. Used at the time of the full moon, it will facilitate lucid dreaming and bring the unconscious to light. Moonstone encourages empathy, compassion and the ability to know who you truly are, deep inside.

How to use Place on relevant parts of the body or chakras. Wear as a ring, although women might need to remove it during a full moon, as the effects may be too strong. Women should also wear a moonstone necklace to synchronize their menstrual cycle with the moon, to know when they are most fertile. Or make a fertility grid with 12 moonstones placed around the bed, with one in the centre underneath. Positioned in the bedroom or under your pillow, the stone also helps with sleep, banishing nightmares and anxiety.

Moonstone gift tip

Hold a smooth pebble of moonstone close to your heart, fill it full of loving energy, then give to someone going through an emotionally tough time.

Muscovite

TYPE OF CRYSTAL This commonly found variety of mica forms in layers of plates, looking like books, flakes, flowers or slabs coming off the main stone. Muscovite is mostly found in Brazil but also the US, Russia, Switzerland, Austria and the Czech Republic. It comes in various colours, including grey, brown, green, pink, red, violet, yellow and white, all with a pearlescent shimmer.

CHAKRA CONNECTION Heart, third eye, crown

ASTRO AFFILIATION Leo, Aquarius

HEALING doubt and insecurity

Mind Muscovite encourages sharp wit, quick thinking and heightened problem-solving abilities, especially with big life decisions or if you are worried about the impact your choices have on those who rely on you. This reflective gem helps you spot your projections onto others, enabling you to see that what you don't like in others is actually the unaccepted parts of yourself. It then assists with the transformation of these traits, releasing insecurity, self-doubt and nervousness, and stimulating unconditional love for yourself and humanity. Anger and resistance to moving forward are let go of with this stone, which helps you explore painful feelings and replace them with appreciation for past lessons and joy for future possibilities.

Body Physically, this crystal releases tension in the body and aligns the energy meridians. It can improve your appearance, giving your hair more shine and your eyes more sparkle, as well as helping you reach the best weight for you. Beneficial for anyone with diabetes, it balances blood sugar, prevents hunger – even while fasting – and regulates the function of the pancreas and kidneys. Muscovite also rehydrates, relieves allergies and combats insomnia.

Spirit A highly mystical crystal, muscovite will help you meditate and activate connection with the angelic realm, spiritual guidance and your higher self. Opening up the heart, third eye and crown chakras, it tunes you into your intuition and psychic awareness. It assists astral travel and can be used in scrying (clairvoyantly seeing) the future.

How to use Place muscovite on your bedside table to bring guidance in your dreams. Stare deeply into a piece of muscovite and see what images appear in the crystal itself or come into your mind's eye from the future. Meditate holding a piece gently in either hand. Place on or near the relevant chakras or parts of the body in need of its help. Stroke over the skin to brighten.

Warning: Muscovite is very brittle, so handle and store with care. Never use water or salt to cleanse it.

Nephrite

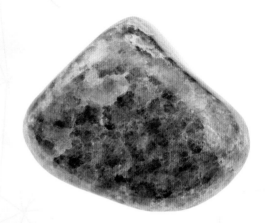

TYPE OF CRYSTAL A type of jade with actinolite, found in masses in Canada, the US and originally China. Also known as greenstone, it comes in shades of green as well as black, cream, light brown, pink or blue. The hardest of the jades, nephrite was the first to be made into ornaments in China, used between 5000BCE and the 1700s, by grinding it rather than carving, as it is so strong. It is the original Chinese jade, as jadeite was not discovered until 1740. Not only used in China, it has also been part of Russian history and is used by the New Zealand Maori and indigenous North Americans.

CHAKRA CONNECTION Heart

ASTRO AFFILIATION Libra

HEALING by calming the mind and soothing the heart

Mind Nephrite helps calm the mind to a point of refreshing stillness and serenity. It encourages you to appreciate everything in your life, and to see the potential of your desires, career goals and purpose.

Body Boosting your overall health and wellbeing, nephrite stimulates the immune system and metabolism, and helps rid the body of viruses and bacterial infections. Beneficial to the adrenal glands, it heals the body of stress-related illness. It also helps soothe colic in infants.

Spirit This variety of jade is good for protection from various causes of mental, physical and spiritual disease. Use it to deepen your meditation practice, guiding you swiftly to stillness.

How to use Carry nephrite with you for protection and good fortune. Meditate holding it in either hand or place on the heart chakra to calm and restore balance to fluctuating emotions.

Novaculite

TYPE OF CRYSTAL Also known as Arkansas stone due to its source in the US, novaculite is a fine-textured yet hard sedimentary stone made of microcrystalline silica quartz. Its name is taken from the Latin *novacula*, meaning razor, due to its sharp, flinty edges. Usually white, but also shades of grey or black, whether lustrous, translucent or opaque, it makes a good whetstone for sharpening metals and was used thousands of years ago for arrow tips and spearheads. It is also found in Russia, Brazil and parts of Africa.

CHAKRA CONNECTION Aligns all; connected to crown and higher chakras

ASTRO AFFILIATION Aquarius, Sagittarius

HEALING by finding the gift in any situation

Mind Giving you the ability to see the positive even in the most negative scenarios, this crystal can lift depression and stop obsessive thinking, which blocks true happiness and fulfilment. It highlights the underlying causes of repetitive doom-mongering, then brings a fresh perspective on events and provides solutions to problems. Let novaculite bring calm to manic thoughts, and light and hope where there is despair. Focus better on your goals with this crystal, and allow it to boost your personal magnetism to attract good financial fortune.

Body Work with this stone to get rid of warts and unsightly moles, and promote healthy, supple skin. It can also relieve allergic reactions and chills, and release trauma from deep within the cells. Novaculite commits you to a new exercise regime or health kick, encouraging you to reach the best of your physical capabilities.

Spirit This gem will energize and align all your chakras, raising your frequency to match its lightness and ground spiritual energy into the body. Opening the crown and etheric chakras, novaculite connects you to the angelic realm and other dimensions so you can journey to them in your mind and learn lessons from other worlds. Its laser-like light can cut cords to ancient spells and curses, as well as emotional and etheric ties to people you no longer want to be associated with (see opposite).

How to use Hold or position over the relevant area or chakra. Meditate lying or sitting with a piece placed on the crown to open up to other dimensions of awareness. Use in a healing grid with other crystals such as nuummite to clear spells, and tugtupite to heal and forgive past relationships and encourage unconditional love. Wear as jewellery to enhance attractiveness.

Cord-cutting ritual with novaculite

This exercise is ideal to do after the death of a loved one, a painful breakup or when you feel the need to draw your energy back from a hectic or upsetting situation.

> Find a calm place, free from interruptions.

> Sit quietly, eyes closed, holding a piece of novaculite in your cupped hands.

> Breathe deeply and let the crystal take you into a state of deep relaxation.

> Call upon your spirit guides and/or guardian angels to help you through this cord-cutting process.

> Visualize yourself with a healing white light all around your body.

> Repeat the affirmation: 'I release any cords to _ _ _ _ _ _ _ _ _ _' – whoever or whatever is weighing you down or negatively affecting your energy. Don't dwell on the reasons; just keep releasing the cords by stating it and seeing the cords being loosened and let go in your mind.

> When you've completed this cord-cutting ritual, slowly open your eyes and connect to your surroundings.

> Smudge all around you with a sage stick to clear any remaining negative energy before having a warm bath to finally clear your energy.

> Drink plenty of water to ground and revitalize.

Nuummite

TYPE OF CRYSTAL Also known as magician's stone or sorcerer's stone, nuummite is the oldest living mineral at almost 4 billion years old, and is found increasingly in Greenland and Canada. Opaque black or very dark brown, it contains iridescent golden flecks.

CHAKRA CONNECTION Root and crown

ASTRO AFFILIATION Sagittarius

HEALING through intense spiritual clearing

Mind Nuummite improves the memory and intellect, its shimmering particles acting as flashes of inspiration about how to make positive changes in your life. This gem removes mental blocks to fulfilment and gives you the strength and willpower to reach your goals. If you've been manipulated or over-protected by others and feel defensive, nuummite clears this and connects you to your sovereign self. It brings respect and integrity, helping you take responsibility for your own protection and stick to obligations and promises while guiding you to let go of that which does not serve you.

Body This mineral enhances vitality, relieves stress and eases pain. It gets rid of insomnia and tension headaches, and soothes the central nervous system. The eyes and ears are helped with this stone, which can treat tinnitus. Insulin is regulated with this gem, helping anyone with diabetes. The throat, brain, spinal cord, kidneys, lymph and blood get a boost with this powerful healer. Even degenerative diseases such as Parkinson's can be aided with nuummite.

Spirit A powerful spiritual healing stone, nuummite links the root and crown chakras, grounding any spiritual healing experience into the body. It activates all chakras, raising your consciousness. When its magic is used respectfully, this intense crystal is highly effective as a wand to pull out negative energy from the auric field. It finds and fills any holes in your aura, made through trauma in this or past lives, and bolsters your energetic shield, blocking psychic attack.

How to use Hold in either hand when meditating or using as a healing tool. Place on relevant chakra or area for alleviating pain or symptoms of ill health. It can be used for psychic surgery on the etheric blueprint for your body, cutting away past-life curses and traumatic memories causing problems in this life. Works well with novaculite to cut through ancient cords, then purify and seal in your energy afterward. Use in a crystal grid combined with other crystals. Wear set in silver as jewellery, especially together with tugtupite, for healing rituals, protection and unconditional love.

Obsidian

TYPE OF CRYSTAL Obsidian is made when molten lava cools so fast it turns into smooth volcanic glass. Found in Mexico, the US and other countries, it comes in many colours, most commonly black, but also brown, blue, blue-green, mahogany, rainbow and with a gold or silver sheen. Some of the colours, including the rough brown-black Apache tears (see page 66), get their own entry in this book, so this covers the general qualities and healing properties of this dynamically powerful stone.

CHAKRA CONNECTION Root primarily; other chakras depending on colour

ASTRO AFFILIATION Sagittarius

HEALING quickly, powerfully and without limitations

Mind This reflective crystal mercilessly highlights any flaws or outdated programming in your thinking, which helps you destroy blockages to abundance, empowerment and fulfilment. Be aware that it can suddenly reveal hidden or unpleasant truths or bring negative emotions to the surface, revealing the root of disease to be examined and cleared. It helps you face your subconscious shadow side with strength and acceptance. Obsidian brings new emotional clarity and expands awareness of who you truly are, enabling you to move forward with ease and confidence.

Body A good detoxifier, this gem promotes healthy digestion, both physically and mentally, of anything that's hard to accept. It dissolves blockages in arteries and stiffness in joints, and relieves the painful symptoms of arthritis, muscle cramps and injuries. Good for circulation, obsidian warms up cold hands and feet. A gem essence can be drunk to help with shock.

Spirit This powerfully protective stone creates an energetic shield around you to combat negativity, repel harmful EMFs and guard against psychic attack when travelling in the spiritual realms. With obsidian's protection, your spirit can journey safely into the unknown while firmly grounded in your body. Stimulating spiritual growth, it helps you actualize your soul purpose in alignment with your deeper truth.

How to use Place obsidian on the appropriate area of the body or chakra to clear. Use in a ball or mirror for scrying the future or simply gaze into a piece with a soft focus. Meditate holding a piece in either hand or with it placed on your altar in front of you. Put a chunk under the bed or pillow to calm mental tension – but remember, the deeper reasons for that stress could also be revealed to you. Place in a room or in front of any electrical device to soak up negativity and harmful EMF rays.

Warning: Clean obsidian under cold running water after every use.

Obsidian - black

TYPE OF CRYSTAL See previous page

CHAKRA CONNECTION Root, sacral, third eye

ASTRO AFFILIATION Sagittarius

HEALING the deep subconscious

Mind Black obsidian powerfully grounds spiritual inspiration into the body, igniting your creativity and manifestation abilities. It forces you to face your subconscious fears and behaviour stemming from the past, including previous lives and ancestral issues holding you back. It repels unloving thoughts, releases mental anguish from former love affairs and supports you through change, bringing strength of mind, self-control and clarity.

Body All the physical healing properties described above apply to black obsidian, especially smoothing digestion. It also helps your survival instincts kick in, whether in a sudden emergency or when overcoming long-term disease.

Spirit Good for shamanic healing ceremonies and removing blockages or illness, black obsidian also enables one to see the future. A common crystal ball material, it is excellent for scrying and meditating with to amplify clairvoyant skills. But make sure you use what you discover for the highest good of all, as this crystal highlights how power is used – and that it must benefit everyone.

How to use As before; but also place on the sacral chakra to ground spiritual energy into the body. Hold above the third eye to help remove mental blockages or conditioning that is holding you back.

Obsidian - mahogany

TYPE OF CRYSTAL This brown-black obsidian, found mainly in Mexico, has a gentler energy than pure black, and is tuned into the Earth for extra grounding ability.

CHAKRA CONNECTION Root, sacral and solar plexus

ASTRO AFFILIATION Libra

HEALING through gentle grounding and supporting

Mind Use mahogany obsidian to activate your purpose and encourage you to meet your goals. It stimulates mental, emotional and spiritual growth while keeping you grounded in reality. Let this crystal give you strength in times of need.

Body This type of obsidian restores physical health and vitality in a slightly gentler way than black obsidian. Worn regularly, it can boost circulation and ease pain. It corrects the spinning energy of the relevant chakras, unblocking stagnation and leading to wellbeing.

Spirit Brown-black obsidian assists deep relaxation in meditation, while protecting you from negative energy and stabilizing your aura. It also releases energy blocks that may be stopping full spiritual expansion.

How to use Wear as jewellery for physical healing benefits. Hold in either hand in meditation or place on an altar in front of you. Position on the appropriate chakra, or each of those mentioned, in turn, to balance energy. Hold over a place of pain for relief.

Obsidian - rainbow

TYPE OF CRYSTAL Found mainly in Mexico, this volcanic glass has coloured bands on its black base.

CHAKRA CONNECTION Root and heart

ASTRO AFFILIATION Libra

HEALING the heart by unhooking others' attachments to you

Mind This gem boosts your happiness, encouraging you to see the wonders of life and beauty in nature. It can also be used in hypnosis, releasing your mind from outdated patterns of thinking to help end addictions or habits that hamper your wellbeing.

Body With its gentle yet protective energy, rainbow obsidian releases stress from the body when worn as a pendant.

Spirit This obsidian, and any of the blue variations, are excellent for divining the future. This crystal will connect you to your spiritual side and tune you into your inner self. It absorbs negative energy from your aura and protects you further by cutting cords to past relationships, healing your heart energy ready to love again.

How to use Wear as jewellery, especially as a pendant. Meditate with it on your altar or held in either hand. Place on the heart while lying down relaxing.

Obsidian - sheen (gold or silver)

TYPE OF CRYSTAL Black obsidian with a silver or gold sheen is found mainly in Mexico.

CHAKRA CONNECTION Root

ASTRO AFFILIATION Sagittarius

HEALING by getting to the root cause of disease

Mind Use this type of obsidian to overcome a sense of futility and give you patience when life doesn't go according to plan. It helps release attachment to the ego, letting spirit lead the way so you can persevere through sudden change, knowing you are still on course.

Body As with all obsidians, this gets to the root cause of any disease; then use other crystals or methods to help heal the issue at its core. Gold sheen, in particular, balances your energy field, helping soothe your nervous system.

Spirit Much like the other obsidians, the sheen variety acts as a mirror to your inner being, helping you align with your spiritual path. Gold sheen is great for scrying and for looking into the past to see the causes of problems.

Silver sheen assists astral travel by keeping your spirit connected to your physical body even while journeying in other realms.

How to use Use in a crystal ball or for crystal gazing to divine the future or explore the past. Hold in either hand during meditation, or lie down and place it next to your root chakra to stay grounded.

Obsidian - snowflake

TYPE OF CRYSTAL This rough greenish-black obsidian has small, snowflake-like, mottled inclusions of white phenocryst. It is found all over the world but mostly in the US, and is commonly sold in small tumbled and polished stones.

CHAKRA CONNECTION Root, sacral

ASTRO AFFILIATION Virgo

HEALING by purifying the mind, body and spirit

Mind This black and white crystal teaches you to appreciate mistakes in your life as much as successes. It releases anger and resentment to bring peace of mind, calming your thoughts and connecting to the present moment, where all is well and you are safe. It allows you to recognize and halt harmful thinking patterns, enabling you to become more centred and focused on the now.

Body Beneficial for a detox and boosting circulation, snowflake obsidian is good for the skin, and treats any vein and bone issues. It unblocks the energy meridian between the stomach and sinuses, clearing issues in these areas. A gem essence is also good for improving the health of the eyes.

Spirit Snowflake obsidian transforms feelings of loneliness into connected independence. This is especially felt during meditation with this gem, when you can surrender to spirit and realize you are never truly alone.

How to use Place on or next to the root or sacral chakra while lying down meditating. Hold in either hand for deep surrender to the present moment. Carry in a pocket. Place on any part of the body in need of its healing. Use an elixir on the skin or eyes.

Onyx

TYPE OF CRYSTAL This smooth, dark and heavy type of chalcedony mostly appears black, although sometimes it can have white banding or a marbled effect, or be grey, red, yellow, brown or blue. Onyx is found in many countries, including Brazil, Mexico, the US, Russia, South Africa and Italy.

CHAKRA CONNECTION Root

ASTRO AFFILIATION Capricorn

HEALING by increasing mental, physical and spiritual strength and protection

Mind A stone for support through tough times – such as when dealing with grief, stress or unhappy relationships – onyx alleviates fears and encourages a more positive outlook. Onyx reduces anxiety and confusion while boosting confidence and awareness of your dualistic thoughts and actions. It can help stop repetitive thinking patterns, habits and addictions, promoting self-control and wise decisions. Use onyx to facilitate celebrating your achievements.

Body Onyx brings strength and stamina to your training, especially if it involves endurance, so you can move healthily away from obesity and feel full of vigour and vitality. It is also believed to help with the process of childbirth. It can relieve the symptoms of allergies, alleviate blood disorders and is beneficial for bones, bone marrow, teeth and feet.

Onyx can take your attention to an area of the body injured in the past, or even in a previous life, to be released through more crystal healing or other therapies.

Spirit This crystal grounds, centres and aligns your energy with higher guidance and universal consciousness or Source energy in everything. It will absorb these energies for use in healing, as well as soak up negative vibrations in your environment. Onyx will spiritually protect you when worn daily or placed in your home. Meditating with it can take you into the future to show you lessons you need to learn, or back to past lives to heal old injuries or sorrows affecting you in the present.

How to use Wear in a ring or bracelet on the left side of the body. In ancient times, wearing onyx as

a pendant was believed to reduce lust and support chastity. Position in any area of the home to soak up negative energy, or carry with you for the same purpose. Keep in your meditation area. Hold in either hand and allow its energy to fill your mind and body, to see where it leads you for healing, using your intuition and imagination.

Opal - common

TYPE OF CRYSTAL This high-vibration, delicate, clear or cloudy crystal often displays a fiery iridescence and comes in all the colours of the rainbow including pink, red, orange, purple and blue, as well as white, brown and black. Some varieties are given separate entries in this book. This entry is for the common opal, usually found in milky white, clear, pink, grey, green/white and red/white masses without iridescence. Found in many countries including Australia, the UK, Mexico, Honduras, much of South America, the US and Canada, opals are often sold as small polished stones; precious gem-quality crystals are expensive.

CHAKRA CONNECTION Sacral, solar plexus and heart in particular, but all chakras depending on colour

ASTRO AFFILIATION Cancer, Libra

HEALING through spontaneity and creative inspiration

Mind A stone to encourage your innate creativity and interest in the arts, opal brings inspiration and spontaneity. It amplifies your personality traits, whether good or bad, bringing the less desirable characteristics up for transformation and helping you fully express yourself. Opal enhances self-worth and enables you to realize your full potential. Long associated with love, loyalty, passion and desire, it can release inhibitions and supercharge eroticism. Emotions may be intensified, scattered or balanced, so you need to be centred when working with this gem.

Body Boosting your vitality, opal gives you the will to live if you have been suffering a long time. It treats Parkinson's disease, fevers and infections. Childbirth can be eased with this crystal nearby, and menstrual issues rectified.

Blood, kidneys and memory are all enhanced with opal. It can also balance insulin levels in diabetics. Wash the eyes in an elixir of opal to soothe and stop irritations and infections.

Spirit With this karmic crystal, what you put out into the world will quickly come back to you, so make sure to exude loving, kind and positive energies. It aids communication with your higher self, divine consciousness and spiritual beings, giving you psychic insight and clairvoyant visions. It can be programmed to make you invisible, which is especially good when doing shamanic work where you need to be protected.

How to use Place on or next to a relevant chakra. Hold in receiving (non-dominant) hand for blessings. Keep on your meditation altar or in your creative work area for inspiration. Wear as jewellery, especially as a ring on the little finger. You can also use opals to heal the energy field of the Earth by sending their frequency to re-energize and stabilize the grid of light around the planet.

Warning: Opals are very soft and can damage easily, so take care when wearing, cleaning and storing. Never use salt or water to cleanse opals.

Opal - fire

TYPE OF CRYSTAL An orange and red opal that shimmers with fiery iridescence and mainly comes from Mexico and Australia.

CHAKRA CONNECTION Third eye

ASTRO AFFILIATION Cancer, Leo, Libra, Sagittarius, Pisces

HEALING by amplifying energy, power and emotions

Mind Fire opal amplifies your personal power, getting your inner flames of motivation and optimism burning. It carries you through change and emotional turmoil with strength and hope. This variety of opal is said to return thoughts and feelings back times three, so be careful when working with it, and make sure you're in a positive frame of mind first.

Body Another crystal for enhancing energy levels, fire opal balances the adrenal glands and stimulates the sex organs. The lower back, abdomen, kidneys and intestines can all be helped with this crystal. It is believed to treat emphysema. Eyesight can be improved too.

Spirit This gem aids the release of grief and upset from past lives or recent events, but can generate explosive emotional outbursts if feelings have been suppressed. It deepens meditation and revitalizes your psychic skills. Fire opal is also a great protector against spiritual and physical danger.

How to use Place on the relevant area or chakra to warm and re-energize. Meditate holding it in both hands or with it placed prominently on your altar. Wear as a pendant to stop burnout and exhaustion. Carry daily for protection.

Opal - green

TYPE OF CRYSTAL Also known as Andean opal, as it is found in Peru, this green variety is found in large masses and is sometimes iridescent.

CHAKRA CONNECTION Heart

ASTRO AFFILIATION Aries, Cancer, Sagittarius

HEALING with gentle balance

Mind Green opal teaches you to how to filter information and re-focus the mind onto what's most important to help solve problems. It reveals deeper meaning to daily reality, enabling you to see the spiritual side of life and recover from emotional upset.

Body Colds and flu are alleviated with green opal, which boosts the immune system and aids cleansing detoxes. It brings down fevers, balances fluctuating temperatures and treats hypothermia. Tune into green opal and it will guide you toward good nutrition for yourself and others.

Spirit This type of opal smooths relationships, raises your spiritual awareness and helps you relax during meditation. It brings you into a calm, centred state and keeps you grounded, especially during

shamanic journeys. Your divination abilities may increase when using green opal, which also helps you remember the messages in your dreams.

How to use Carry with you daily or wear as jewellery, especially a pendant hanging close to your heart. Meditate with it in front of you on your altar or by holding it in cupped hands. Place on the heart chakra while lying down or on any area in need of soothing and balance.

Opal - purple ray

TYPE OF CRYSTAL Also called the violet flame opal or Mexican purple opal, this common opal (without fiery iridescence) is a mixture of white and violet shades.

CHAKRA CONNECTION Crown

ASTRO AFFILIATION Aries, Gemini, Cancer, Virgo

HEALING with gentle release

Mind This crystal helps you through potentially traumatic change, as well as healing shocking times from the past. It transforms anger and fear into love and compassion, giving you the impetus to act on that positive energy. Purple ray opal also helps you discover and digest new concepts and ideas, from physics to spirituality.

Body Digestion and nutrient absorption get assistance from this gem, which also improves your sense of taste and benefits the immune system, the pancreas and eyesight. It can control your temperature, combat hair loss and boost fertility. This crystal can also protect the body from harmful EMFs.

Spirit Purple ray opal clears the aura and creates a protective shield around your energy, helping you firm up boundaries and stay spiritually strong. It brings clairvoyant visions and insight from the spirit world, angelic realm and even your animal guides.

How to use Wear in jewellery, especially earrings or a necklace, to protect and connect to spirit. Meditate holding a piece in cupped hands or place on the crown chakra to activate this spiritual centre on the top of the head. Position in front of any gadget or Wi-Fi router to shield you from its rays.

Pearl

TYPE OF CRYSTAL The protective layers built up around a foreign body inside the shell of an oyster (or sometimes another mollusc) create small, pale stones in white, grey, pinkish and yellowish tones with an iridescent lustre. Found mainly in China, Japan, the Philippines and Sri Lanka, but also in the UK, Austria, France, Germany, Australia and the US, naturally occurring pearls are irregular in shape, whereas man-made pearls are perfectly spherical but do not have healing properties.

CHAKRA CONNECTION Sacral

ASTRO AFFILIATION Gemini, Cancer

HEALING through inner wisdom and Goddess energy

Mind Pearls calm and balance your thoughts and emotions, helping release irritability and ground you in reality. They focus the mind and enhance wisdom, lifting you out of situations that drag you down or lead to antisocial behaviour. These gems help you learn lessons from any situation in life, growing stronger and smarter through trials and tribulations. If you have an important activity or project to do, pearls enable you to see it through to the end.

Body These tiny gems are beneficial for women's health issues including sexuality, fertility and childbirth. They also encourage chastity and purity. Pearls are believed to aid digestion, alleviating bloating and gas. Skin complaints, such as scarring, acne, rosacea and other minor blemishes, can be helped with this gem.

Spirit In Buddhism, Hinduism and Taoism, the 'flaming pearl' is a symbol of inner wisdom and connection with the divine, especially Goddess energies. Pearls can be used to access these qualities in moon rituals. Used by witches as talismans of protection against unwanted otherworldly entities, these gems provide a shield against negativity, balancing your aura and stopping others from draining your energy. Meditating with them encourages us to look inward, to discover and love our true selves and our purpose in life.

How to use Wearing pearls as jewellery means you can always access their abundance, positivity and feminine essence; also, their lustre will be polished by your body's natural oils. Wear them whenever you need extra confidence, or position them in your home or office for continual effects. Meditate holding a pearl in your cupped hands. Place on, or next to, the area of the body in need of energy.

Warning: Always clean pearls with a soft cloth before storing.

Peridot

TYPE OF CRYSTAL Also called chrysolite and olivine, this clear crystal can be red, brown or honey-coloured, but mostly comes in shades of green ranging from light olive to bright apple, sometimes with small black or brown flecks. Found in Afghanistan, Pakistan, Egypt, Russia, the US, Brazil, Sri Lanka, Ireland and the Canary Islands, good-quality gems are often cut and polished into faceted stones for jewellery.

CHAKRA CONNECTION Sacral, solar plexus, but mainly heart

ASTRO AFFILIATION Leo, Virgo, Scorpio, Sagittarius

HEALING through release – of toxins and emotions

Mind Peridot stimulates the mind, eliminates lethargy and brings clarity, enabling you to navigate your path in life much better. Known as the 'release stone', it helps you let go of stress, anger, jealousy or guilt. It stops you from hanging onto something or someone by revealing the illusion that is not serving you – or them. Let peridot release burdens and baggage from the past so you can move forward toward your destiny, quickly and confidently, with renewed purpose. Peridot is also said to balance bipolar disorder and stop hypochondria.

Body Believed to be an antitoxin, peridot acts as a tonic for the body, mind and spirit, cleansing out what is not needed. It can treat major organs, such as the heart, lungs, liver and spleen. It is a healer for cells and the skin as well as the intestinal tract, thymus and gallbladder. It can boost metabolism, alleviate ulcers and IBS, and benefit those with Crohn's disease. Helpful for the eyes, it lessens astigmatism and heals short-sightedness. It can be used to strengthen contractions in childbirth.

Spirit Once used as a talisman to ward off evil spirits, peridot clears and bolsters the aura and helps you detach from external influences, trusting higher guidance instead. In assisting the release of old, negative patterns, this crystal enables you to access a higher frequency. It opens and cleanses the heart and sacral chakras, promoting love and understanding in relationships. Meditating with this gem leads to greater enlightenment and awareness of deeper spiritual truths.

How to use Wear as any kind of jewellery, especially in a choker-style necklace at the throat. Carry in a pocket. Place on or next to the relevant chakras or areas of the body in need of its energy, in particular over the liver in contact with the skin for a full cleanse. Keep on your meditation altar. Hold in your receiving (non-dominant) hand to reap its blessings. Carry with you when working on relationship issues.

Phenacite

TYPE OF CRYSTAL Often colourless or tinted yellow, red, pink or brown, this glassy quartz-like crystal grows in slender prisms, masses and fibrous spherical structures in Madagascar, Zimbabwe, Russia, Brazil and the US.

CHAKRA CONNECTION Third eye, crown

ASTRO AFFILIATION Gemini

HEALING through higher vibrations

Mind This colourless crystal focuses the mind on healing the whole system, giving you all the knowledge you need to bring about mental wellbeing. It enables you to download information from the higher realms, such as the Akashic records, so you can discover and release any disease from any source.

Body This high-vibration stone works on cleansing and purifying the physical and energetic body, bringing about healing wherever it's needed. Its high frequency heals your etheric blueprint, if necessary, which is a precursor to optimum bodily health.

Spirit Good for improving meditation and heightening your spiritual awareness, phenacite assists contact with the angelic realm and Ascended Masters by activating the third eye and crown chakras. It brings spirit down to Earth through you, fostering a deep inner knowledge of what's best for you. It heals the soul and aids the ascension process by raising your energetic frequency even higher.

How to use Phenacite magnifies the energy of other healing gems, so it works well in a crystal grid. Place on relevant chakras or wherever it is needed on the body. Position on top of the head, in a seated meditation, to open up the crown chakra and connect to higher guidance. Wear as a faceted stone in jewellery.

Picture jasper

TYPE OF CRYSTAL Also called picture stone, this brown or tan variety of jasper has darker markings on it that look like ancient pictures or cave drawings. It is found mainly in the US and South Africa.

CHAKRA CONNECTION Third eye

ASTRO AFFILIATION Leo

HEALING through a sense of proportion

Mind In keeping with its name, this unique type of jasper helps you see the bigger picture. It allows deeply buried feelings of grief, guilt, envy, hatred and love to rise to the surface for healing. When released, these repressed emotions will be seen simply as lessons on your path to fulfilment. Picture jasper also aids creative visualization, especially to help grow a business.

Body This gem boosts the immune system and kidney function, flushing out toxins from both. It helps clear up any problems with your skin, too.

Spirit If you can read the images on this stone, it imparts a message from Mother Earth. Past life lessons may come to mind during meditation with picture jasper, seen in proportion to the rest of your journey in this lifetime. It

helps you address any fears about these events and gain comfort and harmony instead.

How to use Place on any area of the body in need of healing. Lie down with picture jasper on your third eye chakra to connect to past lives or sense messages from Mother Earth.

Pietersite

TYPE OF CRYSTAL Fairly recently discovered but easily obtained in Namibia and South Africa, pietersite is a type of tiger's eye. It comes in grey and blue tones, sometimes golden and brown, and is often mottled with iridescent flashes. It is often known as the tempest stone because it connects with tempestuous energy.

CHAKRA CONNECTION Third eye

ASTRO AFFILIATION Leo

HEALING through vision quests and spiritual journeying

Mind This stone serves as a reminder to follow your own path rather than adhering to the rules and beliefs imposed upon you by parents or other authority figures. It clears confusion, strengthens willpower and supports you to speak your truth, while picking up others' honesty or insincerity. It also removes mental blocks and releases past-life promises holding you back in your mind, helping you process old conflicts and buried feelings.

Body Beneficial for the pituitary and pineal (and other endocrine) glands, this crystal balances hormone production governing growth, metabolism, blood pressure, temperature and sex. When you have no time to rest but have illness related to exhaustion, such as chronic fatigue, this stone can help by clearing and revitalizing the energy meridians in the body.

Pietersite is also good for the intestines, helping with digestion and the absorption of nutrients from food. It can also improve the health of the lungs, liver, feet and legs.

Spirit Pietersite highlights the fact that you are a spiritual being having a human experience, and gives you deeply loving guidance. It grounds you to your etheric body, which helps with spiritual journeying. Allow it to take you to the Akashic record to see all your lives recorded there, or travel in your mind's eye on a vision quest or shamanic journey. This crystal helps you access a higher level of awareness, in particular during moving meditations. It awakens the third eye and pineal gland, heightening your psychic intuition, creative visualization and clairvoyance.

How to use Place or hold over appropriate chakras or areas of the body in need of its properties. Meditate holding it in cupped hands, or placed on your third eye for illuminating visions.

Prehnite

TYPE OF CRYSTAL Prehnite is found as massive globular structures, layered plates, tabular and prismatic crystals in Australia, South Africa, India, Mali and the US. Usually slightly transparent, it is coloured a muddy, olive green through bright green to yellow, white or brown, often with small striations. Polishing it gives it a luminous transparency.

CHAKRA CONNECTION Solar plexus, heart, third eye

ASTRO AFFILIATION Libra

HEALING the healer through divine connection

Mind A crystal to clear clutter from your surroundings as well as your mind, prehnite eliminates brain fog and agitation, and encourages calm, peace and harmony with the flow of life. It relieves phobias and fears, eases nightmares and lessens hyperactivity in children, in particular. Working with prehnite will get to the karmic reason for these issues – they are often due to inner feelings of lack, from this or past lives – and restore your faith in the benevolent universe.

Body This serene stone is the healer for healers, as it can help diagnose the causes of disease in the self and others. It supports the kidneys, bladder and thymus gland, and boosts the health of connective tissues all over the body. Use prehnite to relieve gout, anaemia and other blood disorders. It also treats issues in the shoulders, chest and lungs.

Spirit Another high-vibration stone, prehnite is sometimes referred to as 'the stone of prophecy', as it brings clairvoyant visions and psychic precognition, and shows you the way to spiritual growth. It helps with shamanic work, dream recall and visualization. By deepening your meditation practice, prehnite connects you to divine consciousness and the universe's energy grid. It links you in with healing archangel Raphael and other higher beings for guidance, which help you trust in order to manifest unconditional love in your life.

How to use Place on or next to the area of the body in need of its help, or the relevant chakra. Lie down and place on the heart chakra for unconditional love or on the third eye to encourage psychic insight and guidance. Carry in a pocket for shamanic work. Place in your meditation or healing area. Hold in either hand if carrying out a healing session with prehnite.

Preseli bluestone

TYPE OF CRYSTAL This special stone is only found in the Preseli Mountains in Wales, and forms the inner ring of the ancient Stonehenge monument in Wiltshire. Looking like granite, it is in fact mottled and spotted with white plagioclase feldspar, augite and possibly mica, which creates the glittery effect in sunlight. These crystals shine a lustrous blue when wet or polished; when dry, they appear green.

CHAKRA CONNECTION Throat, third eye

ASTRO AFFILIATION Gemini, Pisces

HEALING through connection with the ancestors and ancient knowledge

Mind This stone helps heal the hurt from relationship breakups, bringing peace of mind, calm and compassion. It allows you to leave past attachments behind so you can live in the present. Anxiety and panic attacks subside, phobias disappear and insomnia is no more with this powerful stone nearby. It boosts your willpower, courage and strength to get through even the hardest of times, assisting the fulfilment of your goals and ideals. Meditating with Preseli bluestone brings focus and concentration, clearing the mind of any distractions ready to receive intuitive knowledge. It can also give answers quickly, especially in dreams, and enables you to access and integrate ancient spiritual information.

Body Drink as an elixir or bathe in water containing these stones to promote physical healing and bring the body's energies back into balance. The throat and immune system are especially supported by Preseli bluestone.

Spirit Found only in Britain's spiritual centre, this stone encapsulates the Merlin energy and awakens the shaman in us all. It helps you explore past lives, especially ancient Celtic heritage. It enhances your psychic divination abilities, brings about rebirth and facilitates astral travel. Highly protective, Preseli bluestone makes a good shamanic anchor to ground you during spiritual journeys and connects you to the support and gifts of the ancestors. Magic, psychometry and kinesiology are all supported with bluestone, which also aids communication of even the most complex spiritual ideas, such as the ancient Egyptian knowledge apparently held deep within the stones.

How to use Carry with you when speaking in public, or to boost your sexual attraction. Position under your pillow for intuitive dreaming and psychic insight. Place on or next to the appropriate chakras for healing. Meditate holding a piece in your non-dominant hand to receive ancestral guidance or ancient knowledge. Wear at the throat to boost communication skills. Remove or turn it around to face another way if a headache develops, as it has a strong directional energy.

Purpurite

TYPE OF CRYSTAL This opaque, bright purple, crystal is banded and veined with a metallic inclusion. Although perhaps less popular than other gems, it is easily found in Namibia, France, the US and Western Australia.

CHAKRA CONNECTION Root and crown

ASTRO AFFILIATION Aquarius

HEALING by rejuvenating, awakening and protecting

Mind Another crystal assistance for public speaking, purpurite brings clarity and focus to your thoughts, along with the confidence to communicate them to others. This stone alleviates despair and encourages you to be alert and receptive to new ideas and teachings. It enables you to drop old attitudes that keep you stuck in past ways of thinking and behaving, and move forward afresh.

Body This is a rejuvenating crystal that boosts stamina and helps ease physical, mental and emotional exhaustion. It regulates the pulse, blood flow and the cardio-thoracic system, alleviating bruising, stopping bleeding and purifying the blood.

Spirit Purpurite opens the crown and higher chakras and connects them to the root chakra, stimulating enlightenment and spiritual evolution by grounding elevated consciousness into daily reality. It is highly effective for psychic protection, dispels negative energy from your surroundings and dissolves ill-intent or curses holding you back from spiritual awakening.

How to use Position between you and the source of negative energy or unwanted influence. Wear as jewellery or carry with you for spiritual protection. Use in a healing grid. Hold or place on the relevant chakras or areas in need of healing.

Pyrite

TYPE OF CRYSTAL Also called iron pyrite, this golden or brown lustrous, opaque crystal is commonly known as fool's gold because it looks like gold but isn't as valuable. This iron sulphide is sometimes found as small flecks in another stone, but more often in masses, cubic or dodecahedral crystals, sometimes flattened and known as pyrite suns in Peru, Chile, the US, Spain and the UK.

CHAKRA CONNECTION Solar plexus especially, but all chakras get a boost

ASTRO AFFILIATION Leo

HEALING by blocking harm of any kind

Mind This metallic stone gives sparks of inspiration to your thinking, boosting brain activity and problem-solving thought processes. It improves memory, strengthens willpower and turns the mind to attracting prosperity. Pyrite increases confidence and self-esteem, dispelling frustration, anxiety, lethargy or despair. It helps combine intuitive insights with instinct, and creativity with analysis. Ideas flow freely with pyrite nearby, so place it in your work area to energize your business.

Body Iron pyrite increases blood flow to the brain, so not only does it enhance mental capabilities, it also benefits overall brain health. It allows more oxygen into the bloodstream, benefitting both the circulation and respiratory systems, helping those with

asthma, bronchitis and other lung issues. Pyrite brings better sleep, overcomes fatigue and repairs cell and DNA damage. It enhances the function of digestion, neutralizes the effects of toxins in the body and can help mend bones. This gem quickly brings the root cause of illness into awareness for treatment. It holds the ideal of optimum wellbeing in its energy and can block everything from infectious diseases to radiation from reaching the body.

Spirit Another highly protective crystal, pyrite creates a shield around your energy field and blocks energetic leaks from your aura, keeping you out of harm's way. This stone helps you see the truth behind whatever may be presented by others' actions, and encourages diplomacy. It balances the masculine energy in all of us,

increasing it where needed, to facilitate inspired action, utilize your abilities and achieve success.

How to use Place a piece on your solar plexus chakra area while lying down. Wear in a pouch or choker-style necklace at the throat. Put some under your pillow to stop snoring and encourage undisturbed sleep. Carry in a pocket or purse, or place in a cashbox or on a desk to attract wealth and success in your business.

Pyrolusite

TYPE OF CRYSTAL Found as large, shiny silver, dark grey, blue, brown or black fan-like shapes on brown matrix or granular masses, pyrolusite comes from the US, Brazil, India and the UK.

CHAKRA CONNECTION Sacral

ASTRO AFFILIATION Leo

HEALING by restructuring your life

Mind This is a crystal to enhance your determination and tenacity when going through changes. It brings optimism in the transformation process and confidence in yourself to get to the heart of any issue in your life and heal from it.

Body Another crystal that gets to the root cause of any disease when working with it, pyrolusite is highly supportive of any body work for emotional release, from massage to dancing. It is believed to boost sex drive as well as metabolism. It can improve eyesight, strengthen blood vessels and help treat bronchitis.

Spirit This is a great gem to block psychic attack or negative energy directed toward you. It bolsters the aura and creates a barrier against any person or thing out to manipulate or overpower you. Wear a piece in the presence of an authority figure you don't want to be dominated by and it will help you stick to your guns and stay true to yourself. Pyrolusite can also transform relationships, balancing them. Use it for support during any emotional healing, especially during past-life regressions exploring the karmic cause of illness.

How to use Pyrolusite is delicate, so it can't be worn or placed on the body. Instead, hold it during meditation or whenever needed, next to the relevant chakra or area. Keep a piece in your meditation area for protection from negative energies. Only make it into an elixir using the indirect method (see page 39), then apply topically or drink.

Quartz

TYPE OF CRYSTAL Known as the 'master healer', as it helps with absolutely everything, quartz is the most abundant mineral on Earth. It covers over 70 percent of the planet in one variety or another. Many types - such as angel aura, rose or smoky quartz - get their own entry in this book, although there are many more than can be included here. Pure quartz is transparent and translucent, clear or milky white, and comes in all sizes of hexagonal points, pillars, geodes and clusters, sometimes with inclusions or striations. It is found all over the world, especially in China, Russia, Brazil, Colombia, South Africa, Madagascar and the US.

CHAKRA CONNECTION All chakras, especially the crown

ASTRO AFFILIATION All

HEALING everything

Mind Quartz is a feel-good crystal that lifts negativity from the mind and makes you feel happier. It re-energizes mental capacity, unlocks long-buried memories and helps you concentrate better on any task. With its elevated energy, quartz connects the mind with the physical body so both work at their best. You can programme a piece of quartz to help with anything you want by sending the feeling of the desired result into the gem as you meditate. It will remember it and bring forth opportunities for this goal to be realized the more you sit with it.

Body The 'master healer' quartz helps all ailments and physical issues, healing, harmonizing and stimulating all systems including the chakras, energy meridians and immune system. It is especially good for balance and for rectifying hearing problems such as tinnitus or ear infections. It treats diabetes, boosts heart and spine health, and alleviates the symptoms of MS and ME. It can soothe burns, reduce pain and help with weight loss. A strong radiation blocker, it also removes potentially harmful positive ions from your environment and replaces them with benign negative ones.

Spirit This high-vibration crystal attunes to and amplifies the energy of whoever is using it for healing or spiritual development, protecting that energy at the same time. It cleanses the soul, balances the chakras and raises your consciousness to its highest level, advancing awakening. Quartz placed on your third eye helps you meditate by removing distractions from the mind so you can focus on the pure bliss of stillness beyond. It can bring up past-life memories and help you remember your dreams. It opens the crown chakra so you can clearly receive psychic messages and intuitive guidance from your higher self or the angelic realm, especially about your spiritual purpose.

How to use Use quartz to cleanse and charge other crystals and amplify their energy. Place in a healing grid. Position on any part of the body or next to any chakra to heal. Lie down in meditation and put a quartz next to your crown chakra to open up this area to higher wisdom. Place on your heart chakra to transform emotional blocks into self-acceptance and love. Wear as any kind of jewellery. Carry it with you. Keep it in a room or anywhere protection or energy clearing is required. Sleep next to a piece to have meaningful, memorable dreams.

Cleanse your quartz
regularly by soaking
it in saltwater overnight,
smudging it with sage
smoke or leaving it in the
sunlight; but make sure the
light doesn't pass through
it and start a fire.

Aura quartzes

TYPE OF CRYSTAL The 'aura' varieties of quartz are artificially bonded with gold, silver and/or titanium to produce intense shades of blue, red, yellow and rainbow effects. Although they are created in laboratories, they still have intense energies emitting from the process of bonding pure quartz with precious metals. They have different qualities and energies depending on their colour, but similar properties when bonded with the same substances.

CHAKRA CONNECTION All

ASTRO AFFILIATION All

HEALING: Self-love and communication, relationships and divine connection

AQUA AURA: This combination comes with a manufactured coating on it, including Siberian (blue), rose or ruby (red) and sunshine (yellow). All are bonded with gold. Aqua aura cleanses and heals holes in the aura, plus the throat and third eye chakras, enabling you to fully express your soul essence, birth something new, and fulfil your highest potential. It protects you from psychic attack, brings deep peace in meditation and facilitates channelling, spirit communication and attunement to universal energies. Physically, it boosts the immune system and aids the healthy functioning of the thymus gland. It lifts depression and alleviates sadness, negativity and grief.

ANGEL AURA - ALSO KNOWN AS OPAL AURA: With a lighter rainbow shimmer than rainbow aura, angel aura is created with platinum and silver bonded to quartz. It is a crystal of harmony, peace, optimism and joy that integrates the light body into the physical domain, as well as any spiritual information received during deepened meditation. It cultivates a strong connection with the angelic realm, the Akashic records and divine cosmic awareness. It helps keep you well overall by protecting your energy field and purifying your chakras.

RAINBOW AURA (ALSO CALLED TITANIUM QUARTZ): This is made when quartz is combined with gold and titanium. Like the sight of a rainbow, this crystal uplifts your energy and brings a new excitement for life. Highly beneficial for troubled relationships, it helps release negative projections and emotions such as grief, resentment or jealousy, as well as any past-life karmic ties getting in the way of harmonious relations. It's also good for seeing someone else's point of view and tuning into your own and others' auras. A good illness preventer, it balances the body's fluids, easing water retention, combating dehydration and reducing fever.

How to use For all 'aura' quartzes, hold or place next to the relevant area or chakra for healing. Use with other crystals, such as in a healing grid, to amplify their properties. Wear as jewellery, especially at the throat to encourage heart-centred communication. Meditate holding them in either hand.

ROSE AND RUBY AURA: Created with quartz and platinum to make varying degrees of red, rose aura activates the pineal gland and heals the heart chakra of self-doubt, bringing unconditional love from the universe to you. It rebalances all cells to optimum wellbeing. Deeper red ruby aura quartz opens you up to Christ consciousness, activates heart wisdom and clears the root chakra of any abuse or survival issues. It boosts the endocrine system and overall energy levels, and acts as a natural antibiotic for parasites and fungal infections.

SUNSHINE AURA: A bright yellow combination of gold and platinum bonded with quartz, sunshine aura has a powerful and dynamic energy that activates the solar plexus chakra. It helps you let go of past hurts and traumas. Physically, it relieves constipation and eliminates toxins. It protects and expands your energy field.

SIBERIAN BLUE AURA: This is a lab-regrown combination of quartz and cobalt to create a garish blue gem that activates the throat and third eye chakras. It brings peace and positivity, alleviating depression and connecting you to higher consciousness. Intense psychic visions, telepathic abilities and spirit communication can all increase when working with this stone, which also helps you share this wisdom, speak your truth and be fully heard. An elixir can be used externally to soothe sunburn, ease stiff muscles and neck pain, and reduce inflammation. Drinking this gem essence can treat throat infections, stomach ulcers and other symptoms of stressful living.

Blue quartz

TYPE OF CRYSTAL This natural blue quartz is rare but is found all over the world in threads or patches of clear quartz. See also indicolite quartz, which is also blue, but is created naturally from blue tourmaline inclusions in quartz.

CHAKRA CONNECTION Throat

ASTRO AFFILIATION Taurus, Libra

HEALING connection

Mind A great stone to ignite creativity, blue quartz also dispels fear and brings hope for the future based on your talents. It alleviates depression and helps you gain clarity of mind, get calmly organized and have the self-discipline to follow through with any tasks toward your goals.

Body This gem supports the healthy functioning of the spleen, blood, endocrine and immune systems. It clears the throat and aids detoxification of the whole body, especially calming overstimulated nerves. A rutilated blue quartz is believed to stop premature ejaculation.

Spirit Blue quartz assists spiritual transformation, teaching you more about your true soul nature. Positioned at the throat chakra, it enables you to connect well with others, the universe and divine consciousness to help raise your awareness and heighten your intuition.

How to use Hold during meditation. Position on or next to the relevant chakra or area in need of support. Use in a crystal grid.

Elestial quartz

TYPE OF CRYSTAL Sometimes called etched crystal, this type of quartz is multi-terminated, layered and enfolded, often with internal phantoms and windows of light, in clear, smoky, amethyst, yellow and pink tones. Initially found in Brazil, where it is sometimes known as *jacare* crystal (*jacare* means alligator in Portuguese), it can also be found in India, Namibia, Madagascar and the US.

CHAKRA CONNECTION All, especially crown

ASTRO AFFILIATION Gemini

HEALING through transformation

Mind Acting as a catalyst to transform your emotional state, elestial quartz brings the change necessary to raise your frequency to new heights. It links your emotions to your intellect and helps you get rid of psychological baggage and bust through blockages to better thoughts. Fears, confusion and judgmental attitudes are released with this gem. But be aware: its transformative ways may come about quickly and when you are least expecting them.

Body This multifaceted quartz aids multidimension healing, as it rebuilds your etheric blueprint, determining your health and wellbeing in this life. It sends energy to the head to relieve headaches and any issues with the inner ear, including balance problems, vertigo and tinnitus. Your sense of taste can be enhanced with this gem. It can also assist the restoration of damaged brain cells after long-term alcohol or drug abuse.

Spirit Elestial quartz is a very high-vibration stone. It activates your ascension and develops your spiritual powers by opening your crown chakra and connecting you to the flow of divine energy from the heavens. Meditating with it opens you up to different dimensions, spirit and higher guidance, and awakens your metaphysical abilities. It can also show you past lives, connect you to your ancestors and reveal ancient knowledge to help release karmic ties, facilitating deep soul healing and advancement.

How to use Position on your meditation altar, or hold while meditating. Lie down and place a piece just above your crown chakra to open this connection to divine energy. Use in a crystal grid to enhance the powers of other stones.

Hues of elestial quartz

All elestial quartzes share the above qualities, but different shades exhibit different properties.

Smoky elestial quartz: This crystal is an excellent purifier and Earth healer, as it draws out negative energy from the environment or person and replaces it with positive, high-vibration light. It can protect against psychic attack or geopathic stress, and alleviate pain. It can stop nightmares, lift depression and shield the body against radiation.

Amethyst elestial quartz: Attuned to the violet flame of healing, this powerful gem connects to all spiritual beings for help. It activates the pineal gland, dispels negative energy and brings calm reassurance.

Rose elestial quartz: Linked to the pink flame of unconditional love and compassion, makes it a great heartbreak healer. It releases heavy emotional strife and enables you to love again by reminding you of the divine within everything and everyone.

Faden quartz

TYPE OF CRYSTAL This white or clear quartz usually forms in a tabular fashion, in the crevice between two existing rock formations. It has fractured during its growth and mended again, giving it an obvious string-like or even hollow line running through it. Some of the oldest quartz on the planet, faden quartz is found in countries where there has been a lot of tectonic activity, such as Pakistan and Brazil. Because it is so brittle, faden quartz can only be mined using a delicate hammer-and-chisel technique.

CHAKRA CONNECTION All, especially solar plexus and crown

ASTRO AFFILIATION Scorpio

HEALING by reconnecting breakages in mind, body, spirit and relationships

Mind This crystal gives you strength of mind to keep going through intense times and emotional trauma. It assists with relationship issues and helps overcome family conflict or group discord, enabling you to set clear intentions to heal, trust and be intimate with others, all while retaining your independence. A gem to promote personal growth and heal old thinking patterns, faden quartz helps bond those working on creative or intellectual projects together.

Body Carrying its own healed fracture within it, faden quartz can fix broken and fractured bones, and help repair torn tendons, ligaments or muscles. Any cuts, scabs or bruises can also be treated with this crystal. It supports the spine, encouraging proper alignment. A good crystal for distance healing,

it boosts communication and connection between patient and healer.

Spirit Faden quartz helps fragmented parts of the soul come back to the self and links your entire being with your higher consciousness, healing the aura and harmonizing energy flow through the chakras. It keeps the etheric body connected to the physical during astral travel or spiritual journeying. In past-life regression sessions or visits to the in-between-life state in other realms of your awareness, faden quartz takes you to the root of any disease. It helps you see the bigger picture of your soul's path and learn from lessons in this life.

How to use Place on any area in need of healing. Position on the solar plexus to calm fluctuating

emotions. Lie down and put a piece of faden quartz next to your crown chakra to activate this area, align the chakras and connect you to higher wisdom. This stone can be used in a healing grid to balance unstable energy in the physical body or in the Earth beneath. Carry with you or wear as jewellery for protection, especially if travelling – particularly by air.

Harlequin quartz

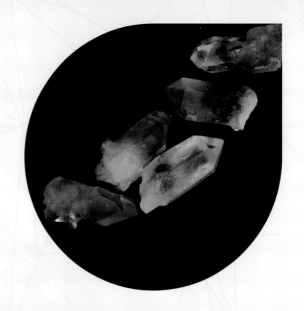

TYPE OF CRYSTAL Also known as hematoid quartz, this variety of quartz has different inclusions - often seen as red dots - from one or more of the following: goethite, hematite, lepidocrocite or titanium. As with most quartzes, this crystal is found all over the world, but harlequin is especially mined in Madagascar and China.

CHAKRA CONNECTION Root

ASTRO AFFILIATION Gemini

HEALING by smoothing relationships

Mind Harlequin quartz alleviates anxiety and aids concentration, even for those with attention-deficit disorder and hyperactivity issues. It boosts communication skills and makes emotions clearer so you can fully express them with honesty and integrity, improving relations between lovers.

Body This stone helps with all the lower parts of the body, including any problems with feet, ankles, knees and legs, as well as the lower back. It helps you feel more grounded, especially during panic attacks and other mind-body disorders where you feel dizzy or unsteady. It can also help stabilize the thyroid and strengthen veins.

Spirit As with all quartzes, you can expect deep connection with the spirit world. But harlequin quartz also encourages meaningful links between people, promoting positive, stable relationships of all kinds. A large harlequin crystal in a room can take away any negativity between people in readiness for more loving energy to come in. It encourages the full expression of universal love.

How to use Place in an area where people gather to transform energy from negative to positive. Position at the root chakra to stabilize energy. Wear as jewellery or carry in a pocket. Meditate holding it or sitting next to a piece on your altar.

Indicolite quartz

TYPE OF CRYSTAL Threads of blue tourmaline inside a clear or white quartz point create blue indicolite quartz, found mainly in Brazil.

CHAKRA CONNECTION Throat

ASTRO AFFILIATION Taurus, Libra

HEALING the soul when passing over or grieving

Mind The combination of quartz and blue tourmaline releases stuck emotions and helps you talk about them. Feelings of sadness and grief are replaced with comfort and even insight into the reasons behind any loss, and an awareness that you are never alone even if someone special to you has gone. Indicolite quartz encourages you to forgive others with tenderness for their mistakes rather than going for revenge or attack as a means to defend yourself. It brings energy and healing to the brain to sharpen memory and cognitive abilities.

Body Healers benefit from using indicolite quartz; it 'jumps' to pinpoint the area of disease in a person so it can be treated. It specifically boosts the pulmonary and immune systems, and helps the thymus and thyroid, kidney, bladder and lungs. Sore throats or larynx infections, sinusitis and eye problems can be cleared up with this crystal. It also balances fluids, soothes burns and alleviates night sweats and insomnia.

Spirit A reassuring gem for anyone dealing with the death of a loved one, indicolite quartz calls in spirit guides to assist anyone passing over and support those left behind. It reassures you that love never dies, as it is always there for you from spirit. If leaving this plane, it helps you see that your soul has learned its lessons, explored its gifts and is now going home to the great All-That-Is. A good stone for facilitating out-of-body experiences and spiritual journeying, indicolite quartz shows you an overview of all your lives and stops negative energy from sticking to you.

How to use Carry with you when needed. Give to anyone passing over to keep with them through their transition to the afterlife. Meditate with it on your altar or held in cupped hands. Place on throat chakra or anywhere that feels congested and in need of healing. Use in a full-body healing treatment to pinpoint areas needing special attention.

Lemurian quartz

TYPE OF CRYSTAL Considered by healers to be the most powerful of all the quartzes, this clear or sometimes frosted hexagonal, pointed quartz is etched with bar-code-like striations on alternate faces. It is rare, but can be found in Brazil, Colombia, Russia, China, Arkansas in the US and Zambia. Golden Lemurian quartz is coloured by iron inclusions and has similar qualities to clear Lemurian quartz. There are also varieties in pink, tangerine, yellow, blue and smoky, with slightly different properties. All of them are profound healers and manifesters that raise your frequency higher and remind light workers to work on their own evolution as well as helping others.

CHAKRA CONNECTION All

ASTRO AFFILIATION All

HEALING your energy with ancient wisdom

Mind These crystals help with manifesting your dreams by teaching that 'thoughts become things' – so make sure you have the best intentions, strong self-belief and inspiring ideas to actualize your full creative potential. They can focus the mind on improving your life by releasing negative thinking, consciously becoming happier and re-energizing your attitude to your goals. Spiritual knowledge can be reawakened by working with these gems.

Body The No. 1 healing crystal, Lemurian quartz accurately focuses and raises your energy so it can help with any condition. It especially alleviates pain or discomfort, removes disease and opens new energy channels in the physical or energetic bodies to bring about healing. Golden Lemurian is good for alleviating stress symptoms, improving heart health and boosting the immune system as a general tonic to wellbeing. Clear Lemurian quartz specifically helps with ME and chronic fatigue by increasing your vitality. It rids the body of infections, treats diabetes and helps with weight loss and obesity. The spine and anything to do with the ears, including balance and tinnitus, get extra support from this crystal.

Spirit This stone of positivity opens your heart to universal love and intense joy. It aids deep concentration and spiritual connection in meditation, allowing you to climb its lines like a ladder to ascension and multidimensional states. It enables you to receive wisdom from ancient civilizations such as Lemuria and Atlantis. Spirit guides from these times may show you an overview of previous lives or take you to past-life memories stored in the Akashic records. Sit in a grid of these gems and you can create a stargate to contact the angelic realm and anchor into reality any insights or guidance you get, including reawakening any latent healing abilities or spiritual skills.

How to use Hold or position wherever needed to clear, revitalize and heal. Sleep with a Lemurian crystal under your pillow to be able to re-enter a dream or, for lucid dreaming, to gain insights or clarity, or to dream a new reality into being. Use in a crystal healing grid with other gems, especially elestial quartz, to open a powerful, healing energy portal bringing in past, present and future scenarios for transformation.

Lithium quartz

TYPE OF CRYSTAL This translucent to opaque quartz is naturally coated or spotted with lithium, manganese, aluminium, iron or kaolinite inclusions. Commonly found in Brazil, its hexagonal terminated crystals come in a lilac-pink to purple colour.

CHAKRA CONNECTION Third eye

ASTRO AFFILIATION Aquarius

HEALING the mind, plants and animals

Mind A natural antidepressant, lithium quartz lifts despair, alleviates stress and eases anxiety, nervousness and behaviour patterns that hinder happiness. Many mental illnesses, such as bipolar disorder and obsessive-compulsive disorder, are helped with this crystal because it gets to the root of any anger or grief stemming from the past, or even from previous lives.

Body This crystal can purify water so, when drunk as an elixir, it gives maximum benefits. It's a highly beneficial pick-me-up whenever your immune system is run down with colds, flu, stomach upsets or infections.

Spirit By balancing the mind and cleansing the chakras, lithium quartz can bring about meaningful dreams full of insightful messages that you're able to interpret. You

may even be shown past-life scenarios that have caused disease, so you can release the karmic ties and feel better again. It also promotes stronger intuition.

How to use Meditate holding a piece of lithium quartz in cupped hands or by sitting in front of some on your altar. Position on your third eye when lying down to activate intuition and encourage important dream recall. For the same effect, sleep with some under your pillow. Wear as jewellery to boost mood. Good for Earth healing in a crystal grid. Place near animals or plants to help them grow healthy and strong.

Phantom quartz

TYPE OF CRYSTAL This is clear quartz that contains a smaller, ghost-like crystal in white or another colour, depending on the mineral of the inclusion. It is found all over the world, but especially in Brazil, the US and Madagascar.

CHAKRA CONNECTION Heart, crown

ASTRO AFFILIATION All

HEALING by activating your own healing abilities

Mind This crystal helps you face your shadow side and see the gifts it has for you. Good for emotional clearing, phantom quartz can restore your mind to calm concentration even through the most turbulent of transitions.

Body Phantom quartz is believed to stimulate your healing skills and encourage planetary restoration. It treats hearing issues, such as tinnitus or blocked ears, to enable you to fully hear again, including messages from Spirit.

Spirit This gem encourages you to focus on your inner self, where you can connect to a deeper cosmic awareness and activate your clairaudience ability. By enhancing your meditation, phantom quartz tunes you into your spirit guides, helps you access the Akashic records and reveal your past lives, releasing you from karmic ties. It can also take you to the state of consciousness in between lives to discover your soul plan for this life. Spend some time looking softly into this crystal and it may bring long-hidden answers to questions you may have about your existence.

How to use Hold in either hand while meditating. Place on or near any chakra or area of the body in need of healing. Wear as jewellery to activate your own healing powers. Use in a healing crystal grid for personal healing or to work on the Earth below.

Different hues of phantom quartz to help with different issues

Amethyst phantom: Clear quartz with a ghost of amethyst helps you understand what is out of balance and far from ease, behind any mental illness, by taking you to the before-life state to see the soul's plan for this life and evaluate the lessons.

Blue phantom: With its blue phantom inclusion, this quartz enhances telepathic communication between people and the spiritual realm. It facilitates divination skills. This gem supports the throat, spleen and blood vessels while giving the endocrine and metabolic systems a boost. It also dispels anger and anxiety.

Green phantom: Chlorite gives this quartz its ghostly green phantom, helping absorb toxins and negative energy from the body, aura and environment. It grounds you and creates a psychic shield around you by aligning the root, solar plexus, heart and third eye chakras. It helps you feel supported and connects to the angelic realm, bringing clear messages of guidance. Bipolar disorder, despair and panic attacks are eased with this crystal.

Orange phantom: Carnelian gives this quartz its orange phantom, bringing with it the power to energize and rejuvenate mind, body and spirit. By stimulating and balancing the sacral, solar plexus, heart and third eye chakras, it ignites your creativity and connection with your higher self. Once you have realized who you truly are, you can bring this insight and inspiration into practical reality. This is a good stone to help overcome addictions and focus on recovery.

Pink phantom: As with many pink-hued crystals, this one also encourages peace and love - the love of the self - enabling you to accept your life, feel fulfilled or make changes where needed. Abandonment issues, alienation and betrayal, plus any feelings of being restricted in your desires, will be eliminated with this gem. Autoimmune diseases such as lupus are believed to be eased using pink phantom quartz, and the heart restored to good health.

Red phantom: A mixture of limonite, hematite and/or kaolinite gives this gem its red ghost, which increases creativity, alleviates frustration and calms the mind. Anything repressed from childhood comes to the surface with this gem, which then heals your inner child, enabling greater joy and determination. Expect to have more energy using this crystal, which revitalizes the body and restores life-force. It can also be used to stabilize the Earth when it's out of balance.

White phantom: This quartz channels light, energy and wisdom through time and space, enabling powerful multidimensional cellular memory healing to take place. It can be used for etheric surgery, taking away the layers of karma from your soul so you no longer feel the detrimental effects. It loosens the negative patterning in your behaviour and connects you with spiritual guides, bringing clairaudience through deepened meditation. Hearing issues can be alleviated too.

Yellow phantom: Intellectually stimulating limonite is the phantom in this quartz. It connects you to your higher mind, brings up memories and reconfigures thought patterns to bring about a higher frequency. Aligning the solar plexus, third eye and crown chakras, this gem provides insight into the psychological issues stemming from past experiences, then aids your realization and assimilation of these soul lessons.

Rose quartz

TYPE OF CRYSTAL This soft, dusky pink, mostly translucent quartz is easily found in crystalline masses in Brazil, South Africa, the US, Japan, India and Madagascar.

CHAKRA CONNECTION Heart

ASTRO AFFILIATION Taurus, Libra

HEALING the heart

Mind The crystal for bringing peace and love into your life, rose quartz helps you understand and experience unconditional love, releasing emotional pain, jealousy or resentment and helping you express any repressed feelings getting in the way of true love. It teaches you how to appreciate yourself through self-forgiveness and knowing you are worth loving exactly as you are. It creates calm reassurance and provides support during a crisis, or when dealing with trauma or coping with heartbreak. In the face of change, it encourages acceptance, especially during mid-life transitions. Program rose quartz with loving intention or affirmation and it will remind you of your wishes, when you sit with it, and bring them into being.

Body Rose quartz boosts heart health and improves circulation, brightening the complexion in the process. Good for detoxifying, it supports the kidneys, spleen and adrenal glands. It is beneficial for fertility, regulates the menstrual cycle and balances sex drive, enabling you to feel less frustration and more turned on. Positioned on the thymus, it helps treat lung and chest issues, such as asthma or coughs. It can alleviate aches and pains, treat varicose veins and ease vertigo. Alzheimer's disease and dementia may also be helped with this stone. An elixir of it can soothe sunburn and other burns or skin issues.

Spirit This gentle gem purifies and opens the heart chakra, facilitating deep inner healing. Allow it to remove any negative vibes between you and others and replace it with affection, harmony and trust. Even if you feel you have never properly received love, this crystal can open you up to experiencing it on a rich, fulfilling level. Use rose quartz to tune into the ever-flowing abundance of the universe, amplify your unique creativity and imagination, and activate your artistic abilities.

How to use Put on or near the heart chakra. Meditate holding in cupped hands. Wear as jewellery, especially in a pendant close to your heart or close to the thymus to regulate it. Place on a bedside table to attract loving relationships, along with amethyst to temper this if too powerful. Position in the relationship corner of a room (right-hand far corner to the doorway) to attract love, or all around the home for positive atmosphere. Add to water to drink an elixir of unconditional love for the self. Gently stroke a rose quartz tumblestone over the skin to smooth complexion.

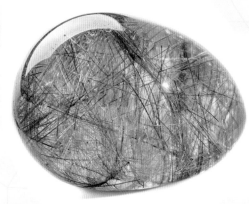

Rutilated quartz

TYPE OF CRYSTAL Rutilated or rutile quartz is clear, smoky or sometimes a gold colour, containing reddish, golden brown or black strands of rutile, which is titanium dioxide. Also known as angel-hair quartz, it is found in points and clusters all over the world.

CHAKRA CONNECTION Solar plexus, third eye, crown

ASTRO AFFILIATION All

HEALING mental health

Mind Another crystal that lifts negativity, rutilated quartz bolsters the brain from mental breakdown and alleviates depression. Any phobias, anxieties or bouts of self-hatred can be dispelled with this quartz. Useful for psychologists and counsellors, it enables us to face darker aspects of our psyche and supports emotional release. It gets to the root cause of mental issues and facilitates positive change. Plus, it helps you clarify your life purpose and act on it with heightened focus and concentration.

Body The vitality inherent in rutilated quartz boosts your energy and immune system, kicks chronic conditions out of your body and even assists with impotence and infertility. It combats ageing and brings about a youthful appearance, helping cells regenerate and tissues mend.

It is believed to be able to absorb mercury poisoning from the blood, nerves, muscles and intestines. Respiratory illnesses such as bronchitis can be treated with rutile quartz, which also expels parasites from the body. The thyroid can be activated and brought back into balance too.

Spirit This powerful vibrational healer lights up the soul and accelerates spiritual development. Allow it to cleanse your aura of negative energy and help you let go of anything blocking your progress. It tunes you into higher wisdom, making it good for scrying the future and channelling spirit guidance. Astral travel and past-life healing are possible with rutilated quartz, which will bring helpful insights from previous lives to current life issues, getting rid of patterns of disease.

How to use Meditate while holding in either hand or positioned on an altar in front of you. Carry it with you. Place or wear at the neck to aid thyroid function, or near the chest to boost the actions of the thymus. Lie down and put a piece of this quartz on the solar plexus chakra to boost energy. Sweep around the outside of your body to clear the aura of negativity. Put a piece on your desk to aid concentration.

Scenic quartz

TYPE OF CRYSTAL This green, brown, cream, clear, red or orange quartz contains magical-looking inclusions of other minerals. Patterns of various substances, including chlorite, feldspar, epidote, rutile, hematite or smoky quartz, along with sand or clay, create what looks like little underwater scenes or gardens inside the quartz. Also known as shaman stone, dream quartz or inclusion quartz, among other names, it is found mostly in Brazil, Uruguay and Madagascar.

CHAKRA CONNECTION All

ASTRO AFFILIATION Pisces

HEALING through your dreams

Mind This crystal lifts your mood and peps up your personality. It helps you focus on accomplishing your goals and manifesting your desires. Let scenic quartz dispel repetitive negative thoughts and feelings that can lead to illness, and help you heal from trauma.

Body A gem essence made with scenic quartz acts as a good general tonic for overall wellbeing. It boosts the immune system and the healthy functioning of the liver, lungs, blood, eyes and various glands. It can alleviate headaches and insomnia, and provide pain relief for sore joints and achy bones. An elixir can be applied to the skin to give a youthful visage. It also helps increase the effects of reiki healing.

Spirit Useful for any shamanic practices, this gem can help you remember messages in your dreams, or be used for remote viewing or activating your psychic powers. Let the imagery in each crystal lead you into a lucid dream, altered state or spiritual journey in your mind. Meditating with it will heal your heart after a breakup and raise your vibration to a higher level.

How to use Drink or use topically as an elixir. Sleep with some under your pillow or next to your bed for dream recall or lucid dreaming. Meditate holding a piece in either hand. Place on the relevant chakra or area of the body in need of healing.

Smoky quartz

TYPE OF CRYSTAL This brown, grey and sometimes yellowish variety of quartz is coloured by natural radiation from the Earth, but very dark and black – and more opaque – versions are often irradiated in a laboratory. Naturally translucent, with darker ends to the points, smoky quartz is found all over the world, particularly in the US, Madagascar and Brazil.

CHAKRA CONNECTION Root, crown

ASTRO AFFILIATION Sagittarius, Capricorn

HEALING by grounding

Mind A great stress reliever, smoky quartz gives you the resolve to move forward through difficult times with positive, pragmatic thinking, and leave behind thought patterns or behaviours from the past that do not help. Positioned in the bedroom, it can stop the mind from racing and help you drift into a deeper sleep. Fear, depression and apathy are alleviated with this stone, which brings concentration and clear communication.

Body By activating the root chakra, smoky quartz boosts your sex drive and helps you express your sexuality to the full. It helps reiki healers channel energy through their hands. This crystal detoxes the body from EMFs and geopathic stress, and aids the absorption of minerals from food into the body. Any issues with your legs, knees, ankles, hips and feet, as well as the abdomen and back, can be alleviated with this crystal. It also eases pain, especially cramps and headaches, strengthens the heart and activates the reproductive system. Naturally irradiated smoky quartz can treat radiation-related sickness and support the body through chemotherapy.

Spirit This is the best crystal for grounding when doing any spiritual work, yet it also helps raise your frequency when meditating. Smoky quartz absorbs any negative or polluting energies from your environment and brings about deep relaxation. It is a great protector from psychic attack, and will bring spirit guides and extra-terrestrial beings' energy into your aura to receive their wisdom. This crystal also reveals the deeper meaning in your dreams.

How to use Position at the root chakra while lying down to clear, heal and activate. Wear as jewellery for long periods of time to de-stress and to absorb negative energy. Carry in a pocket. Meditate holding in either hand to rid the body of electrosmog from technological gadgets. Put around your home to absorb these EMFs as well as bad vibes. Place over area of pain to dissolve it. Aim a point of smoky quartz away from your body into the ground to pull away negative energy. Face a point towards the body to revitalize.

Snow quartz

TYPE OF CRYSTAL Also known as milky quartz or quartzite, this opaque white variety is found, often water-worn, as pebbles, boulders and masses all over the world, with abundant supplies in India and the US.

CHAKRA CONNECTION Crown

ASTRO AFFILIATION Capricorn

HEALING like clear quartz, but in a gentler way

Mind This quartz heightens your wisdom and mental powers, making it good for exam revision and studying. The purity of thought that comes with this crystal releases negative beliefs and clarifies the mind. Thinking before you speak and saying things tactfully are other traits that come with this crystal.

Body Snow quartz can be used in the same way as clear quartz, amplifying and channelling energy to heal mind, body and spirit. But it has a slower, more gentle effect if that is what's needed.

Spirit Let this quartz help you let go of limitations, release draining responsibilities and relinquish victim mentality to enable cooperation and connection with others. Deep inner wisdom, formerly buried by yourself or society, will rise to the surface with snow quartz.

How to use Place or hold wherever it is needed. Meditate holding it in either hand or placed on or next to the crown chakra when lying down. Wear as jewellery. Use in a healing grid.

Tangerine quartz

TYPE OF CRYSTAL A bright orange to red-orange surface coating from hematite gives this quartz its colour. This warm-toned quartz is naturally found in Brazil and Madagascar.

CHAKRA CONNECTION Root, sacral, solar plexus

ASTRO AFFILIATION Leo, Libra

HEALING your self-worth

Mind Tangerine quartz helps you overcome trauma, upset and inner wrangling by encouraging you to let go of limiting, self-sabotaging thoughts and beliefs. It brings about change by making you more self-aware and by providing mental strength, understanding and the courage to move toward your goals and intentions. As your self-worth increases and healing unfolds, happier relationships, more love and increased joy will come to you.

Body Believed to balance acidity in the body, tangerine quartz can help eliminate free radicals and reduce cancerous growths. It benefits the reproductive system, boosting fertility and libido. It also aids weight loss and the absorption of nutrients, especially iron, from food, increasing red blood cells and overall energy. Any issues with intestines or lower abdominal pain can be relieved with this gem.

Spirit This stone gives you spiritual security as it protects from psychic attack and the negative vibes of others. Through this, you can feel deep calm and comfort, which heightens your creativity and sense of playfulness, and improves your relationships. Let this quartz ground your dreams into reality and smooth the path of change.

How to use Wear as jewellery. Keep on your meditation altar. Meditate holding a piece in either hand. Place on or near the chakra or area of the body in need of its help. Position in the relationship area of your room or home (right-hand far corner) to bring love into your life and increase passion.

For *titanium quartz see rainbow aura quartz (page 192)*

Tourmalinated quartz

TYPE OF CRYSTAL This clear quartz variety has black rods of tourmaline growing through it and is found all over the world. The combined effects and properties of quartz and tourmaline make this a powerful crystal for healing.

CHAKRA CONNECTION All

ASTRO AFFILIATION All

HEALING by turning negative energy to positive outcome

Mind Another good stone for lifting you out of depression and alleviating unfounded fears, tourmalinated quartz helps the mind solve problems so you feel and function better. Childhood situations that have left you stuck, or ingrained programming from your upbringing, can be released and healed with this crystal. In fact, any negative thoughts or issues can be turned to positive outcomes with this crystal.

Body Tourmalinated quartz combats stress, tension and nervous exhaustion by regulating the nervous system. It also brings the body, mind and spirit back into balance by aligning the chakras and harmonizing the energy meridians.

Spirit This gem grounds your spiritual awakening into everyday reality, and keeps you anchored in the present moment while meditating. It strengthens your aura against any unwanted energies or toxic input from your environment.

How to use Meditate with it regularly by holding in either or both hands, or positioning on chakras. Place on or next to the appropriate area for healing.

Rhodochrosite

TYPE OF CRYSTAL Found in Argentina, Uruguay, the US, Russia and South Africa, this pink- or white-banded crystal is usually a mixture of pale pink to orangey pink or red, sometimes with cream or brown. It forms in masses or small rhombohedral shapes and is partially translucent and quite soft, so take care when storing it with other stones.

CHAKRA CONNECTION Root, solar plexus, heart

ASTRO AFFILIATION Leo, Scorpio

HEALING a broken heart with unconditional love

Mind Imparting its positive, can-do attitude, rhodochrosite increases your self-worth and guards against mental breakdown and depression. The stresses of modern living – from juggling too many activities to the harmful effects of social media or loneliness – can be alleviated with this soothing crystal. Past hurts that play on your mind can be released with rhodochrosite, which gives you the courage to carry on regardless of any emotional pain you might be going through.

Body This gem gives heart health a boost, regulates blood pressure and improves circulation. It also purifies the kidneys and spleen. Rhodochrosite filters out allergens from the atmosphere, helping those with hay fever, asthma or other respiratory illnesses. Poor eyesight can be corrected and migraines eased, as this stone dilates blood vessels. It is believed to invigorate the sex organs, increase energy and encourage the healthy development of babies in the womb. An elixir can be used to smooth wrinkles and enliven skin tone, eliminate infections and harmonize thyroid function.

Spirit Unconditional love and compassion are the gifts of this gem, which helps you feel more loved, express deeper feelings and heal from trauma, such as sexual abuse. It can expand your consciousness, bring the spiritual realm into material reality through music and art, and even attract a soul mate. Passion and eroticism increase with rhodochrosite in your life. Plus, it can enliven your dreams with messages from spirit.

How to use Place on or near the appropriate chakra or area of the body where emotional pain manifests. For migraines, position at the top of the spine. Wear as a bracelet or pendant. Carry in a pocket. Meditate holding it in your receiving (non-dominant) hand or place on your art workspace to bring new and inspiring creative ideas. Place on bedside table to enliven dreams.

Do not use water or salt to cleanse this crystal, as it is easily damaged.

Rhodonite

TYPE OF CRYSTAL This crystal is usually pink or red, although it's sometimes found in green, yellow or black. It is often mottled, flecked or lined with black veins of manganese. It is found in large masses or tabular crystals in the US, the UK, Australia, South Africa and Madagascar.

CHAKRA CONNECTION Heart

ASTRO AFFILIATION Taurus

HEALING emotional and physical wounds

Mind Shock, panic and confusion after traumatic or upsetting events can be eased with this stone. It helps you see both sides of an argument and brings calm in confusing or dangerous situations. Any self-destructive tendencies, including harbouring resentment, anger or a desire for revenge, can be cleared with rhodonite. It alleviates stress from 21st-century living, quells anxiety and promotes the unity of all humanity.

Body Rhodonite is said to soothe insect bites, reduce scarring and help heal surface wounds. An elixir can be drunk to ease shock and trauma after accidents or injuries. Anything to do with hearing, fertility and bone health can be stimulated with this stone. It also treats inflammation issues, such as arthritis and autoimmune disease, as well as emphysema and stomach ulcers.

Spirit This gem is beneficial for past-life healing, to release feelings of betrayal and abandonment that stop you from living your best life. Lingering negative feelings around codependency and abuse are also cleared away, bringing forgiveness and increased self-love. Repeat a mantra during meditation and rhodonite will raise your soul's frequency to the same vibration, helping you feel more at ease with yourself and aware of loving spiritual guidance.

How to use Position on the chakra or area of the body in need of help. Place or wear over the heart to heal emotional wounds or clear and activate the heart chakra. Meditate holding in cupped hands or sitting in front of a piece on your altar.

Rhyolite

TYPE OF CRYSTAL This combination of quartz, feldspar and nephelite was formed from ancient volcanic activity, flow markings from which can sometimes be seen on the surface. Also known as rainforest rhyolite or green rhyolite, it is spotted or banded, and most often green, white, brown or grey, sometimes with red tones running through it. It is found in Mexico, Australia and the US.

CHAKRA CONNECTION Solar plexus, third eye

ASTRO AFFILIATION Aquarius

HEALING by increasing your mental, physical and spiritual strength

Mind If your mind keeps going back over past events, reminding you of previous hurts and trauma, carry rhyolite with you to help gently release and balance your emotions, and anchor you more firmly in the present. It can eliminate procrastination and guide you during times of change, granting the calmness and strength to move forward through any challenges.

Body Rhyolite boosts the body's natural defences. As an elixir, it is thought to improve muscle tone and strength, and assist the absorption of B vitamins. It can treat diabetes and hypoglycaemia, and dissolve kidney stones. Skin infections, rashes and even varicose veins can be helped with the use of the crystal.

Spirit Your greatest potential, creativity and deep awareness of the soul can be activated with rhyolite. It increases feelings of self-esteem and self-acceptance. This gem encourages a deep state of meditation, enabling you to make journeys in the mind that help you receive spiritual wisdom and heal past-life karma. It can also bring innate mediumship abilities to the fore.

How to use Meditate lying down with it on any area in need of healing or for exploration. Place on the solar plexus to help release emotions. On your third eye, rhyolite can take you into a past-life regression with the right practitioner. Wear as jewellery or carry as a touchstone to bring you into the present.

Ruby

TYPE OF CRYSTAL This precious gem is often used in jewellery, cut and polished to a bright, transparent red crystal. In its raw form, the tabular variety of corundum looks opaque, and can range from pink to deep red. It is found primarily in India, Myanmar, Thailand and Madagascar. Raw ruby has powerful healing properties but does contain aluminium, so use it carefully.

CHAKRA CONNECTION Heart

ASTRO AFFILIATION Aries, Cancer, Leo, Scorpio, Sagittarius

HEALING with improved vigour

Mind Ruby improves mental health, granting heightened creativity, cognitive function and retention of knowledge. Its boost of energy to mind, body and spirit can be too much for some, but it's worth allowing it to motivate you to set some realistic goals and support you through new beginnings. A stone of courageous leadership, ruby helps you make the right decisions and stay positive in times of change, controversy or conflict. It transmutes anger, takes away anything negative from your path, and enables you to concentrate on the way forward.

Body A good gem to use for distance healing, ruby encourages the will to live and increases overall vitality. It activates the pineal gland, which promotes good health. Its vigour boosts sex drive and bolsters the blood, treating anaemia as well as blocked arteries. It regulates the menstrual cycle, supports the reproductive organs and brings good health to a growing embryo. Ruby quickly detoxes lymph glands, improves immunity and boosts the circulation system, restoring the heart to good health. The kidneys, spleen and adrenal glands are all supported with this stone, which can also reduce a fever and rid the body of infectious diseases. It is even believed to protect you from being struck by lightning!

Spirit This crystal increases your passion for life and drive for fulfilment. Stimulating the heart chakra, it brings joy, love and sexual adventures into your life in abundance. Ruby gives you renewed enthusiasm to follow your bliss, shielded from others' ill will or psychic attack. It facilitates positive dreams, astral travel and remote viewing, bringing clear visions and spiritual wisdom. Meditating with it can help you access the Akashic records for deeper insights about your life.

How to use Wear as any kind of jewellery, especially in a ring or a pendant at the heart. In Eastern countries, it is worn on the brow to activate the pineal gland. Carry in a pocket to protect and re-energize. Place under your pillow or mattress to boost a flagging sex life and increase passion. Put a piece on or near the appropriate chakra or area of the body.

Sapphire (blue)

TYPE OF CRYSTAL Sapphire is another form of the very hard and durable crystal corundum (aluminium oxide) in any colour other than red (for ruby, see previous page). It is often recognized in its precious-gem form, as blue, but it can also be found in uncut stones of green, yellow, pink, white, black and violet. The various colours of sapphire are found in many countries, with blue obtained mainly from India, Sri Lanka, Madagascar and Thailand.

CHAKRA CONNECTION Third eye, throat and others, depending on colour

ASTRO AFFILIATION Virgo, Libra, Sagittarius

HEALING all chakras and the Earth

Mind Known as the wisdom stone, sapphire brings peace of mind and encourages you to let go of unwanted thoughts and mental stress. It alleviates depression by elevating your mood and helping you focus on the beauty around you every day. This gem is good for fulfilling your ambitions, giving you the enhanced concentration and calm determination needed to attain your goals and attract lasting prosperity.

Body Restoring balance to the body, this crystal calms overactive organs, bodily systems or hormones, and regulates the performance of various glands, especially the thyroid. Stemming excessive blood flow, sapphire treats any issues to do with the blood, and improves the strength and elasticity of veins. It is also thought to combat ageing and infections, and assist with backache, boils and nausea.

Spirit Wisdom from spirit is given to you with sapphire, which aids connection and communication with the divine. It helps you receive intuitive guidance from your higher self and stay strong on your spiritual path. A stone to aid honest self-expression, it activates the throat chakra when placed there or worn as a necklace, helping you speak your truth with love. It is often used in shamanic ceremonies to transform negative energy, and as a record-keeping stone to enable access to the Akashic records or facilitate astral travel.

How to use Place on or next to the relevant chakra or part of the body in need of its powers. Wear as any type of jewellery, especially in a ring or choker-style necklace to open the throat chakra. Carry in a pocket. Hold in both hands during meditation or place on the third eye while lying down to access ancient wisdom. Heal the Earth by positioning it on the area or on top of a photo of the land and sending its healing rays into the soil.

Other shades of sapphire have the following extra properties:

Green works on the heart chakra to encourage love, loyalty and fidelity, as well as compassion and understanding toward others. It heightens both inner and outer vision, and enables you to recall the messages in your dreams.

Pink sapphire attracts issues into your life to help you evolve spiritually. It clears emotional blockages and enables you to master and integrate your deepest fears and feelings.

Violet, also called Oriental amethyst, brings emotional balance, deepens your meditation practice and attracts more joy into your life. It activates kundalini energy in you, expanding the crown chakra and opening you up to spiritual abilities, including psychic intuition and visions. An elixir can be used as an astringent on the skin to tighten pores.

White is the purest energy of the sapphires. It expands your consciousness to ever greater levels, heightening your spiritual awareness. It also protects your vibrant energy, shielding your burgeoning ascension from any hindrances and bringing a clearer focus on your purpose and potential in life.

Yellow: By stimulating the solar plexus chakra, yellow sapphire ignites the intellect and brings your creativity into practical reality to attract success and abundance. It inspires wonder at the world and an elevated perspective on matters. Wear it as jewellery touching the skin. A gem essence can help with a body detox, supporting the organs that flush out toxins, such as the liver, gallbladder, spleen and pancreas. Coughs, colds and infections in the lungs can also be eased with this stone.

Sardonyx

TYPE OF CRYSTAL This chalcedony quartz, also known as onyx, contains carnelian (the red-brown part) and is layered with swirls or bands of black, white, brown or clear, sometimes even blue, although this is rarer. A richly coloured and opaque stone, sardonyx is found in India, Brazil, Russia, Turkey and the US.

CHAKRA CONNECTION Sacral

ASTRO AFFILIATION Aries

HEALING... relationships

Mind Sardonyx gives you the mental discipline and ability to focus on tasks to attract good luck and happiness. Self-control and tenacity are abilities promoted by this crystal, which alleviates depression and heightens your perception of your life. It helps you process new information, avoid hesitation and have the courage go for your dreams.

Body This gem enlivens the senses, boosts the immune system and metabolism, and brings renewed vigour to your body by increasing the absorption of nutrients from food. It aids the elimination of waste and regulates fluids in the body. It is believed to treat issues with bones and the lungs, too.

Spirit Another good stone of protection, sardonyx brings strength of spirit and integrity. It highlights the need for meaning in your life. It stabilizes existing relationships and brings new friends to you, helping you feel more sociable.

How to use Position anywhere in need of treatment. Place on the stomach area while lying down for a good overall boost of energy and healing. Carry it for luck and relationship help. Meditate while holding in either hand.

Did you know?

In ancient times, sardonyx was used as a stone of strength and protection, where a piece placed in each corner of the home was used to keep away evil. Talismans of this gem were worn to boost energy and the Romans carved Mars, god of war, or Hercules into this crystal to promote courage. It is also mentioned in the Bible Book of Revelation as the first foundation stone in the walls of New Jerusalem.

Scapolite

TYPE OF CRYSTAL The shiny, striated, translucent or opaque masses and prismatic forms of this crystal often show the shimmering visual effect of chatoyancy. It comes in various colours, including blue, grey, yellow and many shades of purple, and can also be colourless. The US, Canada, Norway, Italy, Mexico and Madagascar are the main countries where scapolite can be found.

CHAKRA CONNECTION Third eye, crown

ASTRO AFFILIATION Taurus

HEALING eye issues and blockages to full health and self-realization

Mind This crystal encourages clear, analytical thinking and improves problem-solving. It supports you to make conscious change, releasing trauma from, or worries over, the past, especially if you are blaming yourself or thinking you are not good enough. Scapolite helps you achieve your goals with meticulous thought and planning. It is also thought to aid those with dyslexia.

Body All colours of scapolite are good for eye problems, including cataracts, glaucoma and twitchy eyes. Incontinence can be eased with this crystal. Shoulder aches and pains are alleviated, and bone strength is boosted with this gem, which increases the body's absorption of calcium. Used after an operation, it can speed recovery, stimulating the cells to regenerate. It also works to unblock everything from stagnant energy to clogged-up veins, especially in the legs.

Spirit Clearing all sense of self-sabotage and spurring you on to transform, scapolite will propel you out of spiritual inertia and move you into action. It also blocks anyone wanting to scapegoat you for past wrongs or hinder your progress. Let this stone raise your frequency and support your spiritual evolution.

How to use Meditate regularly holding scapolite in your non-dominant hand. Carry with you, especially if dyslexic. Hold on or next to the relevant chakra or area of the body in need of treating.

Schorl (black tourmaline)

TYPE OF CRYSTAL Schorl is the darkest black variety of tourmaline, which actually makes up around 90 percent of all the tourmaline on the planet (see tourmaline entries for other colours). It is comprised mainly of sodium and iron, along with borosilicate, aluminium, magnesium, lithium or potassium. Formed in hard, long, vertically striated prismatic crystals, it is found in Brazil, India, Pakistan, the US, Germany, the UK and Italy.

CHAKRA CONNECTION Root

ASTRO AFFILIATION Capricorn

HEALING by protecting from radiation and increasing vitality

Mind Schorl helps you feel better, whatever the situation. It promotes a relaxed attitude to life, enhanced practical creativity and open-hearted altruism. This gem alleviates negativity, anxiety and victimhood, and brings about emotional stability. It stimulates the intellect, enlivening your thinking and encouraging self-confidence and personal power.

Body A good grounding stone to connect you to the Earth, schorl stops you from being clumsy and eases the effects of stress. It protects against radiation from electronic gadgets when placed between you and the source. Chronic, debilitating diseases such as arthritis or immune issues can be treated with this stone, which boosts heart and adrenal health. It can also provide pain relief and realign the spine.

Spirit One of the best crystals for grounding during meditation, schorl also keeps you safe while exploring the spiritual realm and purifies your aura from unwanted energetic attachments. Highly protective, black tourmaline blocks psychic attack, ill intent and negative energy. It can transmute bad vibes in the home when placed in an area of discord.

How to use Carry a piece of schorl with you daily to reduce embarrassment. Wear around the neck as a pendant or position between you and an electrical device for protection. Sleep with some in your pillowcase to clear depression or anger from your mind overnight. Place on or near the appropriate area of the body or root chakra for clearing, or position point outwards to draw off bad vibes. Meditate holding a piece in each hand to clear your aura. Sit in meditation within a grid of schorl crystals to stop negative self-talk and clear impurities from mind, body and spirit.

Warning: Schorl should not be made into an elixir, as it contains minerals that could do more harm than good if ingested.

Selenite

TYPE OF CRYSTAL This translucent crystal is a variety of soft, ridged gypsum, sometimes with fine ribbing, other times coarser or patterned, such as the rose-like formations of desert rose or fish-tail-like shaping of angel-wing selenite (see page 221). Named after Selene, the Greek goddess of the moon, it is usually pure white, but also appears in orange, brown, blue and green. Its long, slender wands grow in Mexico, Morocco, Poland, Greece, Russia, Austria, Germany, France, the UK and the US.

CHAKRA CONNECTION Crown

ASTRO AFFILIATION Taurus

HEALING women's libido and fertility

Mind Selenite encourages fidelity and commitment. It can help you see through deception, clear confusion and balance emotions. It brings subconscious thoughts and behaviour into conscious awareness for healing. Better judgment, increased insight and inspiration are available to you with selenite. It can also heal abuse by enabling you to see and learn from the bigger picture of your life's path.

Body This calming crystal works especially well on women's issues, stimulating libido and fertility, and regulating the menstrual cycle. It also supports breastfeeding and healthy child development. It brings alignment to the spine and can increase flexibility. It's a great neutralizer - of mercury poisoning from fillings and of free radicals that can cause cancer. It can also protect against seizures.

Spirit This high-vibration crystal activates the crown chakra, helping you connect with ancestors, angels and Ascended Masters. Meditating often with selenite will bring a deep peace, ignite your psychic skills, and protect your aura. It increases communication with your higher self and the divine, fostering enlightenment the more you work with it. If two people hold a piece of selenite, it can increase telepathy between them. Use a selenite wand to detect energy blocks in chakras, or unwanted energetic aura attachments, then send its pure white light to clear.

How to use Activate a selenite wand by gently stroking it. Place on or near the crown chakra in meditation, by positioning a point next to the top of your head while lying down. Meditate holding in cupped hands or with it placed in front of you on your meditation altar. Sit in a crystal grid made of selenite to clear energy and provide psychic protection. Place in the corners of your home to keep everyone within it safe, or use one large piece to ensure peaceful vibes. You can use selenite to cleanse other crystals by waving it over each one.

Never use selenite as an elixir. Cleanse it gently with water that the full moon has shone into, but never leave it in water or use salt to clean it. It is too soft and delicate, and may dissolve.

Special selenite meditations

To receive psychic insight, lie in meditation with a wand on the heart chakra pointing at your head and another on the floor with the point just touching your crown chakra. Breathe deeply and feel the calm clarity this crystal brings. In your mind, you may meet spiritual beings with messages for you or receive visual symbols or stories about past lives or the future.

Alternatively, sit upright, breathing in deeply and imagining white light filling your body, allowing yourself to relax. Hold your selenite in your left hand and place your right hand underneath the left, cradling your crystal in your lap. Look gently at your selenite and attune yourself to its pure white light.

Next, slowly place your crystal on the top of your head (the crown chakra) and let the white light of the selenite enter the crown. Move the gem to your third eye chakra and hold it there for a few minutes. Know that you are safe and let your mind journey where it wants - to familiar places, through the stars, or channelling beings from other dimensions.

Don't forget to ground yourself after communing with the cosmos by feeling your feet on the floor, taking a few deep breaths and drinking some water.

Angel-wing selenite

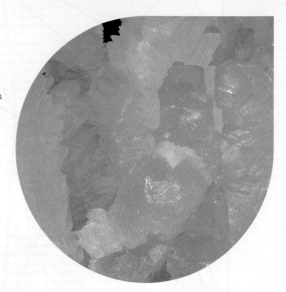

TYPE OF CRYSTAL This type of selenite is clear or white gypsum that forms in shapes that look like feathery angel wings, fish tails or even Christmas trees. Also known as fishtail selenite, it is mainly found in Mexico.

CHAKRA CONNECTION Crown

ASTRO AFFILIATION Taurus

HEALING through angelic connection

Mind This highly calming crystal helps release tension to do with the cycles of life. If a new phase is beginning or something is coming to an end, meditate with angel-wing selenite to bring tranquillity and make space for the change in your mind and heart. It brings fluctuating emotions back into balance so you can focus on practical matters and what you do best.

Body Angel-wing selenite increases vitality and is believed to grant longevity. It calms and heals shattered nerves. It gives a youthful appearance, smoothing wrinkles, diminishing age spots and boosting skin elasticity. In fact, any skin problems, including acne, eczema and psoriasis, are greatly improved with this gem.

Spirit With its angel-wing pattern, this crystal clearly connects you to

the angelic realm, bringing guidance from the archangels or archeia (the female version) just when you need it the most. Spirit guides can also come to the fore when working with selenite, helping you reinvent yourself if necessary. All you ever have to do is ask, and take the time to get quiet enough to hear their wisdom.

How to use As with selenite. Plus, wear as jewellery to encourage longevity.

Warning: Do not make angel-wing selenite into an elixir.

Serpentine

TYPE OF CRYSTAL The masses, layered plates and fibres of this crystal are generally found inside other minerals in China, the UK, Italy, Norway, Zimbabwe, Russia and the US. Serpentine comes in shades of green, brown, red and dark yellow, usually mottled, with a dual appearance, sometimes looking like tree bark or with magnetite inclusions, which create a web-like look.

CHAKRA CONNECTION Heart, crown

ASTRO AFFILIATION Gemini

HEALING with increased energy flow to the body, mind and spirit

Mind Serpentine leads you toward a deeper understanding of the spiritual side of life and an awareness of your rising consciousness. It assists with remembering ancient wisdom, enabling you to help yourself and others heal. It helps you regulate and stay in control of your emotions.

Body Increasing energy flow, this gem is said to bring longevity. It cleanses and detoxes the whole body, especially the blood, and can treat hypoglycaemia and diabetes. Parasites are eliminated with this crystal, which also aids the body's absorption of certain minerals, including magnesium and calcium.

Spirit This crystal encourages your kundalini energy to rise, which clears the chakras, stimulates the crown's connection to divinity

and awakens your spiritual self, bringing psychic skills to the fore. Your artistic abilities can increase when working with serpentine, so whether you're naturally creative or not, try something to stimulate the senses and help you find fun and fulfilment. Meditation is deepened and past lives remembered when using this stone, which grounds you during any spiritual exploration.

How to use Meditate holding serpentine in either hand or place it on the heart chakra while lying down. Place on or next to the relevant chakra or area of the body. Carry with you daily. Wear as jewellery, especially a pendant over the heart.

Shattuckite

TYPE OF CRYSTAL This is a blue variety of plancheite crystal found in fibres or masses in the US.

CHAKRA CONNECTION Throat, third eye

ASTRO AFFILIATION Sagittarius, Aquarius

HEALING communication

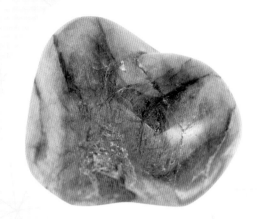

Mind This crystal helps you create your own reality, from having ideas to planning them and finding the motivation and determination to act on them. It eliminates the need for secrecy, especially when sharing any spiritual talents you may be developing in connection with this crystal.

Body An elixir of shattuckite treats minor illnesses, brings the body back into balance and acts as a good general tonic for wellbeing. It eases the painful symptoms of tonsillitis and gives the body the strength to kick it out. It helps blood issues such as haemophilia and assists with clotting to heal wounds and infections.

Spirit A highly spiritual stone, shattuckite raises your vibrational frequency, leading you to ascension. It ignites your esoteric talents, such as clairvoyance, channelling or reading tarot cards or runes – especially when past-life experiences might have caused you to repress these skills. Highly protective, it will stop any spirit you are working with from taking over your body. It also enables you to develop telepathy, commune with extra-terrestrials, and even try automatic writing connected to the purest source of information possible.

How to use Place on the appropriate chakra or area of the body. Meditate lying down with it positioned on the third eye to open up your psychic vision and divination skills. Position near you when doing a reading, channelling or automatic writing to help you tune into messages from spirit guides.

Shungite

TYPE OF CRYSTAL Shungite is a black, charcoal or brown, oily or dull-looking non-crystalline stone – unless it's elite shungite, which has a silvery tint and occasionally gold inclusions. Top-grade shungite is only found in the Shunga region of Karelia, in Russia, while the regular stone is found in Austria, India, Kazakhstan and the Congo. Both varieties are up to 98 percent carbon and contain fullerenes, which conduct electricity yet shield from EMFs and radiation from modern technology.

CHAKRA CONNECTION All

ASTRO AFFILIATION Cancer

HEALING by absorbing harmful pollutants from your body and the environment

Mind Using shungite can help keep worries, anxiety and depression at bay, as its cleansing energy removes negativity from your mind, body, spirit and environment. If you suffer from insomnia or other effects of stress, sleeping next to shungite can reduce these symptoms. It also encourages you to let go of any thought patterns or emotions holding you back.

Body The fullerenes in shungite contain powerful antioxidants that absorb and eliminate harmful pollutants in our environment and our bodies, protecting especially from EMF radiation from mobile phones, laptops or Wi-Fi routers. Shungite-infused water can prevent and reduce the effects of colds, detoxify the body, and aid recovery from illness. Its gem essence is also beneficial post-injury or post-surgery to help repair tissue and maintain healthy cell growth. Testing of this mineral has also revealed that it can absorb pesticides, free radicals and bacteria from the body.

Spirit This stone activates all the chakras, raising your vibration and keeping negative energy away. It brings relief from emotional stress and spiritual upset, and is good for balancing and purifying your feelings. Meditating while holding it will give your body a strong healing connection to the Earth.

How to use Soak a chunk of the duller shungite in a glass bottle of water overnight to purify the water and fill it with the mineral's healing antioxidants. Drink a cup at least two times a day for a boost to the immune system. Place a stone or pyramid of shungite at the back of an electrical device or stick a disc to the back of a mobile phone to soak up the potentially damaging EMFs. Carry one with you if travelling through airports to protect you from the same energy emitted by security scanners. Place a shungite sphere or pyramid by your bed to combat the effects of stress. Wear as a pendant to protect and clear your energy field. Meditate holding a piece to cleanse your aura and keep negativity away.

Smithsonite

TYPE OF CRYSTAL Looking like layers of lustrous, silky bubbles forming in masses or as crusts, smithsonite is found in a variety of colours, mainly soft, light blue, turquoise shades, lavender and pink, but also green, brown, yellow and light grey. It is found in Mexico, the US, Australia, Greece, Italy and Namibia.

CHAKRA CONNECTION Throat, crown

ASTRO AFFILIATION Virgo, Pisces

HEALING through psychic communication

Mind This stone calms the mind and releases mental stress, halting a potential breakdown when life gets too much. It supports anyone who has been emotionally abused or had a tough, loveless upbringing, healing the wounded inner child by dissolving hurt and subtly helping you feel better. It brings kindness, harmony and balance to relationships, tact and diplomacy to tricky situations.

Body A great strengthener of the immune system, smithsonite also treats issues with the sinuses and digestion. Its tranquil energy transforms infertility and encourages birth. It can bring elasticity back to muscles and veins, soothe skin issues and help with osteoporosis. It helps bring an end to alcoholism by gently releasing the root cause of this addiction and encouraging those affected to stick to their recovery programme.

Spirit Smithsonite activates psychic powers and enables you to deduce the truth of messages if holding a piece while receiving spirit communication or intuitive guidance. Divining with tarot cards, runes or other esoteric methods is greatly enhanced by this crystal. A piece placed on your crown chakra links you directly to the angelic realm so you can sense or even see wisdom from the archangels or archeia. Lavender-violet smithsonite also heals unresolved past-life trauma and death, directing the soul to rebirth and healing in this life.

How to use Carry with you always. Place on the area of the body in need of its energy. Position on or next to the crown chakra to align the energy centres and open you up to Spirit. Pink smithsonite can be placed over the heart or thymus to heal heartbreak and strengthen the whole body. Create a grid of this gem around the four corners of your bed, with a piece under your pillow and one on your bedside table to create a calm, healing space for sleep and treatments.

Sodalite

TYPE OF CRYSTAL Looking a bit like lapis lazuli but a lighter, denim blue with white or black spots or striations, sodalite forms in masses, nodules and occasionally individual prismatic crystals. It is mined in Brazil, Bolivia, Canada, the US, Greenland, Norway, Russia and Germany, with some rare singular crystals found on Mount Vesuvius, in Italy. It is sometimes discovered attached to rocks ejected from volcanoes.

CHAKRA CONNECTION Throat, third eye

ASTRO AFFILIATION Sagittarius

HEALING self-worth and overall mental health through improved communication

Mind Sodalite connects you to your higher mind, linking intellect and logic with intuition and idealism. It sparks ideas for creative expression in a bid to share your truth with the world, and improves all forms of communication, especially written. This crystal promotes objectivity and integrity, and encourages speaking up for what you believe in, boosting self-esteem and deepening trust in yourself and your perception. It calms emotions, alleviates panic attacks and confusion, and curbs oversensitivity or defensiveness. Shadow traits, such as guilt or control, and worn-out mental programming, can rise to the surface without self-judgment but rather to explore and release on the journey to authenticity.

Body This crystal brings the body back into balance, regulating metabolism, treating diabetes and boosting the immune system. It clears the lymph system and related organs, reduces high blood pressure and fevers, and improves calcium and fluid absorption. The throat, larynx and vocal cords are all supported with this stone. A piece of sodalite in the bedroom helps clear electromagnetic pollution, treat radiation damage and relieve insomnia.

Spirit With its connection to higher wisdom, sodalite improves psychic skills and brings intuitive insights to help you understand where you are on your spiritual path. Meditation deepens considerably when sitting and holding sodalite.

How to use Wear as jewellery, especially earrings or a necklace, for long periods of time. Place on or next to the chakra or area of the body in need of treating. Hold in non-dominant hand during meditation to receive its blessings. Position next to where you write, paint or create to inspire ideas. Place at your bedside.

Warning: Sodalite contains aluminium, so use with care.

Spinel

TYPE OF CRYSTAL Spinel is a small, sparkling crystalline, usually red, but also other colours, sometimes with inclusions. The bright red, pink, white, clear, yellow, orange, brown, black, blue and violet gems are often clear, and either a small pebble or terminated. They are obtained in India, Pakistan, Sri Lanka, Myanmar and Canada.

CHAKRA CONNECTION Root for red stone; other chakras depending on colour

ASTRO AFFILIATION Aries, Sagittarius

HEALING by renewing energy

Mind Spinel supports and encourages the mind, body and spirit during tough times, and soothes the emotions after an upset or traumatic event. It reveals your positive traits and pushes you to share them, helping you achieve success but at the same time keeping you humble and appreciative.

Body This tiny stone packs a punch of energy, rejuvenating and renewing cells, systems and an attitude to life that adds beauty and promotes longevity. It restores strength and vitality.

Spirit Expect an uplift of spirit and a sense of awakeness as the kundalini energy rises from the base of your spine, opening all chakras, with the aid of spinel. Your whole being will feel light, energized and connected to the great All-That-Is.

How to use Place on or next to the root chakra in meditation – or, if you are lucky enough to have all the colours, place them on the relevant chakras. Wear as jewellery of any kind. Carry with you, especially during harsh times. Hold in either hand when meditating or healing.

Warning: Spinel contains aluminium, so use with care.

Other shades of spinel relate to different chakras and traits

Black connects to Earth energy, giving you stamina to get through problems, plus protection and grounding when your kundalini energy rises.

Brown also connects to the Earth, cleansing the aura at the same time.

Red activates the root chakra.

Orange activates the sacral chakra, balancing the emotions and stimulating intuition and creativity. This sunny gem is thought to treat infertility.

Yellow: The solar plexus chakra gets aligned when using this crystal. This ignites the intellect and empowers the soul to go for its dreams.

Green opens the heart chakra, increasing feelings and actions of love, kindness and compassion.

Blue calms the libido and encourages clear communication with others. It aligns the throat chakra and aids in channelling spirit.

Violet and clear spinel both activate the crown chakra, connecting you to a higher wisdom and bringing visions from spirit – all leading to enlightenment. Violet is good for astral travel to guide you to the highest outcome.

Spodumene

TYPE OF CRYSTAL This clear or yellow-tinted crystal forms in flat prismatic shapes, with vertical striations, in Pakistan and Afghanistan. It is also found in blue, as pink or lilac kunzite, green hiddenite, and two- or three-toned gems.

CHAKRA CONNECTION Heart, third eye, crown

ASTRO AFFILIATION Scorpio

HEALING with heart-centred higher-consciousness connection

Mind This gem gives the intellect a boost, making it helpful for studying. Its drive for intelligence takes away childishness and promotes responsibility. It assists in controlling wild emotions, aiding calm self-expression and increasing confidence. Depression, addiction and obsessive-compulsive disorder can be treated with this stone. It brings comfort and self-worth, and removes thoughts that hinder your progress.

Body Spodumene works to release the energy blocks that can lead to disease. It supports good heart and lung health, lowers blood pressure and combats the effects of stress and pollution on the body. Skin gets an extra-youthful appearance with this gem, which can also help us resist unhealthy cravings. Women's menstrual cycles, period pains and hormones are all balanced, too.

Spirit This stone can enhance your sexuality and spiritual understanding of attraction and love. Another crystal for protection, it lifts negative energy from your environment and helps you stay centred during meditation. Activating the upper chakras, spodumene connects you with higher consciousness, spiritual awareness and the great oneness behind all life.

How to use Hold in cupped hands while meditating. Carry as a touchstone. Wear as earrings or any other kind of jewellery. Place on or next to appropriate chakras when lying down relaxing.

Stibnite

TYPE OF CRYSTAL This metallic dark grey or silver crystal is a toxic sulphide mineral called antimony that forms long, needle-like columns, fans and shards that look like wands. Also called antimonite, it is found in areas of China, Uzbekistan, Japan, Romania, Brazil, Canada and the US. Heavily striated and ridged, its surface tarnishes, so it needs to be handled with care and should *not* touch the skin.

CHAKRA CONNECTION Root, sacral, solar plexus and crown

ASTRO AFFILIATION Scorpio, Capricorn

HEALING through powerful transformation

Mind This stone helps you cope with daily pressures and big life changes. When you feel overwhelmed, it promotes endurance. It also prepares you for unexpected events, giving you the mental strength and optimistic outlook to deal with anything that comes your way and find the gift in the experience. Its transformational qualities can be intense to mind, body and spirit, but it enables you to quickly make the right decisions and discover the best direction to go on your path to fulfilment. On the other side of turmoil is stability and success. Use its power to attract all you desire toward you; just make sure what you want is the highest outcome.

Body Stibnite is believed to treat stomach or oesophagus issues and rid the body of infections – cold sores in particular. It's a good gem to help reduce stiffness and improve physical flexibility as well as mental and spiritual adaptability.

Spirit Connecting the root, sacral and solar plexus chakras, this magical mineral creates a shield of protection around the body to keep you safe from unwanted entities when journeying into the spiritual realms. A powerful shamanic tool, stibnite tunes you into your power animal and connects to the energy of the wolf, in particular, bringing you its perception and protection as you travel in altered states of awareness. Its wands can be used to cut emotional and energetic ties with people, severing clingy relationships for good and releasing past-life contracts with others.

How to use Use as a wand to sweep the aura clear and cut energetic ties. Make an elixir using the *indirect method only*. Hold next to the relevant chakras to create a protection shield. Use in a crystal healing grid to sit in. Meditate lying down with a piece placed on top of clothing next to the chakras or on the floor near the crown for vision quest, astral travel or shamanic journeying.

Warning: Wash hands well after use and clean skin thoroughly if this crystal touches your skin, as it is highly toxic. Do not make stibnite into an elixir at all.

Stichtite

TYPE OF CRYSTAL This crystal is a variation of chromite that contains serpentine in its waxy, opaque, plate-like layers. Its colours range from deep purple to lilac and light pink. It is found in Tasmania, South Africa, Canada and the US.

CHAKRA CONNECTION Heart

ASTRO AFFILIATION Virgo

HEALING by activating kundalini energy to heal the heart

Mind By keeping your mind and emotions tuned into your true loving self, stichtite aids in reframing perpetual negative thinking and beliefs to improve your wellbeing. It guides you to the root cause of any issues around food and gives you the resilience to get past these problems. Hyperactivity or attention-deficit disorder can be greatly reduced using this stone.

Body This powerfully protective stone is of great benefit when recovering from illness or surgery, stabilizing blood pressure as well as brain chemistry. It activates new neural pathways to stave off dementia, Alzheimer's or Parkinson's disease. It can relieve stress headaches and calm frayed nerves. Helpful for discovering the cause of eating disorders and food allergies, it soothes the digestive system. Stichtite supports healthy gums and teeth, boosts skin suppleness and reduces stretch marks.

Spirit Stichtite activates kundalini energy to rise up the spine from the root to the heart chakra, protecting as well as expanding your heart centre to attract and share love and encourage self-love. This releases trapped emotions from your heart, allowing you to fully feel everything, which will lead to more positive experiences. This crystal facilitates the full expression of your true self, as per your soul contract for this lifetime. It is a good stone to have on hand if you live alone to help you feel a sense of calm companionship with your surroundings.

How to use Carry it with you and touch it regularly for comfort; or, if you have ADHD, it can calm emotions and anxiety. Use in a crystal healing grid. Hold or place over the heart chakra for healing or lie down with one piece on the heart area and another next to the root chakra to activate kundalini energy. Wear as a pendant over the heart.

Sugilite

TYPE OF CRYSTAL Also known as luvulite, lavulite and royal azel, this slightly sparkly, opaque violet stone has bands of other colours running through it, including other shades of purple, brown and white. It is quite rare, and is found only in South Africa and Japan.

CHAKRA CONNECTION Third eye, crown

ASTRO AFFILIATION Virgo

HEALING the mind-body connection for optimum wellbeing

Mind Sugilite helps you live your truth and discover the answers to life's eternal questions, such as 'Who am I?' and 'Why am I here?'. It lifts grief and despair, and imparts self-forgiveness and acceptance, even for those who feel they don't belong, or have paranoid thoughts or schizophrenia. Enhancing loving communication, this gem helps groups get along better, overcoming conflict with ease. It works on the mind to stop nightmares, increase positive self-talk and even seems to reconfigure how different brains understand the world, such as with dyslexia and autism. It enables you to face difficulties by grounding you in the present moment.

Body This stone promotes your healing abilities, and strengthens the whole mind-body connection for improved wellbeing. The manganese in sugilite acts as an effective pain reliever for all areas of the body. It also supports the adrenal, pituitary and pineal glands, while the lighter shades of sugilite are thought to purify the blood and lymph glands. Aligning nerves and brain, sugilite aids motor-neurone issues such as epilepsy.

Spirit Another 'love stone' that brings the beholder spiritual love and deep wisdom, sugilite aligns and activates all the chakras so that energy flows freely. Meditating with this crystal connects you to Spirit and your higher self, heightening your psychic awareness and your ability to channel. It can take you back to past lives or the in-between life state, or on any spiritual journey, to find out the cause of disease. This gem assists those sensitive to others' and the Earth's vibrations, helping you to stay positive, shining light into even the darkest moments.

How to use Position on or next to the relevant chakras, especially the third eye, to lift mood or mindset. Hold next to heart or lymph glands for cleansing, on forehead for headaches, or on any other area of the body in need of treating. Keep in your meditation space or on your altar. Hold in either hand while meditating. Wear as earrings or a necklace. Carry in a pocket. Place underneath your pillow or on your bedside table for increased wellbeing and to help with learning difficulties.

Sulphur

TYPE OF CRYSTAL This bright yellow, opaque mineral has sparkling pieces of crystal inside it and on its surface. It comes from volcanic regions of the Earth, such as Italy, Sicily, Greece and South America. Sulphur, with its potent, egg-like odour, is used in matches, fertilizer and medicines, but the crystalline or powdered version can produce toxic gases when heated, and will dissolve in water. It must never be ingested.

CHAKRA CONNECTION Solar plexus

ASTRO AFFILIATION Leo

HEALING flare-ups – of emotions, skin conditions and swellings

Mind This mineral brings balance to the mind, stopping the unhelpful, constant internal chatter and grounding you in the present. It quashes violent thoughts and actions, assists good reasoning and inspires the imagination to come up with creative solutions to problems. Sulphur enables you to become more aware of your negative personality traits, then soften them. It does the same for the attitude of the wilful teenager, or any stubborn, rebellious soul who will not adhere to rules – even those that are for their own good.

Body With its volcanic energy, sulphur helps anything that erupts: negative emotions, fevers and infections as well as skin flare-ups, including boils, insect bites and acne. It can reduce tissue swelling and joint inflammation when placed over the painful area. It can also re-energize the body after illness or when feeling exhausted. However, use with extreme caution: sulphur gases can seriously irritate the eyes as well as harm the respiratory tract, creating asthma-like symptoms or damaging the brain and reproductive organs. Handle with gloves and use only when necessary.

Spirit Sulphur is exceptional at absorbing negative energies and emotions and clearing away blocks to spiritual development and the soul's progress. It gives your self-esteem a boost and connects you more deeply with your inner feelings and reasons behind certain actions, which, in turn, can activate your unexplored psychic skills.

How to use Place on the solar plexus chakra. Put a piece of sulphur in any room to absorb negative energy and increase self-worth. Hold over area of swelling or eruption to reduce symptoms – wash hands after touching. It can be used externally to treat skin issues but must never be ingested as it causes vomiting and diarrhoea.

Warning: Never leave sulphur near a fire or a lamp, where it might heat up; its fumes are highly toxic if inhaled. Do not use salt or water to cleanse sulphur, or it will disintegrate. Do not make sulphur into an elixir at all, and never take it internally.

Sunstone

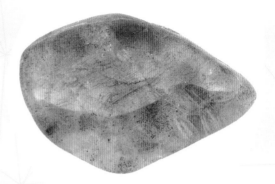

TYPE OF CRYSTAL This shimmery orange, yellow-orange or red-brown crystal is a type of oligoclase, a variety of the feldspar mineral plagioclase. It is either opaque or transparent and often has iridescent inclusions of hematite and goethite. Specialist shops typically sell small tumbled and polished stones made from sunstone found in India, Norway, Greece, Canada and the US.

CHAKRA CONNECTION Sacral, solar plexus, crown

ASTRO AFFILIATION Leo, Libra

HEALING with sunny optimism and positivity

Mind This cheerful crystal restores enthusiasm for life, even during depression and low mood. Shining its regenerative light even in the darkness of winter, sunstone alleviates seasonal affective disorder especially, encouraging you to nurture yourself. It rids the mind of procrastination, fears and stress, and replaces these with positivity and optimism. Any sense of failure is banished, while confidence and self-worth flourish, enabling you to say no and mean it, rather than always pleasing others at the expense of yourself. Programme sunstone with your affirmations to see them manifest.

Body Stimulating self-healing abilities, sunstone gives vitality, strength and longevity. It alleviates most aches and pains in the body, including issues with the cartilage, feet and spine. It soothes chronic sore throats, treats rheumatism and stomach ulcers, and rebalances the nervous system and any out-of-kilter organs.

Spirit By clearing and activating all chakras, sunstone revives your spiritual energy to bring good fortune and allow your true self to shine. During meditation, it protects you from negative entities and connects you to the uplifting power of the sun, to carry you happily through each day. It cuts draining energetic ties to your aura from other people, such as controlling parents or partners, empowering you to be fully independent and sure of your intuition.

How to use Place on the appropriate chakras, especially the solar plexus, to transmute heavy or hidden emotions. Use in a crystal grid for healing mind, body and spirit. Hold in either hand to meditate or keep in a sacred space for positive energy. Carry it at all times. Wear as jewellery, ideally in the sunshine for maximum effect.

Super seven

TYPE OF CRYSTAL Also known as melody stone or sacred seven, this crystal comprises seven different types of quartz: clear, amethyst, goethite, lepidocrocite, rutile, cacoxenite and smoky quartz. With all these gems mixed within its original mass, super seven is usually purple but with areas of red, orange, brown, white, black and colourless. It is rare, and is found only in the US and one particular mine in Brazil, but new sources are being found, whether with all seven stones combined or fewer (super six or five).

CHAKRA CONNECTION All

ASTRO AFFILIATION All

HEALING by activating your own healing powers and raising the vibrational frequency of all humanity

Mind This nurturing crystal gives you great clarity about your purpose, encouraging you to go for your goals and ideas to do with the New Earth. It reminds us that we are part of the web of humanity on this planet, soothing any mental disease. It instils a sense of peace and safety, especially in communities where there may be fear of violence or unrest, bringing about elevated connection and cohesion in groups.

Body Super seven naturally has vast curative properties that stimulate the body's natural healing abilities, and it can be used to treat remotely. It harmonizes all the systems and organs in the body, boosts the immune system and improves the health of the skin and bones.

Spirit With all these powerful crystals combined in one, super seven has a supremely high vibration, which can be felt in the hand if held for a while. It activates all the chakras and brings a deep sense of bliss to meditation. The amethyst part of it protects you, smoky quartz grounds you, while clear quartz amplifies your energy, raising your frequency ever higher. It connects you deeply to divine consciousness and the spiritual realm. This, in turn, heightens your psychic awareness, guiding you to develop intuitive talents, such as telepathy, clairvoyance and clairaudience, and the ability to see auras.

How to use Meditate in front of a piece of super seven on your altar or by holding it in the non-dominant hand to receive its blessings. Lie down and place super seven next to your crown and root chakras to activate all the energy centres, or position one on your third eye to connect to spiritual awareness. Use it in crystal grids, as it amplifies the energy of all other crystals, maximizing their healing potential. Push a healing grid of super sevens into the ground where Earth healing needs to take place.

Tanzanite

TYPE OF CRYSTAL Only found in Tanzania, this is a rare variety of zoisite that forms in masses or prismatic, striated formations. These clear, lavender-blue, lilac or violet gemstones, which change colour when looked at from different angles, are often faceted and used in expensive jewellery.

CHAKRA CONNECTION Throat, third eye, crown

ASTRO AFFILIATION Gemini, Libra, Sagittarius

HEALING in readiness for spiritual ascension

Mind This gem calms the mind, alleviates anxiety and lifts depression. It brings trust in things working out for the highest good. It synchronizes the head and the heart, helping you live a life of compassion for yourself and others, combined with elevated thinking about your true path and potential. If you feel overworked, let tanzanite help you take more time for yourself.

Body Tanzanite boosts hearing and supports kidney and nerve health, bringing respite from exhaustion. It supports the chest, throat and head, and enlivens the skin and eyes.

Spirit This consciousness-raising crystal aids spiritual development in many ways. It helps you deepen your meditation practice and live more in the present, every day. Tanzanite can connect you to your spirit guides, Ascended Masters and the angelic realm, accelerating your psychic gifts and ascension process. Allow this gem to guide you on spiritual journeys and link you into the Akashic records for increased past-life awareness and karmic healing.

How to use Place on the relevant chakras. Keep on your meditation altar. Meditate holding in either hand. Use in a crystal healing grid. Carry in a pocket. Wear with care as a necklace or earrings, as it can overstimulate sensitives. If it increases psychic or telepathic information to an uncomfortable level, remove the jewellery and replace it with smoky quartz or hematite to protect yourself from unwanted energy. Position next to the bed to further your spiritual development while you sleep.

Tektite

TYPE OF CRYSTAL Tektite is formed when meteorites crash into the Earth, fusing molten space matter and planet particles, which cool into this glassy stone. It can be black, brown, green moldavite (see page 161) and Libyan gold glass, as it's known. China and Thailand have the most of this rare gem.

CHAKRA CONNECTION Third eye, crown

ASTRO AFFILIATION Aries, Cancer

HEALING by boosting fertility of all kinds

Mind Tektite activates reason and helps you absorb and retain higher knowledge and spiritual wisdom. It gives you insight into the truth of matters and the action you need to take. Tektite helps you learn lessons from less-than-favourable life experiences, knowing it's all for your growth. It also balances the masculine and feminine sides of your personality.

Body Worn as a talisman in ancient times for fertility of all kinds, tektite brings this force into the mind, body and spirit. It boosts circulation and the healthy function of capillaries. It can bring down a fever and halt disease transmission. This crystal has also been used for psychic surgery, drawing out illnesses from the body.

Spirit This is a good stone to meditate with when just beginning, to help reach and maintain a peak experience. It rebalances the spinning of the chakras and activates the third eye. It increases telepathic and psychic skills, gifting visions and a connection to other worlds and dimensions. Yellow Libyan gold tektite works especially well for distant healing.

How to use Hold or position on or next to the appropriate chakra or area of the body. Carry it with you. Meditate holding a piece in cupped hands or placed on the third eye while lying down, or on the crown chakra when seated.

Tiger's eye

TYPE OF CRYSTAL Tiger's eye a variation of quartz with the reflective effect of chatoyancy. It is usually gold, brown or yellow with lighter or darker shimmering bands, giving it the look of a cat's eye. The blue version is called hawk's eye (see page 127), while the red is falcon's eye, and you can get stones containing all the colours. All types are found in South Africa, the US, Mexico, India and Australia.

CHAKRA CONNECTION Solar plexus, third eye

ASTRO AFFILIATION Capricorn

HEALING mental illness and personality disorders

Mind A feel-good stone that dispels depression, tiger's eye brings self-confidence and creative thinking, releases negative beliefs and clears any obstructions to fulfilment. It imparts calm in any crisis, especially helping counsellors and mediators with their work to bring peace to fraught relationships. This gem resolves internal conflicts, shifts inadequacy and gets to the root of issues such as self-criticism or pride. Enhancing personal power and sharpening the mind, it pushes you into action by increasing your decision-making skills and clarifying your intentions to help achieve your goals. It makes you aware of your true talents and encourages integrity, enabling you to go for what is needed to accomplish the highest manifestation of your desires, which tiger's eye brings into physical reality with abundance.

Body This crystal helps manifest a healthier lifestyle, boosting your determination and giving you the energy to succeed at a fitness plan. It is believed to be beneficial for broken bones, assisting their healing. It stimulates the digestive system, alleviating disorders in this area, such as nausea or flatulence, and treats any throat issues. Not surprisingly, tiger's eye helps the eyes, especially boosting night vision. It also supports the reproductive organs and encourages addictive personalities to make the changes needed to release their dependency and curb cravings.

Spirit Combining the elevated frequency of the sun with the grounded energy of the Earth, this is a high-vibration protective stone, once carried as a talisman to ward off curses and harmful intent. Tiger's eye is another gem to heighten your intuition, and can be used for distance healing in meditation. It is believed to bring equilibrium between the yin and yang sides of your personality.

How to use Place on any area of the body for healing. Position on the solar plexus while lying down for spiritual grounding, or on the third eye to boost psychic gifts, balance the lower chakras and activate kundalini rising from the root chakra. Wear as a bracelet on the right arm or as a pendant for short periods. Carry it with you for abundance. Hold in the receiving/non-dominant hand while meditating, or sit in front of a piece on your meditation altar. Place a piece in a prominent position in the home to soothe fractious family relationships and bring harmony.

> Red/falcon's eye relates to the root chakra more than the above, so supports healthy sexuality and boosts the workings of the reproduction organs. It can also treat sunburn. Emotionally, it brings balance to out-of-control feelings.

Tiger iron

TYPE OF CRYSTAL This crystal is a combination of tiger's eye, jasper and hematite, banded in red, yellow/brown and black/grey and generally found in Australia. Raw tiger iron looks mostly dull and rusty, whereas polished, tumbled stones are beautifully striped and shiny.

CHAKRA CONNECTION Root

ASTRO AFFILIATION Leo

HEALING physical, emotional and mental exhaustion

Mind Tiger iron uplifts the mind to bring relief from emotional burnout or relationship stress. It helps you think about what you need to make a change and gives you the drive to do it, especially if danger threatens and you have to act quickly. Let tiger iron guide you to simple, practical solutions to problems.

Body A powerful combination stone, tiger iron ignites your survival instinct and boosts vitality, lifting the energy of even the most exhausted. It supports the health of muscles, aiding absorption of B vitamins and natural steroid production. This special stone fortifies the blood, releases toxins and balances the red-white cell ratio, assisting those with anaemia. The feet, hips and legs are all supported with this crystal.

Spirit Meditating with tiger iron enhances your artistic abilities, bringing out latent creative talents to guide you toward deeper enjoyment of life.

How to use Place next to the root chakra while lying down relaxing for increased energy and motivation. Meditate while holding a piece in cupped hands. Carry with you in a pocket or wear in contact with the skin to have its quick-thinking and -acting powers with you wherever you go.

Topaz

TYPE OF CRYSTAL Often found faceted into small, precious gemstones in expensive jewellery, polished topaz is crystal clear and comes in various colours including yellow (imperial topaz), blue, colourless, brown, green and (very rarely) red-pink. It is usually found in the US, Brazil, Mexico, Pakistan, India, Sri Lanka, South Africa and Australia.

CHAKRA CONNECTION Solar plexus (yellow), throat and third eye (blue), and crown (all colours)

ASTRO AFFILIATION Leo, Sagittarius, Pisces

HEALING joyfully

Mind Stimulating thoughts and creative ideas, this crystal tunes you into your thinking processes, enabling you to observe your mind, know your truth and share it with honesty and openness. It's perfect for artistic types, as it guides you to express your inner wisdom and life experiences in a positive way. Topaz brings clear communication without arrogance or obsession, but with confidence and generosity. It encourages empathy and integrity, and helps you set clear boundaries to regain self-control and improve your self-esteem. It also balances the emotions and helps you receive love and support from a variety of sources.

Body Topaz directs its energy to wherever it is needed most. Plus, it aligns the body's meridians, manifesting good health all around. The liver, gallbladder and endocrine glands are especially supported with imperial topaz, while an elixir of blue topaz is thought to brighten the eyes. Topaz restores your sense of taste, aids digestion and boosts metabolism. It assists anyone with anorexia to restore their relationship with food.

Spirit This bright crystal brings forgiveness, joy and abundance into your life, cleansing your energy field of negativity. It connects you to the higher planes of awareness, speeding up your spiritual awareness and helping you trust in the universe as a benevolent force. Topaz encourages you to relax in the present moment, from where everything can manifest, especially with the aid of affirmations and positive visualizations, which this gem generates.

How to use Wear in a ring on the ring finger. Place on the solar plexus or third eye chakra while lying down. Position on or next to the area in need of healing energy. Keep blue topaz on your meditation altar for communication with the divine. A topical gem essence can be made from topaz and used on the skin to promote a clear complexion.

Warning: Topaz contains aluminium and fluorine, so do not ingest it.

TIGER IRON • TOPAZ

Tourmaline

TYPE OF CRYSTAL Tourmaline is a crystalline silicate mineral made up of boron compounded with other elements, including aluminium, iron, magnesium, sodium, lithium and potassium. This combination creates a variety of colours, each with their own healing properties. It can be clear, light pink, dark pink, watermelon, red, brown, green, blue (see indicolite quartz, page 198), blue-green, yellow and black (see schorl, page 218). It may be opaque or transparent, is usually shiny, and is found in long, striated wand-like formations or hexagonal masses in several countries including many in Africa, plus the US, Brazil, Australia, Afghanistan, Sri Lanka and Italy, depending on variety. The properties mentioned here are general, for all types of tourmaline. See separate entries for the different varieties and their specific healing attributes.

CHAKRA CONNECTION All

ASTRO AFFILIATION All, depending on colour

HEALING by cleansing, purifying and transforming energy

Mind This powerful mental healer balances both hemispheres of the brain, linking logic with intuition, creativity with intellect. It encourages deep self-reflection to help understand yourself and others better, benefitting those with paranoid thoughts. Tourmaline can transform negative thinking into positive, replacing fears and victim mentality with self-confidence, compassion and inspiration. Red tourmaline (rubellite), as well as the brown and yellow varieties, helps you examine the emotional issues around a depleted libido.

Body Wands of tourmaline are fantastic healing tools, releasing muscle tension, aligning the spine and rebalancing energy meridians. They can be used to point to problems on the body, pick out solutions from a range of options, and direct energy to clear blockages and heal specific areas. This crystal supports anyone with dyslexia, as it boosts hand-eye coordination and helps with information translation. Brown tourmaline regenerates the whole body, clearing intestinal blockages and treating skin issues. See other colours for the various ailments and afflictions they assist.

Spirit Tourmaline is an energy transformer, changing dark, dense or heavy vibes into a lighter, more elevated frequency - in yourself, others and your environment. It aligns all the chakras and creates a protective energetic shield around the body so you are safe from unwanted entities during spiritual exploration or rituals. It can be used to scry the future, letting you know which direction to go on your path.

How to use Place on or next to the chakra or area of the body in need of cleansing. Point the tip of a wand in the direction you want energy to flow along the meridians. Wear as any kind of jewellery. Meditate in front of tourmaline on your altar or by holding in either hand. Tune into a wand and ask it to point to the right option from a range of choices either in front of you or written down on pieces of paper.

Warning: It is best not to make tourmaline into an elixir, as it contains a mixture of minerals, including iron and aluminium, that can be harmful if ingested.

Bubblegum/pinktourmaline

TYPE OF CRYSTAL Also called bright pink tourmaline, this is a shocking pink variety with increased lithium and manganese, giving it its rosy glow. It might look artificial but is usually natural, with vertical striations on its clear, prismatic crystals. There are different variations of pink and red gems, including elbaite, rubellite and liddicoatite found in the US, Brazil and Pakistan. All pink and red tourmalines have a similar energy connected to the heart, increasing love, creativity, stamina and vitality in all areas.

CHAKRA CONNECTION Heart

ASTRO AFFILIATION Scorpio, Sagittarius

HEALING the heart through self-love and divine wisdom

Mind Sharpening the intellect and sparking ideas, inventions and creativity, bubble-gum tourmaline likes to give you a new challenge. Any self-defeating or self-deprecating attitudes are quashed and replaced with calm, confidence and joy. Beneficial for talking therapists, pink tourmaline helps them have empathy without absorbing others' pain or problems. Its bright colour is believed to boost and protect mental health.

Body Bubble-gum tourmaline enables you to receive healing energies. It supports the heart, lungs and skin to function at their best. It also balances the endocrine system, regulating hormones. It protects your energy levels from depletion, keeping your vitality high.

Spirit This crystal cleanses the heart chakra, releasing past emotional pain and encouraging self-love before you attract love from another. Meditating with it connects you to the deep spiritual love and wisdom of divine consciousness, which brings peace and trust that all will work out for your highest good. An aphrodisiac when worn as a pendant over the heart, it ensures you are safe to love freely and express yourself sexually.

How to use Wear bubble-gum tourmaline as jewellery, especially a necklace or bracelet, to attract romance, and on dates to help them go well. Carry with you to promote universal compassion. Hold in either hand when meditating or place on the heart area while lying down relaxing. Drift off into a love-filled meditation, allowing the wondrous bliss from the universe to wash through you, clearing away any negative emotions and filling you with divine love.

Elbaite/multicoloured tourmaline

TYPE OF CRYSTAL This tourmaline contains all colours. Its name comes from its place of origin: the Italian island of Elba. It is also found in Afghanistan, Pakistan, Russia, Mozambique, Brazil and the US.

CHAKRA CONNECTION Crown

ASTRO AFFILIATION Libra, Sagittarius

HEALING through wholeness of mind, body and spirit

Mind This variety of tourmaline enhances the imagination and inspires creativity. It elevates your thinking to encourage exciting new ideas for your life.

Body Synchronizing the mind-body-spirit connection, elbaite helps the body reach optimum working order. The immune system and metabolism are both given a boost with this gem.

Spirit Multicoloured elbaite brings prophetic dreams and visions to you and acts as the gateway to higher spiritual realms. Gaze gently into a piece of this crystal to journey deep into yourself, as well as other worlds, where messages of wisdom may be revealed.

How to use Place on or next to the heart chakra or area of the body in need of restoration. Put a piece of this gem on your bedside table or under your pillow to encourage prophetic imagery in your dreams and positivity in your life. Wear as a pendant to bring wholeness.

Verdelite/greentourmaline

TYPE OF CRYSTAL Verdelite is the variety of tourmaline that ranges from very light to dark green, and is found in Pakistan and Brazil.

CHAKRA CONNECTION Heart, third eye

ASTRO AFFILIATION Capricorn

HEALING by nurturing and finding solutions

Mind This tourmaline is highly beneficial for the brain, turning around negative thinking and instigating new ideas. It helps you choose the most constructive solution to any problem. It is also able to assist with getting over abuse and coming to terms with issues with father figures. It calms the mind to enable better sleep and relaxation. Panic attacks, claustrophobia and hyperactivity can be soothed with this gem.

Body With its green colour, it's no surprise that this gem links to gardening and plant wisdom, teaching you the healing power of herbalism, flower remedies and cultivating healthy crops for wellbeing and nourishment. It relieves exhaustion and strengthens the nervous system in readiness for a higher vibration brought on when working with this crystal. Green tourmaline can treat issues to do with the heart, thymus, brain, immune system and eyes. It aligns the spine and eases muscle strains. It also helps you lose weight and encourages the body to detox.

Spirit Verdelite enhances visualizations, revitalizes creativity and encourages a sense of openness and compassion for all. Feelings of tenderness, patience and belonging can be yours once green tourmaline has opened your heart chakra and healed your heart, renewing your enthusiasm for life.

How to use Position on or next to the heart chakra or any area where it is needed. Wear as a bracelet or necklace. Meditate while holding in the receiving (non-dominant) hand to attract its blessings. Carry in a pocket, purse or wallet for prosperity. Keep in a garden shed, greenhouse or with potted plants to encourage growth.

Watermelon tourmaline

TYPE OF CRYSTAL Resembling a slice of watermelon, this clear and banded variety of tourmaline usually has a green or blue exterior, and a pink or red centre. It can have reversed colours or be lime green with a white centre. An expensive gemstone, it is often cut into jewellery after it has been obtained from Pakistan or Brazil.

CHAKRA CONNECTION Heart

ASTRO AFFILIATION Gemini, Virgo

HEALING through love

Mind Alleviating stress of the mind, body and spirit, this crystal dissolves past pain and problematic emotions, and brings patience and tenderness. It guides you toward diplomacy in troubled relationships, speaking thoughtfully and with increased tact and clarity. It lifts depression and dispels fears, engendering trust in yourself and others. It helps you understand situations, state your intentions boldly, and bring about peace and joy.

Body This gem is good for the heart - especially the lime-green-with-white-middle variety, which is thought to treat most heart conditions. Lung health also gets a boost with this gem, while the reversed version of it helps the body heal after accidents, quickens the reflexes and increases nutrient absorption from food. It is believed to help regenerate nerves, even in the case of paralysis or multiple sclerosis.

Spirit Watermelon tourmaline is known as the 'super activator' of the heart chakra, aligning it to higher wisdom to ignite your innate creativity. This crystal opens you up to unconditional love from all angles. It fosters a deep connection with nature in all its glory and helps you find deep peace.

How to use Position on or next to the heart chakra. Wear as jewellery, especially over the heart or in earrings. Carry with you, especially outdoors. Sit on the ground somewhere tranquil outside and hold a piece of watermelon tourmaline in either hand to tap into nature's calm stillness and abundance.

Tugtupite

TYPE OF CRYSTAL Discovered in Greenland in 1962, tugtupite is also called reindeer blood; Inuit legend says it was formed from the blood of a birthing reindeer. It is, in fact, a rare silicate mineral containing aluminium beryllium, chlorine and sodium, and is now also found in Canada and Russia. It displays a unique quality called tenebrescence, meaning its colour changes from white, light pink or pale red, sometimes with black, to a much deeper crimson colour when exposed to light. Under ultraviolet light it fluoresces bright red. Synthetic tugtupite exists, but it has few of the healing qualities of the real thing.

CHAKRA CONNECTION Heart, throat, third eye, crown

ASTRO AFFILIATION Cancer, Leo, Libra

HEALING by feeling and sharing unconditional love

Mind With its soft energy, this crystal calms anxiety, stress and worries about poverty, and instead brings self-love, abundance and clarity about your life's purpose. It bolsters your conscience, helping you solve dilemmas, and turns rage at the world or at others into creativity and compassion. Tugtupite makes you aware that it is your responsibility to look after your mental wellbeing – no one else can do it for you. This gentle gem integrates heart and mind, igniting passion and attracting romance. Kept close to your heart, tugtupite allows you to cultivate true intimacy and emotional honesty while deflecting pulls on your heartstrings by others.

Body This crystal increases your libido and fertility. It regulates hormones and balances metabolism. With its link to the heart, this is the area of the body it heals the most, along with stabilizing blood pressure and cleansing the blood. Its bright glow lifts low mood, and helps treat seasonal affective disorder.

Spirit Tugtupite expands and clears the heart chakra, deepening feelings and expressions of love in everything you do. It connects this wide-open, compassionate heart to higher awareness, raising your frequency and activating your light body so you can share this love with the world. It activates a deep inner peace through meditation. It's also highly protective, blocking others' resentment or anger directed at you, and cutting cords from harmful relationships or past-life trauma (especially when combined with nuummite). It guides you to forgive yourself and others for mistakes. Use it to send unconditional love and healing energy to war zones or other areas of strife.

How to use Position on or next to the heart chakra while lying down relaxing, to expand heart energy and activate all upper chakras. Wear as a pendant over the heart chakra. Place under the right armpit to protect yourself from others' negativity. Position on or next to any area of the body in need of its energy. Put a piece of tugtupite on a map or photo of an area you'd like to send healing energy to, and send this frequency there in your mind's eye while meditating. Sit holding a piece in cupped hands, drop your gaze onto it and allow its warm, loving vibration to fill your whole being, bringing you into a state of deep peace.

Warning: Do not use salt to cleanse tugtupite, as it is far too delicate.

Turquoise

TYPE OF CRYSTAL Used in jewellery and amulets since ancient times, turquoise is a master healer and protector found all over the world, including in China, Mexico, Peru, the US, Russia, Europe and much of the Middle East. As its name suggests, this crystal is turquoise in colour, sometimes more green or blue. Turquoise is always opaque, often with dark or light veins, and forms in masses, crusts and occasionally short prismatic shapes. Some turquoise is actually dyed howlite, so make sure you're using the real crystal for healing purposes. Turquoise should be received as a gift, not bought for oneself.

CHAKRA CONNECTION Throat, third eye

ASTRO AFFILIATION Scorpio, Sagittarius, Pisces

HEALING by purifying and protecting mind, body and spirit

Mind Turquoise works to purify and elevate the mind, clearing suspicion, self-sabotage and martyrdom. It removes all such negative thinking and replaces it with deep inner peace and calm. It encourages empathy, alertness and ambition. Eliminating depression, this gem increases mental strength and highlights creative solutions to problems. By balancing the throat chakra and your emotions, it helps you express yourself honestly and effectively, both verbally – especially supporting anyone speaking in public – and through writing.

Body A fantastic healing stone, turquoise protects the body and clears the effects of external pollutants, such as EMF smog from technological gadgets or anything that causes allergies and asthma. Colds, flu, bronchitis and any

issues with the lungs are alleviated with this stone, which also helps the eyes, including getting rid of cataracts. It relieves exhaustion, regenerates tissue and aids the absorption of nutrients from food. Boosting the immune system, it detoxes the body and reduces acidity and inflammation, making it a great gem for those suffering from rheumatism, arthritis or gout. It helps with wounds, whiplash and post-operation recovery. An elixir of turquoise can be used topically treat rashes, itches and other skin issues.

Spirit A crystal to enhance communication in your relationships and with the spirit realms, turquoise heightens your intuition and expands your psychic skills. It aligns all the chakras and links the spiritual with the physical, grounding you during meditation.

It facilitates astral travel and past-life exploration, helping you release old vows holding you back from your life purpose.

How to use Place on or next to the throat or third eye chakra, or on any part of the body in need of treatment. Wear as a necklace to calm nerves and protect. Carry it with you. Meditate with it regularly by holding in either hand or sitting in front of it on your meditation altar. Make into a gem essence and drink or apply topically.

Warning: Turquoise contains copper and aluminium, and should not be ingested. An elixir should only be used topically.

Ulexite

TYPE OF CRYSTAL Commonly known as TV stone, this crystal is a magnifier. It is transparent and soft, with a silky texture, or white and fibrous, sometimes slightly striated. Naturally formed in rounded masses that look like puff balls, it is abundant in the US.

CHAKRA CONNECTION Third eye, crown

ASTRO AFFILIATION Gemini

HEALING physical and spiritual vision

Mind This crystal clears mental fog, bringing clarity to thought processes and curbing overblown expectations. It takes your mind straight to the reason for any problems, showing you objective solutions. Ulexite heightens the imagination and boosts creativity, especially in business matters and brainstorming sessions. It supports you through changes that may be unwanted, enabling you to transform your thinking, if necessary.

Body Tackling the root cause of diseases, this gem aids detoxification. It improves eye health, promoting clear vision. Ulexite can also be made into a gem essence to smooth wrinkles and improve skin tone.

Spirit Allow ulexite's clarity to bring focus and objectivity to your inner world and spiritual development, instead of getting carried away with mystical magic that may not feel true for you. Meditating with this gem enables you to look deeply into your soul to reveal your spiritual path. It can also help you analyze psychic visions or dreams. It heightens telepathy and helps you see if others are acting from the heart.

How to use Place on the third eye to bring clear thinking and intuitive visions, or over closed eyes to improve eyesight. Wear as jewellery, especially earrings. Gaze into a piece of ulexite for enhanced meditation and telepathy. Carry with you for constant clarity. Place in the centre of a table to bring elevated and imaginative ideas. Make into an elixir in cold water only, as warm water will dissolve it. Do not leave ulexite submerged for long, and only apply the gem essence topically.

Unakite

TYPE OF CRYSTAL This mixture of red, pink or peach-coloured feldspar, mossy green epidote and sparkling quartz make up this type of jasper. It is sold in rough or tumbled and polished stones and mined in South Africa and the US.

CHAKRA CONNECTION Root, solar plexus, heart

ASTRO AFFILIATION Scorpio

HEALING the past with renewed spirituality

Mind Unakite brings balance to emotions, supporting them with spirituality, which especially helps anyone going through grief or loss – of a person, a relationship, a goal or an idea of how their life should have been. It helps you accept past experiences and come back to the present. Unakite also gives you the willpower to combat addiction.

Body This stone helps you discover the root cause of an illness so you can resolve it. It treats the reproductive system, boosts fertility and aids the healthy development of a baby in the womb. Beneficial for those recovering after an operation or illness, unakite improves sleep and encourages healthy growth of skin tissue and hair. It also helps you put on weight if needed.

Spirit Unakite helps insights about the past come to light, to enable you to release spiritual blockages. Past-life healing can be undertaken with this gem, bringing about a rebirth as you reframe your soul's journey. Connecting the root and heart chakras, this gentle gem guides you forward on your spiritual path from a place of loving acceptance of what is. Placed on the third eye, it opens up your psychic vision and is helpful for scrying the future.

How to use Place on or next to the relevant chakra or area of the body. Carry in a pocket or keep some in a bowl at home to calm issues before they explode. Make into an elixir and apply to the skin or scalp. Hold in either hand while meditating to ground energy. Position on bedside table or place a piece under your pillow to improve sleep. Include unakite in a bag of 12 tumble stones, and pick one out to answer a question; the answer will be about healing from the past, transformation and rebirth.

Vanadinite

TYPE OF CRYSTAL This mineral forms when an ore with lead in it becomes oxidized and turns into small, transparent crystals on a matrix. The bright gems come in shades of brown, yellow, orange or red. It's generally only available from specialist crystal stores, and is found in Morocco and the US.

CHAKRA CONNECTION Sacral

ASTRO AFFILIATION Virgo

HEALING energy and mental chatter

Mind This crystal both stimulates and calms the mind, lessening internal chatter and helping you focus on planning and pursuing your goals. It heightens all thinking processes and gives you the motivation to act on your dreams. It allows rational thinking, creative insight and inner guidance to produce something special.

Body Vanadinite helps you conserve energy and learn how not to squander it, keeping your vitality high for longer periods of time. It supports the health of the bladder and the lungs, assisting those with asthma and any other breathing difficulties and teaching various breathing techniques to boost lung capacity. It's a good gem to combat chronic exhaustion, too.

Spirit With its links to the lungs, vanadinite promotes breathing methods that deepen meditation, such as a longer exhale than inhale, or counting and holding the breath. These techniques help ground your spirit into physical reality during heightened spiritual experiences. Vanadinite also aligns the chakras and makes you more at ease with the energy around you - including your own. Sitting with this stone helps you reach a profound stillness connected to the flow of universal consciousness, bringing inner peace and psychic visions. It can also be used to facilitate spiritual journeying.

How to use Place on the sacral chakra while lying down. Meditate in front of a piece on your meditation altar. Put a piece under a mattress or pillow, or on a bedside table, to wake up fully revitalized. Rub an elixir - made using the indirect method - over the chest area to help lung issues. Drink the indirectly prepared gem essence for a few weeks to encourage acceptance of your physicality.

Warning: Vanadinite contains lead and is poisonous. Do not make it into an elixir other than via the indirect method, and handle it with care.

Variscite

TYPE OF CRYSTAL Usually green, grey or white, sometimes with veins, this opaque mineral forms in large masses, nodules or small encrustations on a matrix. It is found in Australia, the US, Bolivia, Germany, Austria and the Czech Republic.

CHAKRA CONNECTION Heart, third eye

ASTRO AFFILIATION Taurus, Gemini, Scorpio

HEALING by supporting carers

Mind Variscite gives encouragement, guiding your mind out of despair and confusion and toward clear thinking, hope and trust that all is well and you are exactly where you are supposed to be. It wants you to show your authentic self to the world, without the need to pretend, and calms fears about expressing your feelings and ideas. It also supports sobriety while not losing your sense of fun.

Body A stone for caregivers, variscite imparts courage to patients to keep going through life even though they are ill. It has a lively vibe that boosts depleted energy and restores a fraught nervous system. It treats abdominal troubles such as distension, gas, gastritis and ulcers. Inflammation issues due to the body being too acidic, such as gout and rheumatism, are alleviated with this stone. Beneficial

for men's health, variscite treats impotence and prostate issues and helps skin elasticity. It also supports healthy veins and reduces constricted blood flow.

Spirit This gem opens the heart chakra, bringing peace and unconditional love into your life. It facilitates past-life exploration, showing you visions of relevant soul experiences and allowing feelings about them to rise to the surface for healing, clearing the foundation of any disease that stems from these lives. From these insights comes a broadened perception of your life as it is now.

How to use Place over the heart chakra or next to any area of the body in need of treatment. Position on the third eye chakra while lying down to bring about past-life visions. Wear as a pendant over

the heart area for long periods of time. Hold in the left hand while meditating or treating a patient if you are a carer. Put a piece under your pillow for peaceful, worry-free sleep.

Warning: Variscite contains aluminium, so use with care.

Vivianite

TYPE OF CRYSTAL This iron phosphate mineral was found in 1817 in Cornwall, UK by John Henry Vivian - hence its name. It is usually deep green, blue or sometimes colourless, small, transparent or metallic, and is found in clusters or blades, sometimes bent. It is mined in Bolivia, Brazil, Mexico and the US.

CHAKRA CONNECTION Heart, third eye

ASTRO AFFILIATION Cancer, Capricorn

HEALING the eyes

Mind This stone enables you to see truths that you may have been avoiding, helping you come to terms with an awareness of something unacceptable, something you now can't unsee, in either yourself or others. If anyone has been stopping you from seeing clearly, vivianite removes them, along with any delusions you may have about the future. It guides you to set and stick to realistic goals, giving you tenacity and strength to keep going, even through troubled times. It can revitalize stale relationships and lift you out of the doldrums with a stimulating challenge. This crystal also improves memory, helps you live in the moment and raises the mind to a higher frequency, especially when paired with moldavite.

Body Of particular benefit to chronic eye conditions, vivianite also soothes flare-ups of eye issues such as conjunctivitis, iritis and cataracts. It removes free radicals from the body and helps with the absorption of iron, increasing your overall vitality. The liver and heart are supported by this stone, which also brings about alignment of the spine. Improved memory is another of the gifts of this gem, making it good for combating senility.

Spirit Vivianite activates the third eye, heightening your intuition and guiding you into other dimensions for healing insights and visions during meditation or lucid dreaming. It turns negativity in your aura to peace and acceptance. Let this stone help you discover your soul purpose and integrate your shadow side, making you aware of things you may not want to look at in yourself and accepting all parts of you on the spiritual path. It also connects to crop-circle energy, enabling you to tune into their magical energy for Earth wisdom.

How to use Place on the third eye or heart chakra while lying down for visioning. Combine with rose quartz on the heart to heal deep subconscious wounds. Use in a crystal healing grid. Hold in either hand while meditating. Meditate with vivianite in the centre of a crop circle or while gazing at a photo of one to see what mystical messages they hold. To treat the eyes, place a crystal on top of a clean tissue on closed eyelids only, for however long you wish.

Zircon

TYPE OF CRYSTAL Often mistaken for synthetically produced cubic zirconia, which has no metaphysical properties, zircon is a red, brown, yellow, green, or clear crystal. It is found as short, square prismatic crystals, often octahedral, in Pakistan, Sri Lanka, Ukraine, Canada, the US and Australia.

CHAKRA CONNECTION Throat, third eye, crown

ASTRO AFFILIATION Leo, Virgo, Sagittarius

HEALING by raising awareness of the unity of humanity

Mind This crystal calms your thinking, lifts depression and boosts self-esteem. It builds mental stamina, giving you the tenacity to follow your purpose, and a sense of constancy and dependability in relationships. Zircon brings clarity of mind and enables you to differentiate between what's important and what isn't, following the most virtuous path happily. Working with this gem releases hurt from old partnerships, including any jealousy or possessive feelings not fully addressed, to help attract new potential loves. It teaches about the unity of humanity and rids the emotional body of the effects of prejudice, racism or victimization.

Body Healing a variety of conditions, zircon supports the pineal gland, liver, bones and muscles. It helps relieve sciatica, cramps, vertigo and insomnia, and regulates a woman's menstrual cycle. This crystal also alleviates allergies and the effects of poisoning.

Spirit Zircon promotes the awareness that you are a spiritual being having a human experience, and that everything is unified by oneness. It cleanses the aura, encourages unconditional love for yourself and others, and bolsters your magnetism, all of which enable you to attract all you want into your life. But with this crystal on your altar, it is spiritual growth that you want most. It connects you deeply to your intuition, improves communication with divine wisdom and amplifies Source energy.

How to use Place on or next to the relevant chakras or areas of the body - cramped muscles, for example - where it is needed. Use in a crystal healing grid. Carry in a pocket. Wear as jewellery, especially earrings or a necklace. Place on a bedside table to improve sleep. Hold in your receiving (non-dominant) hand, or sit in front of a piece on your meditation altar. As you gaze into it, feel yourself fill with unconditional love for yourself and all humanity.

Warning: If you are epileptic or wear a pacemaker, beware, as zircon may cause dizziness.

Other hues of zircon

Brown is good for grounding your energy and centring your thoughts.

Red activates the root chakra, stimulating libido and boosting vitality when stressed.

Orange works on the sacral chakra, increasing creativity and beauty while combating jealousy and protecting against injury, especially when travelling.

Yellow stimulates and clears the solar plexus chakra, increasing alertness and sexual energy, and lifting depression. It also attracts love and business success.

Green opens the heart chakra and brings abundance of all kinds to you.

Zoisite

TYPE OF CRYSTAL An opaque gem with sparkling pieces inside it, zoisite ranges from light to dark green but also comes in various colours under different names. It can be colourless, white, yellow, red, pink (called thulite), blue, brown and lavender-blue (tanzanite). This striated crystal is often found in masses combined with ruby in Tanzania, Kenya, Madagascar, Sri Lanka, Cambodia, India, Russia, the US and Austria. This is a general explanation for the green variety.

CHAKRA CONNECTION Heart

ASTRO AFFILIATION Taurus, Gemini

HEALING by spurring action

Mind Zoisite combats feelings of laziness and spurs you into action to rectify any problems in your life and manifest what is true for you, rather than anything influenced by others or society. It removes blocks on your path to fulfilment. Suppressed emotions rise to the surface with this gem, ready for exploration and full expression, turning negative influences and destructive tendencies into positive and constructive plans.

Body Beneficial after illness, operation or chronic stress, this gem aids recovery and detox. It boosts the immune system, helps cells regenerate and reduces inflammation and acidification in the body. Highly beneficial to the bowels, this crystal alleviates flatulence and gas pains. The heart, lungs, spleen and pancreas are all supported by zoisite, which also treats issues with the reproductive organs, increasing fertility.

Spirit Enabling you to connect to the spiritual dimensions, zoisite opens the heart chakra, which strengthens all relationships, whether in the human plane or higher realms of awareness. Through meditation, introspection and other self-development, this crystal helps you find your true inner self.

How to use Position on or next to the heart chakra. Carry it with you. Hold in either hand while meditating. Place directly on the skin on the area of the body that needs its energy. Wear as a necklace, touching the skin, for long periods, as it takes time to have an effect.

Glossary

Akashic records - A spiritual concept of a kind of library that exists beyond time and space where all lives past, present and future are recorded. They can be visited in spiritual journeys for increased past-life awareness and karmic healing.

Angelic realm - The spiritual/energetic dimension where angels, beings of light, reside; this realm can be tapped into during meditation with crystals.

Ascended Masters - Highly evolved spiritual beings, such as Buddha or Jesus, who may or may not have incarnated on the Earth but are helping with humans' ascension process and the evolution of the Earth.

Ascension - The process whereby humans on Earth are raising their vibration to a higher frequency, from three-dimensional to five-dimensional, through various activities of spiritual development.

Astral travel - Also known as an out-of-body experience or soul journey, this is where the soul is able to leave the physical body and travel to other realms of awareness.

Aura - The energetic field around a living object.

Biomagnetic field/sheath - Energy radiating out of all living things, as seen by Kirlian photography.

Clairaudience - Hearing messages and guidance about the future.

Clairsentience - Sensing messages or guidance about the future.

Clairvoyance - Receiving visions of the future, usually in the mind's eye.

Chakra - The energy centre in the etheric body of a human where two energy meridians cross.

Channelling - A technique of directly passing on information from beings in the spirit realm through speaking or writing messages.

Chatoyancy - An optical reflectance effect seen in certain gemstones looking like a cat's eye.

Dis-ease vs disease - Dis-ease means more unease than illness, such as symptoms caused by blocked emotions, negative feelings and physical imbalances.

Etheric field/body - Also known as an aura, this is the subtle biomagnetic field around the body.

Elixir/gem essence - A crystal or stone soaked in water to create a method of healing.

Electromagnetic frequency or EMF - The energetic frequency given off by electrical devices, such as mobile phones, computers and Wi-Fi routers, as well as power lines, that can have a harmful effect on our bodies.

Feng shui - The ancient Chinese art of energy flow in the home; in feng shui, furniture and objects are positioned in certain places to enhance health and wellbeing.

Grounding - Connecting to the Earth to stabilize and balance spiritual energy.

Hand, dominant or giving - This is the hand in which to place a crystal when *sharing* energy and healing with others. It's the hand a person writes with.

Hand, non-dominant or receiving - This is the hand that is *not* used for writing; place a crystal in this hand to *receive* energy or healing.

Higher self - A person's elevated consciousness that connects to God/Source/divine energy/ universal consciousness, which all things come from. Connecting to the higher self through meditation enables you to be guided on the path Source energy has for you.

Inner child - The part of a person's personality that remains childlike or damaged from childhood abuse, and needs healing.

Intuition - An inner sense of knowing

information - often received from a higher consciousness or spirit guide through the third eye chakra - or experienced as a 'gut feeling' about someone or something.

Kundalini - Life force, creative or sexual energy in the body that rises up from the root chakra, activating all chakras and energizing the whole system.

Ley lines - Subtle energy lines that run between ancient spiritual sites or significant points on the landscape, detectable through dowsing with a pendulum.

Life force - Divine energy, often called *chi* or *prana*, that animates all living creatures.

Lucid dreaming - The ability to control your dreams, often with a purpose of spiritual journeying or spiritual development.

Meridian - The energy pathways that run up and down the body, as used in acupuncture and reflexology. Humans have 12 such meridians associated with each organ.

Reiki - A type of energy healing that directs universal life force toward healing someone or something, usually through the hands or via intention in the mind.

Scrying - Divining/seeing images of the future or secrets of the past in a crystal or crystal ball.

Shamanic work - Working with the spirit world to bring about positive transformation by eliminating negativity in whatever form it may take.

Striations - Lines on a crystal that are usually raised or of a different colour.

Spirit guide - A spiritual being of higher consciousness that guides you along your path or toward your purpose, usually through intuition, creative inspiration or messages in your dreams.

Further reading

BOOKS

Crystal Healing Essentials by Cassandra Eason (Foulsham and Co Ltd, 2002)

Crystals for Healing - The Complete Reference Guide by Karen Frazier (Althea Press, 2015)

The Crystal Bible by Judy Hall (Godsfield Press, 2003)

The Crystal Bible 2 by Judy Hall (Godsfield Press, 2009)

The Crystal Healer by Marianna Sheldrake (The CW Daniel Company Ltd, 1999)

The Complete Guide to Manifesting with Crystals by Marina Costello (Earthdancer, Findhorn Press, 2009)

The Modern Guide to Crystal Healing by Philip Permutt (Cico Books, 2021)

WEBSITES

crystaldigest.com

crystalhealingforwomen.com

crystalshop.co.uk

crystalvaults.com/crystal-encyclopedia

earthlore.com

gemselect.com/gem-info

meanings.crystalsandjewelry.com

mycrystals.com

naturalpedia.com

thecrystalcouncil.com

wikipedia.com

Index of crystals